The New Oxford Bo

Jon Stallworthy was educated at Rug
tier Force, and at Magdalen Colleg
Newdigate Prize for Poetry. His books include two critical studies
of Yeats's poetry; two biographies: *Wilfred Owen* (which won the
Duff Cooper Memorial Prize, the WH Smith Award and the E.M.
Forster Award) and *Louis MacNeice* (which won the Southern Arts
Literary Prize); editions of Wilfred Owen's *Complete Poems and
Fragments* and *War Poems*; and two critical studies of war poetry:
*Anthem for Doomed Youth: Twelve Soldier Poets of the First World
War* and *Survivors' Songs: From Maldon to the Somme*. Most
recently he has published *War Poet*, a selection of his own war
poems. He has been a Professor of English Literature at Cornell
and Oxford, and is now a Senior Research Fellow of Wolfson
College, Oxford, and a Fellow of the British Academy.

The New Oxford Book of War Poetry

Chosen and Edited by

Jon Stallworthy

OXFORD
UNIVERSITY PRESS

OXFORD
UNIVERSITY PRESS

Great Clarendon Street, Oxford, OX2 6DP,
United Kingdom

Oxford University Press is a department of the University of Oxford.
It furthers the University's objective of excellence in research, scholarship,
and education by publishing worldwide. Oxford is a registered trade mark of
Oxford University Press in the UK and in certain other countries

First published 1984
Second published 2014
First published in paperback 2015

Impression: 1

Published in the United States of America by Oxford University Press
198 Madison Avenue, New York, NY 10016, United States of America

British Library Cataloguing in Publication Data
Data available

Library of Congress Cataloging in Publication Data
Data available

ISBN 978-0-19-870447-8 (Hbk.)
ISBN 978-0-19-870448-5 (Pbk.)

Printed and bound in Great Britain by
Clays Ltd, St Ives plc

CONTENTS

CONTENTS

CONTENTS

CONTENTS

CONTENTS

CONTENTS

CONTENTS

CONTENTS

CONTENTS

CONTENTS

CONTENTS

CONTENTS

CONTENTS

CONTENTS

CONTENTS

INTRODUCTION

'POETRY', Wordsworth reminds us, 'is the spontaneous overflow of powerful feelings', and there can be no area of human experience that has generated a wider range of powerful feelings than war: hope and fear; exhilaration and humiliation; hatred—not only for the enemy, but also for generals, politicians, and war-profiteers; love—for fellow soldiers, for women and children left behind, for country (often) and cause (occasionally).

Man's early war-songs and love-songs were generally exhortations to action, or celebrations of action, in one or other field, but no such similarity exists between what we now more broadly define as love poetry and war poetry. Whereas most love poems have been in favour of love, much—and most recent—war poetry has been implicitly, if not explicitly, anti-war. So long as warrior met warrior in equal combat with sword or lance, poets could celebrate their courage and chivalry, but as technology put ever-increasing distance between combatants and, then, ceased to distinguish between combatant and civilian, poets more and more responded to 'man's inhumanity to man'. Not that heroic societies were oblivious to the domestic consequences of their heroes' 'brain-spattering, windpipe-slitting art'. *The Iliad* (3)[1] ends with Andromache watching from the walls of Troy, as her husband's broken body is dragged away behind his killer's chariot: 'she mourned, and the women wailed in answer'. Similarly, as the hero's funeral pyre is lit at the close of the Old English epic, written 1,500 years later,

> his ancient wife with braided hair,
> Grief-stricken raised a song of lamentation
> For Beowulf; repeatedly she said
> That sore she dreaded evil days would come,
> Much carnage, war's alarms, captivity
> And ignominy. Heaven swallowed up the smoke.[2]

Hers, however, is not the last word. That is spoken by Beowulf's warriors, 'his hearth-companions':

> It was their part to mourn, bewail their king,
> Recite an elegy and acclaim the man;
> They praised his prowess, and his mighty deeds

---

[1] Numbers in brackets refer to poems in this anthology.
[2] Mary E. Waterhouse, trans., *Beowulf in Modern English*, 1949, p. 108.

> They fittingly extolled, as right it is
> A man should honour his kind lord in words....
> They said that of all earthly kings he was
> Gentlest of men and kindest unto all,
> To men most gracious and most keen for praise.[3]

Such societies recognized the cost of warfare, but the code to which they subscribed counted it a necessary price for the pursuit of 'praise', honour, renown. This was to be acquired by generosity in peace, mighty deeds in war, loyalty to the living and loyalty to the dead.

That heroic tradition died, and another was transplanted to English soil, when King Harold's foot-soldiers were cut down on a ridge above Hastings by the cavalry of William, Duke of Normandy. Less than a hundred years before, one of the last Old English poets had chanted or declaimed in a Saxon hall the poem we know as 'The Battle of Maldon' (12). And three hundred years after Harold and his housecarls had gone the way of Byrtnoth and his thanes, the first new English poet introduced to a more cultivated audience

> A knight... a worthy man
> That fro the timė that he first bigan
> To riden out, he lovėd chivalry....

The intervening years had seen Duke William's son Henry, in the words of the Anglo-Saxon Chronicle, 'dubbed a rider', married to a Saxon girl, and the two people and the two languages fused and intermingled. Under the influence of the troubadours, the Church, and the new learning out of Italy, *chivalry* had come to mean more than *cavalry*, that other derivative of the Latin *caballarius*, a horseman. The descendant of Duke William's superbly efficient but hardly sophisticated *chevalier* could, like Chaucer's Squire,

> Wel... sitte on hors, and fairė ride;
> He coudė songės make, and wel endite,
> Juste and eek daunce, and wel portraye and write.

The Universities of Oxford and Cambridge had been founded before Chaucer was born, and in his lifetime the first of the so-called 'public schools', Winchester, opened its doors to the sons of noblemen and gentlemen. By 1440, when Eton was founded, the word *gentleman* had come to denote a clearly defined social status, inferior to nobility and superior to the yeomanry, but not necessarily dependent on ancestry. These schools and those others later modelled on them grafted the

---

[3] Ibid., p. 109.

'classical learning of the monastic schools upon the chivalric training in honour, in sport, in military exercise, in social intercourse, in courtesy and generosity, in reverence and devotion, of the schools of Christian knighthood'.[4]

Chaucer had seen military service—had been captured and ransomed—in France, where two centuries later fought and was wounded Henry Howard, Earl of Surrey, who returned to translate Books III and IV of the *Aeneid* into blank verse. Raleigh served in the Huguenot army at Jarnac and Moncoutour; Gascoigne saw military service in Holland; Donne took part in the Earl of Essex's two expeditions to Cadiz; Davenant was knighted by Charles I at the siege of Gloucester; Lovelace served in the Scottish expeditions of 1639; and the Earl of Rochester showed conspicuous courage in the Second Dutch War of 1665-6.

The chivalric tradition, transmuted into the courtly tradition of the High Renaissance, required proficiency in the arts of war as well as in such peaceable arts as music and poetry. The courtier-poet was expected to serve his king in much the same way as the Anglo-Saxon *scop* took his place in the shield-wall with his lord. The Earl of Surrey left a moving elegy to his Squire (20); Gascoigne, a rueful account of his capture and ransom (21); and Donne condensed his experience of Cadiz into an epigram (23). Considering how many courtier-poets had experience of battle, however, the reader in a later century—when war poems are commonly written by those who have never seen a battlefield—may be surprised by how rarely Renaissance poets write of war. Conventions had changed. Love had become the subject proper to a poet. On the rare occasion when the blast of war blows through a poem, it is likely to be the carefully orchestrated overture to a protestation of devotion, such as Lovelace, the dashing Cavalier, offers 'To Lucasta, Going to the Wars' (25). Paradoxically, the convention that proclaimed the subject of warfare too gross for the polite art of poetry sanctioned, and indeed required, a select use of military terminology in the imagery of the love lyric. Cupid is an archer. The besieging lover, having no shield proof against his darts, can only hope that his Beloved in a spirit of Christian compassion will surrender.

During the eighteenth century, soldiering reached the low place in British society that it was to hold until the Great War; an occupation despised by the middle and working classes as a disgrace hardly less than prison. If an eighteenth-century poet wrote of war—which he

---

[4] F. J. C. Hearnshaw, 'Chivalry and its place in History', *Chivalry*, ed. Edgar Prestage, 1928, p. 22.

seldom did—it was as a remote phenomenon. So John Scott of Amwell declares (36):

> I hate that drum's discordant sound,
> Parading round, and round, and round:
> To me it talks of ravaged plains,
> And burning towns, and ruined swains,
> And mangled limbs, and dying groans,
> And widows' tears, and orphans' moans;
> And all that Misery's hand bestows,
> To fill the catalogue of human woes.

As the French Revolution made its contribution to that catalogue, warfare once more became a subject of interest to British poets. The Napoleonic wars moved Sir Walter Scott and Thomas Campbell to patriotic outpourings (37). Coleridge and Wordsworth, on the other hand, 'hailed the rising orb of liberty'. Both were subsequently disillusioned, and in Book 4 of *The Prelude* Wordsworth writes movingly of his meeting with a battered veteran of Wellington's armies. No poet of the Romantic period, however, was more alive to the horrors of war than Byron; alive not only to the sufferings of the combatants but to the domestic consequences. The eyes of the dying Gladiator in *Childe Harold* are

> with his heart and that was far away;
> He recked not of the life he lost nor prize,
> But where his rude hut by the Danube lay,
> *There* were his young barbarians all at play,
> *There* was their Dacian mother—he, their sire,
> Butchered to make a Roman holiday....

Byron, as a schoolboy at Harrow, had been steeped in the classics. He visited Greece in 1809 and 1810 and the first two cantos of *Childe Harold*, based on his experiences, launched a tidal wave of literary philhellenism.

By the time of the Greek Revolution in 1821, the educated public in Europe had been deeply immersed in three attractive ideas—that Ancient Greece had been a paradise inhabited by supermen; that the Modern Greeks were the true descendants of the Ancient Greeks; and that a war against the Turks could somehow 'regenerate' the Modern Greeks and restore the former glories.[5]

Invoking the example of Leonidas and his 300 Spartans, commemorated in Simonides' epigram (4), Byron sounded the call to arms:

[5] William St Clair, *That Greece might Still be Free*, 1972, p. 19.

> Must *we* but weep o'er days more blest?
>   Must *we* but blush?—Our fathers bled.
> Earth! render back from out thy breast
>   A remnant of our Spartan dead!
> Of the three hundred grant but three,
> To make a new Thermopylae.

His love for the land of Pericles and Homer proving stronger than his hatred of war, he set off for Greece with half a dozen military uniforms and a couple of helmets, gilded, crested, and bearing the family motto: 'Crede Byron'.

Like every other philhellene who took that road, he was to learn how unrelated were the reality and the dream. Those more fortunate, who returned with their lives, brought tales of betrayal and brutality, squalor and needless suffering, that anticipate the war correspondents' revelations from the Crimea thirty years later. The philanthropic spirit of the age that urged Florence Nightingale to the hospitals of Scutari found expression in anti-war poems by Thackeray (62) and others, but these were counterbalanced by many sounding a savage note, and the one poem from the Crimean War to have survived in the popular memory celebrates a heroic exploit. Significantly, since Tennyson's imagination had long been engaged with the chivalric world of King Arthur and his knights, it was the *cavalry* charge of the Light Brigade in 1854 that spurred him into song (60).

It is one thing to 'Honour the charge' of professional cavalrymen of one's own country against foreign gunners thousands of miles away; but quite another to watch one's own countrymen—many of them boy civilians in uniform—killing and maiming each other. Walt Whitman was drawn into the American Civil War by a brother, wounded in the battle of Fredericksburg, who was in need of nursing. He remained, long after his brother was better, a non-combatant witness to the horrors of war, tending the wounded (67):

> Bearing the bandages, water and sponge,
> Straight and swift to my wounded I go...

He regards them as '*my* wounded', seeing the results of cavalry action from a markedly *un*-Tennysonian perspective:

The neck of the cavalry-man with the bullet through and through I examine,
Hard the breathing rattles, quite glazed already the eye, yet life struggles hard,
(Come sweet death! be persuaded O beautiful death!
In mercy come quickly.)

His eyes unclouded by the chivalric vision, his tongue untrammelled by the chivalric diction and rhetoric, he perceives 'in camp in the daybreak grey and dim' what Siegfried Sassoon and Wilfred Owen were to perceive in the trenches of the Western Front:

Young man I think I know you—I think this face is the face
  of the Christ himself,
Dead and divine and brother of all, and here again he lies.

While America was forging a new society in the fires of Civil War, Britain was making one of those cautious adjustments to the old society by which she had avoided civil strife for three hundred years. Thomas Arnold, as headmaster of Rugby from 1827 to 1842, had revitalized the public school system. Perceiving that the country and the empire needed more—and more efficient—civil servants and managers than the aristocracy and landed gentry could supply, he and the head-masters of the many Anglican boarding schools that opened their gates in the 1850s sought to make 'Christian gentlemen' of the sons of the middle classes. The ethos of these schools was essentially chivalric. As readers of *Tom Brown's Schooldays* will remember, schoolboy fights were elevated into gentlemanly duels, and on the playing fields the same code of etiquette called for 'fair play' and 'the team spirit'. Each school was dominated by its chapel, which suited the philistine respectability of the devout bourgeois, and the curriculum was dominated by Latin, and to a lesser extent, Greek. In 1884 there were twenty-eight classics masters at Eton, six mathematics masters, one historian, no modern language teachers, and no scientists. As late as 1905, classics masters still formed more than half the teaching staff.

The poet-spokesman for the public schools at the end of the nineteenth century was Henry Newbolt. The title of his poem 'Clifton Chapel' acknowledges a debt to Matthew Arnold's 'Rugby Chapel', but whereas the headmaster's son addresses his father and 'the noble and great who are gone', Newbolt exhorts a new generation of imperialists:

To set the cause above renown,
  To love the game beyond the prize,
To honour, while you strike him down,
  The foe that comes with fearless eyes;
To count the life of battle good,
  And dear the land that gave you birth,
And dearer yet the brotherhood
  That binds the brave of all the earth.

*   *   *

God send you fortune: yet be sure,
  Among the lights that gleam and pass,

> You'll live to follow none more pure
> Than that which glows on yonder brass:
> '*Qui procul hinc,*' the legend's writ,—
> The frontier-grave is far away—
> '*Qui ante diem periit:*
> *Sed miles, sed pro patria.*'[6]

In a more famous or notorious poem, 'Vitaï Lampada' (84)—a title taken from Lucretius, meaning '[They pass on] the Torch of Life'—he envisaged the public-school ethic at work on a frontier far away:

> The river of death has brimmed his banks,
> And England's far, and Honour a name,
> But the voice of a schoolboy rallies the ranks:
> 'Play up! play up! and play the game!'

Newbolt's repeated celebration of the imperialist officer and gentleman, carrying to his country's battlefields a sporting code acquired on the playing fields of his public school, parallels a poetic reappraisal of the private soldier initiated by Kipling's *Barrack-room Ballads* (82) and sustained by Housman's *A Shropshire Lad* (91).

Requirements for a commission in the army had altered radically since the 1850s. 'In place of the old patronage system came, first, limited competition—examination for the select few whom the authorities had personally nominated—and then, in 1870, open competition.'[7] The year 1870, of course, saw the outbreak of the Franco-Prussian War that inaugurated the era of violence in international politics, precipitating further army reforms, the rapid mechanization of warfare, and the growth of imperialist ideologies. Malvern van Wyk Smith has shown how in Britain, at the start of the Boer War, militarist and pacifist doctrines were clearly defined and opposed; and how, because the Education Acts of 1870 and 1876 had made the army that sailed for South Africa the first literate army in history, the British Tommy sent home letters and poems that anticipate those his sons were to send back from the Western Front.[8]

These factual and often bitter accounts of combat, to say nothing of the greater poems by Thomas Hardy (85), had been forgotten by 1914 when that War we still—many wars later—know by the adjective Great was greeted in some quarters with a curious gaiety and

---

[6] 'He who lies far from this place ... died before daybreak: but he was a soldier and he died for his country.'

[7] Rupert Wilkinson, *Gentlemanly Power: British Leadership and the Public School Tradition*, 1964, p. 10.

[8] *Drummer Hodge: The Poetry of the Anglo-Boer War*, 1978.

exhilaration. Rupert Brooke captured the mood of that moment in a sonnet to which he gave the paradoxical title of 'Peace' (103). His first line 'Now, God be thanked Who has matched us with His hour'—and the 'hand' and the 'hearts' that follow—reveal one of his sources: the hymn, and ironically it is a hymn translated from the German, beginning

> Now thank we all our God
> With heart, and hands, and voices....

Shortly before Brooke's death, the Dean of St Paul's read aloud in a sermon from the Cathedral pulpit another of his 'war sonnets', 'The Soldier' (105). So the soldier poet was canonized by the Church, and many other poets—civilians and soldiers alike—found inspiration for their battle-hymns, elegies, exhortations, in the well-thumbed pages of *Hymns Ancient and Modern*.

Most of the British poets we associate with the years 1914 and 1915 had a public-school education and this, more than any other factor, distinguishes them from those we associate with the later phases of the war. The early poems return again and again to the appallingly ana-chronistic concept of war as a game; a concept most clearly articulated by E. B. Osborn, in the introduction to his best-selling anthology *The Muse in Arms*, published in 1917. He wrote:

Modern battles are so vast and so extended in both space and time that composed battle-pieces, such as have come down to us from the far-off centuries of archery and ballad-making, may no longer be looked for. The thread on which all such pictures are strung—the new impressions such as 'The Assault' [a poem by Robert Nichols] and old ballads such as 'Agincourt, or the English Bowman's Glory'—is the insular conception of fighting as the greatest of all great games, that which is the most shrewdly spiced with deadly danger. The Germans, and even our allies, cannot understand why this stout old nation persists in thinking of war as a sport; they do not know that sportsmanship is our new homely name, derived from a racial predilection for comparing great things with small, for the *chevalerie* of the Middle Ages. In 'The English Bowman's Glory', written before any of our co-operative pastimes were thought of, the fine idea is veiled in this homely term:

> Agincourt, Agincourt!
> Know ye not Agincourt?
> Oh, it was noble sport!
>   Then did we owe men;
> Men, who a victory won us
> 'Gainst any odds among us:
>   Such were our bowmen.

Light is thrown on this phase of the British Soldier's mentality by the verse ... he writes in honour of the games and the field-sports in which he acquired the basal elements of all true discipline—confidence in his companions and readiness to sacrifice the desire for personal distinction to the common interest of his team, which is, of course, a mimic army in being.

The legacy of the public-school classroom was as significant for the poets as that of the playing field. Paul Fussell rightly points out in his stimulating book, *The Great War and Modern Memory*, that the British soldier tended to look at the war through literary spectacles. He evidences the popularity of Quiller-Couch's *Oxford Book of English Verse*, but surprisingly overlooks the extent to which the public-school poets' attitude to war was conditioned by their years of immersion in the works of Caesar, Virgil, Horace, and Homer. A reading of these authors would leave no intelligent boy in any doubt that war was a brutal business, but by setting 'The Kaiser's War' in a long, and dare one say a time-honoured tradition, the classics encouraged a detached perspective—quite apart from offering the soldier, by analogy, the intoxicating prospect of a place in history and literature. In the poems of 1914 and the first half of 1915, there are countless references to sword and legion, not a few to chariot and oriflamme, but almost none to gun and platoon. Siegfried Sassoon writes, in a poem of 1916, 'We are the happy legion'; while Herbert Asquith begins his elegy, 'The Volunteer' (100),

> Here lies a clerk who half his life had spent
> Toiling at ledgers in a city grey,
> Thinking that so his days would drift away
> With no lance broken in life's tournament.
> Yet ever 'twixt the books and his bright eyes
> The gleaming eagles of the legions came,
> And horsemen, charging under phantom skies,
> Went thundering past beneath the oriflamme.

A similar vision prompted Rupert Brooke, under orders for the Dardanelles, to write to Asquith's sister, Violet:

Do you *think* perhaps the fort on the Asiatic corner will want *quelling*, and we'll land and come at it from behind and they'll make a sortie and meet us on the plains of Troy? ...

I've never been quite so happy in my life, I think. Not quite so *pervasively* happy; like a stream flowing entirely to one end. I suddenly realize that the ambition of my life has been—since I was two—to go on a military expedition against Constantinople.[9]

---

[9] Geoffrey Keynes, ed., *The Letters of Rupert Brooke*, 1968, pp. 662–3.

INTRODUCTION

On the troopship, he and his friends read Homer to each other, and in
a verse-letter from the trenches, Charles Hamilton Sorley remembers
how Homer sung

> Tales of great war and strong hearts wrung,
> Of clash of arms, of council's brawl,
> Of beauty that must early fall,
> Of battle hate and battle joy
> By the old windy walls of Troy....
> And now the fight begins again,
> The old war-joy, the old war-pain.
> Sons of one school across the sea
> We have no fear to fight....[10]

The poems of these young men move us, as human documents, more
than many better poems. They illustrate the hypnotic power of a long
cultural tradition; the tragic outcome of educating a generation to face
not the future but the past. By the end of 1915, Brooke, Sorley, and
many lesser public-school poets were dead. Sassoon, it is true, sur-
vived to follow Sorley's lead and break the code of his upbringing—
and all honour to him. By publicly protesting in 1917 against the
continuance of the war, and by lashing the leaders of Church and
State and the Armed Forces in his poems, he rejected the obedience to
authority that is one of the prime tenets of the public-school system.
The poets who followed him—Owen, Rosenberg, Gurney—had no
such conventions to reject. They went to war, as Whitman had done,
with no Homeric expectations, and set themselves to expose what
Owen called

> The old Lie: Dulce et decorum est
> Pro patria mori.

One, indeed, had Whitman in mind. 'When I think of *Drum Taps*,'
wrote Rosenberg three months before he was killed, '[*my* poems] are
absurd.'

It is often assumed that chivalry died with the cavalry, scythed by
machine guns, in the Battle of the Somme. Auden, characterizing the
past in his poem 'Spain 1937' (198) wrote:

> Yesterday the belief in the absolute value of Greek;
> The fall of the curtain upon the death of a hero...

---

[10] *Marlborough and Other Poems*, 1919, pp. 82–3.

The curtain may have fallen, but it was to rise and fall again. It is a commonplace that traditions die hard, and none die harder than military ones. Leaving Oxford in 1940 to join a cavalry regiment, Keith Douglas embellished a photograph of himself in uniform—humorously, it must be said—with the scrolled caption 'Dulce et decorum est pro patria mori'. Two years later, chafing at his enforced inactivity behind the lines while his regiment was engaging Rommel's tanks in the Western Desert, Douglas drove off—in a two-ton truck and direct disobedience of orders—to join them; earning thereby his batman's commendation: 'I like you, sir. You're shit or bust!' His subsequent achievement as a poet was to celebrate the last stand of the chivalric hero (224),

> the doomed boy, the fool
> whose perfectly mannered flesh fell
> in opening the door for a shell
> as he had learnt to do at school.

In 1915, on the Western Front, Julian Grenfell had written of the cavalryman (108) that

> In dreary, doubtful waiting hours,
> Before the brazen frenzy starts,
> The horses show him nobler powers;
> O patient eyes, courageous hearts!

So Douglas, in his fine elegy, 'Aristocrats' (226), takes the horse as the natural symbol for his anachronistic hero, and in its last line we seem to hear the last echo from the Pass at Roncesvalles: 'It is not gunfire I hear but a hunting horn.' The poem succeeds where most poems of 1914 and 1915 fail. It is sharply focused, acknowledging both the stupidity and the chivalry, the folly and the glamour of cavalrymen on mechanical mounts duelling in the desert. Douglas's language, finely responsive to his theme, fuses ancient and modern: his heroes are 'gentle'—like Chaucer's 'verray parfit gentil knight'—and at the same time 'obsolescent'.

Sidney Keyes was killed on his first patrol in North Africa, but in such poems of 1942 as 'Orestes and the Furies' and 'Rome Remember' he sees the Gorgon-head reflected in the classical shield he had acquired at a public school. He wrote:

> I am the man who groped for words and found
> An arrow in my hand.

Not a rifle, but an arrow. Henry Reed celebrated the rifle in the first of his 'Lessons of the War' (214), but the ironic detachment of these superb meditations on war and peace owes something to the poet whose lines, saucily emended, stand as epigraph to the sequence:

Vixi puellis nuper idoneus
Et militavi non sine gloria.

wrote Horace (*Odes*, iii. 26), which may be roughly rendered:

Lately, I have lived among girls, creditably enough,
and have soldiered, not without glory.

By changing *puellis*, to *duellis*, exchanging girls for battles, Reed cunningly announces and encapsulates the theme of his Lessons.

By no means all British poets of the Second World War came from public schools, and many more spoke a language that had more in common with Owen and Rosenberg. None, however, offers so sharp a contrast to the work of Douglas and Keyes as the American infantry-man-poets Louis Simpson and Lincoln Kirstein. Simpson tells us that after the war he suffered from amnesia, eventually broken by dreams of battle that—as with Owen—released his poems. He has, indeed, other resemblances to Owen—admiration for the soldier's endurance, com-passion for his suffering, of which he writes with something of the same reverberant simplicity (242):

Most clearly of that battle I remember
The tiredness in eyes, how hands looked thin
Around a cigarette, and the bright ember
Would pulse with all the life there was within.

In his long poem 'The Runner', Simpson's college-boy anti-hero Dodd is humiliated by the rest of his platoon for a momentary act of cowardice; although like the Youth in *The Red Badge of Courage* he redeems himself subsequently. Cowardice, a taboo subject to poets in the chivalric tradition, is a theme of Kirstein's *Rhymes of a PFC*, the first poem of which ends:

The rage of armies is the shame of boys;
A hero's panic or a coward's whim
Is triggered by nerve or nervousness.
We wish to sink. We do not choose to swim.

Where Douglas had asked, in 'Gallantry' (224), 'Was George fond of little boys?' and had answered

... who will say: since George was hit
we never mention our surmise.

Kirstein writes openly and tenderly of homosexual love. Similarly, he
and Simpson share—and show in their poems—what Simpson has
described as 'the dog-face's suspicion of the officer class, with their
abstract language and indifference to individual, human suffering'. It is
interesting that he identifies the general infantryman with the animal
that used to run beside the huntsman-cavalryman's horse. Simpson
and Kirstein speak for the civilian stuffed into uniform not very tidily
and against his will. They write of a wider range of military experience—
not excluding cowardice and homosexuality—because they write as
men rather than as soldiers conscious of soldierly tradition.

What may be termed the anti-heroic tradition is at least as old as
Falstaff. It makes sporadic appearances in eighteenth-century English
poetry, but does not oust its older rival until transplanted to America in
the next century. A civil war fought by large numbers of conscripted
civilians, a high proportion of them literate (but few versed in classical
literature), was a new kind of conflict, and America's produced a new
kind of poetry. Its principal poets, Whitman and Melville, were
civilians and they established a perspective and a tone that would be
adopted by those that followed them, combatant and civilian alike: so
James Dickey, veteran of a hundred combat missions, begins 'The
Firebombing' (250): 'Homeowners unite'. That, surely, is the one
hope for the human race. Only if the poets' perception that we are
all civilians gains universal acceptance will we be spared the fulfilment
of Peter Porter's dark prophecy, 'Your Attention Please' (292).

The poems in this anthology have, with few exceptions, been
arranged chronologically by conflict. Thus, Tate's 1928 'Ode to the
Confederate Dead' (78), appearing with other poems of the American
Civil War, comes before earlier evocations of the Franco-Prussian War
by Rilke (79) and Rimbaud (80). The exceptions to this arrangement
are mainly such nineteenth-century versions of heroic epic as Arnold's
'Sohrab and Rustum' (58), that tell us more about the period of their
composition than that of their historical origin.

Long poems pose a special problem in an anthology of this kind, and
I have preferred to print extracts than to omit them altogether as, for
reasons of space, I felt obliged to omit dramatic poetry. It would have
been unthinkable to exclude, for example, representative passages
from the Greek and Latin epics that have so influenced war poetry
in English. Translations from other literatures have been admitted
when—but only when—they seem to me English poems in their
own right.

The resulting selection necessarily includes many more 'horse-face' poems than 'dog-face' ones, and I am aware that the latter category could have been swelled by the addition of popular ballads such as appear in the 'Soldiers and Sailors' section of Frederick Woods's excellent *Oxford Book of English Traditional Verse*. I decided, however, that they show to better advantage in that context than they would in this.

Many friends helped in the preparation of the anthology, and I am particularly indebted to Miss Jacqueline Doyle, Professor Steven Fix, Professor Ephim Fogel, Professor Anthony Hecht, Professor Alan Heuser, Dr Dominic Hibberd, Professor Mary Jacobus, Professor Gwyn Jones, Mrs Judith Luna, Professor Kevin McManus, Professor Stephen Parrish, Mrs Jacqueline Simms, and Mr Charles Tomlinson. I am also grateful to the Royal Society of Literature, in whose transactions, *Essays by Divers Hands* (new series, vol. xli, edited by Brian Fothergill, 1980), a version of this essay appeared.

JON STALLWORTHY

Cornell University, 1984

THIRTY YEARS ON

THIS Oxford Book has been on active service for thirty years, one hundredth part of the history of warfare to which poets have borne witness. At no point in that history did man's inhumanity to man generate more eloquent testimony from more poets than in the two world wars of the last century, the Second no less than the First. Indeed, when account is taken of the memorable British, American, and European voices of 1941–45 and the aftermath of that conflict, the widespread ignorance of Second World War poetry is disturbing. Why it persists is a question cultural historians should address and a curriculum imbalance that educationalists should urgently correct. Too many schoolchildren (and too many teachers) need to be reminded how warfare—and poetry—have changed since 1918. For three-quarters of a century, hostile fire from the sky has been as common as fire from the ground; and poetry has sought to regain territory 'lost' to prose fiction, frequently with prosaic results. The Second World War produced at least as many potent poems as the First, but, like any war, many more that were impotent.

To demonstrate the qualitative range of poems prompted by warfare, and to suggest why many fail, a brief case-study of the poetry of the Vietnam War may be instructive.[1] This falls, more starkly than the poems of any earlier conflict, into two principal categories: those written by so-called 'Stateside' poets, who never left America, and those of the 'Vets', the veterans, who did. The Stateside poems can themselves be divided into two categories: first, the poetry of first-hand witness to the moral and other effects of the war on *America*—poems by Allen Ginsberg, for example; second, the poetry of second-hand witness to the war in *Vietnam*—too much of it like this:

[1] Some of what follows first appeared in 'The Fury and the Mire', in Jon Stallworthy, *Survivors' Songs from Maldon to the Somme* (Cambridge: Cambridge University Press, 2008), an essay that was itself indebted to Subarno Chattarji, *Memories of a Lost War: American Poetic Responses to the Vietnam War* (Oxford: Clarendon Press, 2001).

THIRTY YEARS ON

Women, Children, Babies, Cows, Cats

'It was at My Lai or Sonmy or something,
it was this afternoon. . . . We had these orders,
we had all night to think about it—
we was to burn and kill, then there'd be nothing
standing, women, children, babies, cows, cats. . . .
As soon as we hopped the choppers, we started shooting.
I remember . . . as we was coming up upon one area
in Pinkville, a man with a gun . . . running—this lady . . .
Lieutenant LaGuerre said, "Shoot her." I said,
"You shoot her, I don't want to shoot no lady."
She had one foot in the door. . . . When I turned her,
there was this little one-month-year-old baby
I thought was her gun. It kind of cracked me up.'[2]

This was written by a great poet—Robert Lowell—but I cannot be
alone in thinking it is not a great poem. In fact, I think it embarrassing
in its blend of black demotic ('I don't want to shoot no lady') with
the literary ('we hopped the choppers', and the coy 'Lieutenant
LaGuerre'). The speaker does not persuade me he mistook the baby
(so neatly foreshadowed in his orders) for a gun; or that 'It kind of
cracked [him] up'. It would tell us—even if we did not know that
Lowell never served in Vietnam—that his testimony is second-hand.
In this, it is strikingly unlike his poignant and powerful poem 'Fall
1961' (270), which bears first-hand witness to a father's fear in the
midst of the Cuban missile crisis:

> All autumn, the chafe and jar
> of nuclear war;
> we have talked our extinction to death.
> I swim like a minnow
> behind my studio window.
>
> Our end drifts nearer,
> the moon lifts,
> radiant with terror.
> [. . .]
> A father's no shield
> for his child [. . .]

If you feel more for the American father and his child than for the
Vietnamese mother and baby, it might be that the poet felt more. Few

---

[2] Frank Bidart and David Grewanter (eds.), *Robert Lowell: Collected Poems* (London: Faber and Faber, 2003), p. 596.

parents can feel as much pity and terror for a mother and baby seen in a newspaper or a television screen as for a threatened child of their own.

It does not follow, however, that a poem of first-hand witness will necessarily be better—more moving because more focused—than one of second-hand witness. Tennyson did not see the Charge of the Light Brigade (60) other than with his mind's eye, but his lifelong absorption in Arthurian legend and chivalry enabled him to take his place, imaginatively, with the 'Noble six hundred'. He feels—and enables us to feel—fury, and horror, and pity, and amazed admiration. Thomas Hardy did not see the Boer War burial party 'throw in Drummer Hodge, to rest / Uncoffined—just as found', but his lifelong absorption in the little world of Wessex enabled him to take his place, imaginatively, at the boy's graveside:

> Young Hodge the Drummer never knew—
> Fresh from his Wessex home—
> The meaning of the broad Karoo,
>   The Bush, the dusty loam,
> And why uprose to nightly view
>   Strange stars amid the gloam.

There is no fury in Hardy's 'Drummer Hodge' (88), but only profound pity and sadness—as for the son he never had. These poems of second-hand witness have an immediacy and power equal to any of first-hand witness, being the work of great poets, each with a lifelong imaginative investment in his subject. But such poems are rare. The second-hand testimony of lesser poets, lacking such investment, is seldom impressive and often embarrassing.

For demographic and social-historical reasons, the ratio of poets to other servicemen and women serving in Vietnam was less than in either world war. Most American intellectuals disapproved of the Vietnam War, and men of military age, particularly white men of military age, could avoid conscription by signing up for university education. And many did. The ratio of Stateside poets to battlefield poets was, therefore, greater than in either world war. There were hundreds of armchair poets pretending, like Lowell, to first-hand witness and/or degrees of moral commitment to which they were not entitled. Few were as good as Lowell, and collectively they deserved the savage rebuke offered by one front-line veteran of the Second World War, Anthony Hecht. Hecht wrote of one such (fortunately unidentified) armchair poet:

> Here lies fierce Strephon, whose poetic rage
> Lashed out on Vietnam from page and stage;

Whereby from basements of Bohemia he
Rose to the lofts of sweet celebrity,
Being, by Fortune, (our Eternal Whore)
One of the few to profit by that war,
A fate he shared—it bears much thinking on—
With certain persons at the Pentagon.[3]

The knock-out punch of the last line should not blind us to the lightning jab of the first: 'Here *lies* fierce Strephon'. Is he lying in the grave or telling lies, or both? The fury driving this poem is directed, I assume, not at a Stateside poet bearing true witness to the impact of the war on America, but one pretending to first-hand witness of combat in Vietnam. Hecht's rebuke comes with the moral authority of a poet burdened with the responsibility of bearing witness to the ultimate brutality of the Second World War. He served with the Infantry Division that discovered Flossenburg, an annex of Buchenwald, an experience that changed his life and his poetry.

The charge against a poem like Lowell's 'Women, Children, Babies, Cows, Cats' is that, far from shocking an exposed nerve, it has the numbing effect of second-hand journalism, thereby contributing to the insensitive apathy that enables us to turn, unmoved, from our newspaper's coverage of disaster to that of a football match. Hecht's rebuke to 'fierce Strephon' points up the further disturbing fact that many of those protesting against the war made money from appearances on 'page and stage'.

The situation and the poetry of the combatant 'Vets' could not have been more different. Their poems of first-hand experience often have a raw power, but I know of none that lives in the memory like Hecht's 'More Light! More Light!' (253). A problem for many American poets then aspiring to be war poets was that, rightly perceiving it to be an unjust war, they could not participate as servicemen or women; and lacking first-hand experience, could not write convincingly of the war 'on the ground'. Given some of their trumpeted expressions of moral commitment to the anti-war cause, it is perhaps surprising that none of them felt strongly enough to follow the example of W. H. Auden who, in January 1937, prompted a banner headline of the *Daily Worker*: 'FAMOUS POET TO DRIVE AMBULANCE IN SPAIN.' Explaining his decision to a friend, he wrote: 'I shall probably be a bloody bad soldier but how can I speak to/for them without becoming one?'[4]

[3] Anthony Hecht, *Anthony Hecht in Conversation with Philip Hoy* (Oxford: Between the Lines, 1999), p. 77.
[4] W. H. Auden, quoted in E. R. Dodds, *Missing Persons* (Oxford: Clarendon Press, 1977), p. 133.

One American poet *did* follow Auden's example. John Balaban went to Vietnam, but not as an ambulance-driver. He went as a Conscientious Objector to work in an orphanage (for children orphaned by his country's war), learnt Vietnamese, and stayed after the war to teach in a Vietnamese university. His poems of those years have a fine grain, a specificity of detail, rare in the many poems bearing first-hand witness to an armchair reading of newspapers or the watching of television news. As with the war poems of earlier wars, many of Balaban's best were written after the guns had fallen silent, most notably 'In Celebration of Spring' (280). That poem speaks of 'Our Asian war' and, of course, it *was* an American war, but not all its poets were American. Britain had its 'Stateside' contingent of armchair witnesses, and one— so far as I am aware, only one—poet-witness to the war on the ground: James Fenton. In the 1970s, Fenton was a freelance reporter in Indo-China and a foreign correspondent in Germany for the *Guardian*. Like Hecht a poet of the School of Auden, his German experience fuelled one of the great English-language poems of the holocaust. *A German Requiem*.[5] This was published in 1981, the same year as one of the great English-language poems of the South-East Asian wars, his 'Dead Soldiers' (282). The power and poignancy of each derives from Fenton's first-hand experience of human suffering, but the poignancy is sharpened by his deployment of grimly comic detail and a refusal to lapse into mawkish solemnity.

What do these and other war poems achieve? In that their subject is tragedy, they can—when made with passion and precision—move us (as Aristotle said) to pity and terror; also, I suggest, to a measure of fury. And just as we go to a performance of Shakespeare's *King Lear* or Britten's *War Requiem* for pleasure, we return (or at least I return) to Homer or Owen or Auden for the pleasurable satisfaction that masterpieces afford.

In the short term, one must doubt whether the poems about Vietnam had any significant effect on the course of the war. Certainly the (much better) poems of 1914–18 and 1939–45 had no significant effect on the course of the two World Wars. In the longer term, however, war poems *have* through history had a significant effect in shaping their societies' attitudes to warfare. The epics of heroic ages—*The Iliad, Beowulf*—encouraged the pursuit of glory with their celebration of courage and skilful swordplay. Over the centuries, all that changed. More British poems of the First World War confirmed 'The Old Lie:

---

[5] James Fenton, *The Memory of War* (Edinburgh: The Salamander Press, 1982), pp. 9–19.

Dulce et decorum est/Pro patria mori' than challenged it; but, with few exceptions, they have been relegated to the dustbin of history. The poets whose work has survived sing a very different song: one that has played a significant part in introducing subsequent generations to the realities of modern warfare.

The poems of the Second World War have had less impact—not because they were less good, but because the reading public has become increasingly attuned to prose, and because the Word (prose as well as verse) has increasingly lost ground to the Image. Our knowledge of the wars in Iraq and Afghanistan derived as much from newspaper and television images as from the spoken or written word. Many poems from or about those wars have been published on both sides of the Atlantic and beyond, but all the precedents suggest that the definitive poems from those conflicts have yet to be written—with, I suggest, one exception, Peter Wyton's 'Unmentioned in Dispatches' (289). As and when others emerge, I believe they are as likely to come from the hand of a frontline medic or war correspondent as from a professional soldier.

I am grateful to the Oxford University Press for commissioning me to recruit reinforcements; and to Fran Brearton, Sandie Byrne, Subarno Chattarji, Santanu Das, Hannah Field, Peter and Sian France, Margit Kail, Tim Kendall, Nancy Macky, Carol O'Brien, and Mary Jo Salter for their help and advice.

NOTE ON DATES USED

In this anthology, the date of composition, where that can be established, is given in italics at the end of the poem (ranged right); where that date is unknown, the date of first book publication is given in roman (ranged left).

Wolfson College, Oxford, 2014

THE BIBLE

from *The Book of Exodus*

Then sang Moses and the children of Israel this song unto the Lord, and spake, saying, I will sing unto the Lord, for he hath triumphed gloriously: the horse and his rider hath he thrown into the sea.

The Lord is my strength and song, and he is become my salvation: he is my God, and I will prepare him an habitation: my father's God, and I will exalt him.

The Lord is a man of war: the Lord is his name.

Pharaoh's chariots and his host hath he cast into the sea: his chosen captains also are drowned in the Red sea.

The depths have covered them: they sank into the bottom as a stone.

Thy right hand, O Lord, is become glorious in power: thy right hand, O Lord, hath dashed in pieces the enemy.

And in the greatness of thine excellency thou hast overthrown them that rose up against thee: thou sentest forth thy wrath, which consumed them as stubble.

And with the blast of thy nostrils the waters were gathered together, the floods stood upright as an heap and the depths were congealed in the heart of the sea.

The enemy said, I will pursue, I will overtake, I will divide the spoil; my lust shall be satisfied upon them; I will draw my sword, my hand shall destroy them.

Thou didst blow with thy wind, the sea covered them: they sank as lead in the mighty waters.

Who is like unto thee, O Lord, among the Gods? who is like thee, glorious in holiness, fearful in praises, doing wonders?

Thou stretchedst out thy right hand, the earth swallowed them.

Thou in thy mercy hast led forth the people which thou hast redeemed: thou hast guided them in thy strength unto thy holy habitation.

The people shall hear, and be afraid: sorrow shall take hold on the inhabitants of Palestina.

Then the dukes of Edon shall be amazed; the mighty men of Moab, trembling shall take hold upon them; all the inhabitants of Canaan shall melt away.

Fear and dread shall fall upon them; by the greatness of thine arm they shall be as still as a stone; till thy people pass over, O Lord, till the people pass over, which thou hast purchased.

Thou shalt bring them in, and plant them in the mountain of thine inheritance, in the place, O Lord, which thou hast made for thee to dwell in, in the Sanctuary, O Lord, which thy hands have established.

The Lord shall reign for ever and ever.

Translated from the Hebrew by William Tyndale

2   from *The Second Book of Samuel*

The beauty of Israel is slain upon thy high places: how are the mighty fallen!

Tell it not in Gath, publish it not in the streets of Askelon; lest the daughters of the Philistines rejoice, lest the daughters of the uncircumcised triumph.

Ye mountains of Gilboa, let there be no dew, neither let there be rain, upon you, nor fields of offerings: for there the shield of the mighty is vilely cast away, the shield of Saul, as though he had not been anointed with oil.

From the blood of the slain, from the fat of the mighty, the bow of Jonathan turned not back, and the sword of Saul returned not empty.

Saul and Jonathan were lovely and pleasant in their lives, and in their death they were not divided: they were swifter than eagles, they were stronger than lions.

Ye daughters of Israel, weep over Saul, who clothed you in scarlet, with other delights, who put on ornaments of gold upon your apparel.

How are the mighty fallen in the midst of the battle! O Jonathan, thou wast slain in thine high places.

I am distressed for thee, my brother Jonathan: very pleasant hast thou been unto me: thy love to me was wonderful, passing the love of women.

How are the mighty fallen, and the weapons of war perished!

Translated from the Hebrew by William Tyndale

HOMER

c.900 BC

3   from *The Iliad*, book 16

Zeus who gathers cloud said: 'Come, dear Phoebus,
wipe away the blood mantling Sarpedon;
take him up, out of the play of spears,
a long way off, and wash him in the river,
anoint him with ambrosia, put ambrosial
clothing on him. Then have him conveyed
by those escorting spirits quick as wind,
sweet Sleep and Death, who are twin brothers. These
will set him down in the rich broad land of Lycia,
and there his kin and friends may bury him
with tomb and stone, the trophies of the dead.'
    Attentive to his father, Lord Apollo
went down the foothills of Ida to the field
and lifted Prince Sarpedon clear of it.
He bore him far and bathed him in the river,
scented him with ambrosia, put ambrosial
clothing on him, then had him conveyed
by those escorting spirits quick as wind,
sweet Sleep and Death, who are twin brothers. These
returned him to the rich broad land of Lycia.

from *The Iliad*, book 22

Achilles with wild fury in his heart
pulled in upon his chest his beautiful shield—
his helmet with four burnished metal ridges
nodding above it, and the golden crest
Hephaestus locked there tossing in the wind.
Conspicuous as the evening star that comes,
amid the first in heaven, at fall of night,
and stands most lovely in the west, so shone
in sunlight the fine-pointed spear
Achilles poised in his right hand, with deadly
aim at Hector, at the skin where most
it lay exposed. But nearly all was covered
by the bronze gear he took from slain Patroclus,
showing only, where his collarbones
divided neck and shoulders, the bare throat
where the destruction of a life is quickest.
Here, then, as the Trojan charged, Achilles
drove his point straight through the tender neck,
but did not cut the windpipe, leaving Hector
able to speak and to respond. He fell
aside into the dust. And Prince Achilles
now exulted:

        'Hector, had you thought
that you could kill Patroclus and be safe?
Nothing to dread from me; I was not there.
All childishness. Though distant then, Patroclus,
comrade in arms was greater far than he—
and it is I who had been left behind
that day beside the deepsea ships who now
have made your knees give way. The dogs and kites
will rip your body. His will lie in honour
when the Achaeans give him funeral.'

Hector, barely whispering, replied:

'I beg you by your soul and by your parents,
do not let the dogs feed on me
in your encampment by the ships. Accept
the bronze and gold my father will provide
as gifts, my father and her ladyship
my mother. Let them have my body back,

4

so that our men and women may accord me
decency of fire when I am dead.'

Achilles the great runner scowled and said:

'Beg me no beggary by soul or parents,
whining dog! Would god my passion drove me
to slaughter you and eat you raw, you've caused
such agony to me! No man exists
who could defend you from the carrion pack—
not if they spread for me ten times your ransom,
twenty times, and promise more as well;
aye, not if Priam, son of Dardanus,
tells them to buy you for your weight in gold!
You'll have no bed of death, nor will you be
laid out and mourned by her who gave you birth.
Dogs and birds will have you, every scrap.'

Then at the point of death Lord Hector said:

'I see you now for what you are. No chance
to win you over. Iron in your breast
your heart is. Think a bit, though: this may be
a thing the gods in anger hold against you
on that day when Paris and Apollo
destroy you at the Gates, great as you are.'

Even as he spoke, the end came, and death hid him;
spirit from body fluttered to undergloom,
bewailing fate that made him leave his youth
and manhood in the world. And as he died
Achilles spoke again. He said:

'Die, make an end. I shall accept my own
whenever Zeus and the other gods desire.'

At this he pulled his spearhead from the body,
laying it aside, and stripped
the bloodstained shield and cuirass from his shoulders.
Other Achaeans hastened round to see
Hector's fine body and his comely face,
and no one came who did not stab the body.
Glancing at one another they would say:

'Now Hector has turned vulnerable, softer
than when he put the torches to the ships!'

5

And he who said this would inflict a wound.
When the great master of pursuit, Achilles,
had the body stripped, he stood among them,
saying swiftly:
                          'Friends, my lords and captains,
of Argives, now that the gods at last have let me
bring to earth this man who wrought
havoc among us—more than all the rest—
come, we'll offer battle around the city,
to learn the intentions of the Trojans now.
Will they give up their strongpoint at this loss?
Can they fight on, though Hector's dead?
                                                        But wait:
why do I ponder, why take up these questions?
Down by the ships Patroclus' body lies
unwept, unburied. I shall not forget him
while I can keep my feet among the living.
If in the dead world they forget the dead,
I say there, too, I shall remember him,
my friend. Men of Achaea, lift a song!
Down to the ships we go, and take this body,
our glory. We have beaten Hector down,
to whom as to a god the Trojans prayed.'

Indeed, he had in mind for Hector's body
outrage and shame. Behind both feet he pierced
the tendons, heel to ankle. Rawhide cords
he drew through both and lashed them to his chariot,
letting the man's head trail. Stepping aboard,
bearing the great trophy of the arms,
he shook the reins, and whipped the team ahead
into a willing run. A dustcloud rose
above the furrowing body; the dark tresses
flowed behind, and the head so princely once
lay back in dust. Zeus gave him to his enemies
to be defiled in his own fatherland.
So his whole head was blackened. Looking down,
his mother tore her braids, threw off her veil,
and wailed, heartbroken to behold her son.
Piteously his father groaned, and round him
lamentation spread throughout the town,
most like the clamour to be heard if Ilium's
towers, top to bottom, seethed in flames.
They barely stayed the old man, mad with grief,

6

from passing through the gates. Then in the mire
he rolled, and begged them all, each man by name:

'Relent, friends. It is hard; but let me go
out of the city to the Achaean ships.
I'll make my plea to that demonic heart.
He may feel shame before his peers, or pity
my old age. His father, too, is old,
Peleus, who brought him up to be a scourge
to Trojans, cruel to all, but most to me,
so many of my sons in flower of youth
he cut away. And, though I grieve, I cannot
mourn them all as much as I do one,
for whom my grief will take me to the grave—
and that is Hector. Why could he not have died
where I might hold him? In our weeping, then,
his mother, now so destitute, and I
might have had surfeit and relief of tears.'

These were the words of Priam as he wept,
and all his people groaned. Then in her turn
Hecabe led the women in lamentation:

'Child, I am lost now. Can I bear my life
after the death of suffering your death?
You were my pride in all my nights and days,
pride of the city, pillar to the Trojans
and Trojan women. Everyone looked to you
as though you were a god, and rightly so.
You were their greatest glory while you lived.
Now your doom and death have come upon you.'

These were her mournful words. But Hector's lady
still knew nothing; no one came to tell her
of Hector's stand outside the gates. She wove
upon her loom, deep in the lofty house,
a double purple web with rose design.
Calling her maids in waiting,
she ordered a big cauldron on a tripod
set on the hearthfire, to provide a bath
for Hector when he came home from the fight.
Poor wife, how far removed from baths he was

7

she could not know, as at Achilles' hands
Athena brought him down.
                     Then from the tower
she heard a wailing and a distant moan.
Her knees shook, and she let her shuttle fall,
and called out to her maids again:
                          'Come here.
Two must follow me, to see this action.
I heard my husband's queenly mother cry.
I feel my heart rise, throbbing in my throat.
My knees are like stone under me. Some blow
is coming home to Priam's sons and daughters.
Ah, could it never reach my ears! I die
of dread that Achilles may have cut off Hector,
blocked my bold husband from the city wall,
to drive him down the plain alone! By now
he may have ended Hector's deathly pride.
He never kept his place amid the chariots
but drove ahead. He would not be outdone
by anyone in courage.'

                    Saying this, she ran
like a madwoman through the megaron,
her heart convulsed. Her maids kept at her side.
On reaching the great tower and the soldiers,
Andromache stood gazing from the wall
and saw him being dragged before the city.
Chariot horses at a brutal gallop
pulled the torn body toward the decked ships.
Blackness of night covered her eyes; she fell
backward swooning, sighing out her life,
and let her shining headdress fall, her hood
and diadem, her plaited band and veil
that Aphrodite once had given her,
on that day when, from Eetion's house,
for a thousand bridal gifts, Lord Hector led her.
Now, at her side, kinswomen of her lord
supported her among them, dazed and faint
to the point of death. But when she breathed again
and her stunned heart recovered, in a burst
of sobbing she called out among the women:

8

'Hector! Here is my desolation. Both
had this in store from birth—from yours in Troy
in Priam's palace, mine by wooded Placus
at Thebe in the home of Eetion,
my father, who took care of me in childhood,
a man cursed by fate, a fated daughter.
How I could wish I never had been born!
Now under earth's roof to the house of Death
you go your way and leave me here, bereft,
lonely, in anguish without end. The child
we wretches had is still in infancy;
you cannot be a pillar to him, Hector,
now you are dead, nor he to you. And should
this boy escape the misery of the war,
there will be toil and sorrow for him later,
as when strangers move his boundary stones.
The day that orphans him will leave him lonely,
downcast in everything, cheeks wet with tears,
in hunger going to his father's friends
to tug at one man's cloak, another's khiton.
Some will be kindly: one may lift a cup
to wet his lips at least, though not his throat;
but from the board some child with living parents
gives him a push, a slap, with biting words:
"Outside, you there! Your father is not with us
here at our feast!" And the boy Astyanax
will run to his forlorn mother. Once he fed
on marrow only and the fat of lamb,
high on his father's knees. And when sleep came
to end his play, he slept in a nurse's arms,
brimful of happiness, in a soft bed.
But now he'll know sad days and many of them,
missing his father. "Lord of the lower town"
the Trojans call him. They know, you alone,
Lord Hector, kept their gates and their long walls.
Beside the beaked ships now, far from your kin,
the blowflies' maggots in a swarm will eat you
naked, after the dogs have had their fill.
Ah, there are folded garments in your chambers,
delicate and fine, of women's weaving.
These, by heaven, I'll burn to the last thread
in blazing fire! They are no good to you,
they cannot cover you in death. So let them

9

go, let them be burnt as an offering
from Trojans and their women in your honour.'

Thus she mourned, and the women wailed in answer.

Translated from the Greek by Robert Fitzgerald

SIMONIDES
c.556–*c*.468 BC

4   *Thermopylae**

Go tell the Spartans, thou that passest by,
That here, obedient to their laws, we lie.

Translated from the Greek by William Lisle Bowles

ANONYMOUS
4th century BC

5   *Hymn to the Fallen*

'We hold our flat shields, we wear our jerkins of hide;
The axles of our chariots touch, our short swords meet.
Standards darken the sun, the foe roll on like clouds;
Arrows fall thick, the warriors press forward.
They have overrun our ranks, they have crossed our line;
The trace-horse on the left is dead, the one on the right is wounded.
The fallen horses block our wheels, our chariot is held fast;
We grasp our jade drum-sticks, we beat the rolling drums.'

Heaven decrees their fall, the dread Powers are angry;
The warriors are all dead, they lie in the open fields.

---

* At Thermopylae, a narrow pass between mountain and sea, 6,000 Greeks including 300 Spartans fought off a vast army of invading Persians in 480 BC.

They set out, but shall not enter; they went but shall not come back.
The plains are empty and wide, the way home is long.
Their tall swords are at their waist, their bows are under their arm;
Though their heads were severed their spirit could not be subdued.
They that fought so well—in death are warriors still;
Stubborn and steadfast to the end, they could not be dishonoured.
Their bodies perished in the fight; but the magic of their souls is
    strong—
Captains among the ghosts, heroes among the Dead!

Translated from the Chinese by Arthur Waley

VIRGIL

70–19 BC

6   from *The Aeneid*, book 12

And now Aeneas charges straight at Turnus.
He brandishes a shaft huge as a tree,
and from his savage breast he shouts: 'Now what
delay is there? Why, Turnus, do you still
draw back from battle? It is not for us
to race against each other, but to meet
with cruel weapons, hand to hand. Go, change
yourself into all shapes; by courage and
by craft collect whatever help you can;
take wing, if you so would, toward the steep stars
or hide yourself within the hollow earth.'
But Turnus shakes his head: 'Your burning words,
ferocious Trojan, do not frighten me;
it is the gods alone who terrify me,
and Jupiter, my enemy.' He says
no more, but as he looks about he sees
a giant stone, an ancient giant stone
that lay at hand, by chance, upon the plain,
set there as boundary mark between the fields
to keep the farmers free from border quarrels.
And twice-six chosen men with bodies such
as earth produces now could scarcely lift
that stone upon their shoulders. But the hero,

anxious and running headlong, snatched the boulder;
reaching full height, he hurled it at the Trojan.
But Turnus does not know if it is he
himself who runs or goes or lifts or throws
that massive rock; his knees are weak; his blood
congeals with cold. The stone itself whirls through
the empty void but does not cross all of
the space between; it does not strike a blow.
Just as in dreams of night, when languid rest
has closed our eyes, we seem in vain to wish
to press on down a path, but as we strain,
we falter, weak; our tongues can say nothing,
the body loses its familiar force,
no voice, no word, can follow: so whatever
courage he calls upon to find a way,
the cursed goddess keeps success from Turnus.
The shifting feelings overtake his heart;
he looks in longing at the Latin ranks
and at the city, and he hesitates,
afraid; he trembles at the coming spear.
He does not know how he can save himself,
what power he has to charge his enemy;
he cannot see his chariot anywhere;
he cannot see the charioteer, his sister.
In Turnus' wavering Aeneas sees
his fortune; he holds high the fatal shaft;
he hurls it far with all his body's force.
No boulder ever catapulted from
siege engine sounded so, no thunderbolt
had ever burst with such a roar. The spear
flies on like a black whirlwind, carrying
its dread destruction, ripping through the border
of Turnus' corselet and the outer rim
of Turnus' seven-plated shield; hissing,
it penetrates his thigh. The giant Turnus,
struck, falls to earth; his knees bend under him.
All the Rutulians leap up with a groan,
and all the mountain slopes around re-echo;
tall forests, far and near, return that voice.
Then humble, suppliant, he lifts his eyes
and, stretching out his hand, entreating, cries:
'I have indeed deserved this; I do not
appeal against it; use your chance. But if

there is a thought of a dear parent's grief
that now can touch you, then I beg you, pity
old Daunus—in Anchises you had such
a father—send me back or, if you wish,
send back my lifeless body to my kin.
For you have won, and the Ausonians
have seen me, beaten, stretch my hands; Lavinia
is yours; then do not press your hatred further.'

Aeneas stood, ferocious in his armour;
his eyes were restless and he stayed his hand;
and as he hesitated, Turnus' words
began to move him more and more—until
high on the Latin's shoulder he made out
the luckless belt of Pallas, of the boy
whom Turnus had defeated, wounded, stretched
upon the battlefield, from whom he took
this fatal sign to wear upon his back,
this girdle glittering with familiar studs.
And when his eyes drank in this plunder, this
memorial of brutal grief, Aeneas,
aflame with rage—his wrath was terrible—
cried: 'How can you who wear the spoils of my
dear comrade now escape me? It is Pallas
who strikes, who sacrifices you, who takes
this payment from your shameless blood.' Relentless,
he sinks his sword into the chest of Turnus.
His limbs fell slack with chill; and with a moan
his life, resentful, fled to Shades below.

Translated from the Latin by Allen Mandelbaum

HORACE
65–8 BC

7   from *The Odes*

(1)

Disciplined in the school of hard campaigning,
Let the young Roman study how to bear

Rigorous difficulties without complaining,
And camp with danger in the open air,

And with his horse and lance become the scourge of
Wild Parthians. From the ramparts of the town
Of the warring king, the princess on the verge of
Womanhood with her mother shall look down

And sigh, 'Ah, royal lover, still a stranger
To battle, do not recklessly excite
That lion, savage to touch, whom murderous anger
Drives headlong through the thickest of the fight.'

The glorious and the decent way of dying
Is for one's country. Run, and death will seize
You no less surely. The young coward, flying,
Gets his quietus in the back and knees.

Unconscious of mere loss of votes and shining
With honours that the mob's breath cannot dim,
True worth is not found raising or resigning
The fasces at the wind of popular whim.

To those who do not merit death, exploring
Ways barred to ordinary men, true worth
Opens a path to heaven and spurns on soaring
Pinions the trite crowds and the clogging earth.

Trusty discretion too shall be rewarded
Duly. I will not suffer a tell-tale
Of Ceres' sacred mysteries to be boarded
Under my roof or let my frail boat sail

With him; for, slighted, often God confuses
The innocent with the evil-doer's fate.
Yet Vengeance, with one lame foot, seldom loses
Track of the outlaw, though she sets off late.

(II)

Pompeius, chief of all my friends, with whom
I often ventured to the edge of doom
    When Brutus led our line,
    With whom, aided by wine

And garlands and Arabian spikenard,
I killed those afternoons that died so hard—
    Who has new-made you, then,
    A Roman citizen

And given you back your native gods and weather?
We two once beat a swift retreat together
    Upon Philippi's field,
    When I dumped my poor shield,

And courage cracked, and the strong men who frowned
Fiercest were felled, chins to the miry ground.
    But I, half-dead with fear,
    Was wafted, airborne, clear

Of the enemy lines, wrapped in a misty blur
By Mercury, not sucked back, as you were,
    From safety and the shore
    By the wild tide of war.

Pay Jove his feast, then. In my laurel's shade
Stretch out the bones that long campaigns have made
    Weary. Your wine's been waiting
    For years: no hesitating!

Fill up the polished goblets to the top
With memory-drowning Massic! Slave, unstop
    The deep-mouthed shells that store
    Sweet-smelling oil and pour!

Who'll run to fit us out with wreaths and find
Myrtle and parsley, damp and easily twined?
    Who'll win the right to be
    Lord of the revelry

By dicing highest? I propose to go
As mad as a Thracian. It's sheer joy to throw
    Sanity overboard
    When a dear friend's restored.

Translated from the Latin by James Michie

ANEIRIN
6th century

from *The Gododdin**

Men went to Gododdin, laughing and chaffing,
Savage in battle, lances aligned.
A brief year in peace they stay quiet.
Bodgad's son, his hand-craft wrought slaughter.
Though they go to churches for shriving,
The old and the young, the bold and the meek,
True is the tale, death confronted them.
Men went to Gododdin, laughter-loving.
Assailants in a war-host, keen for combat,
They would slaughter with swords, in short order.
A pillar in combat, bountiful Rheithfyw.

Men went to Catraeth, in high spirits their war-band.
Pale mead their portion, it was poison.
Three hundred under orders to fight.
And after celebration, silence.
Though they go to churches for shriving,
True is the tale, death confronted them.

Men went to Catraeth, mead-nourished war-host,
Strong, vigorous – wrong should I not praise them –
With great dark-socketed crimson blades.
Close-ranked, stubborn, the warhounds fought.
Of Brennych's war-band I'd have thought it a burden:
Should I leave one in human form alive.
I lost a comrade, I was steadfast,
Ready man in combat, hard for me to leave him.
The hero sought no father-in-law's dowry,
Cian's young son from Maen Gwyngwn.

Men went to Catraeth at dawn:
Their fears had been left behind.

---

* Sometime around 600 AD, Mynyddawg Mwynfawr, a king of the North British people known as the Gododdin, assembled 300 Celtic warriors and feasted them for a year at his court in Edinburgh, before leading them south. At Catterick in Yorkshire they encountered the English hosts and in the ensuing battle all, or all but a handful, were killed.

Three hundred clashed with ten thousand.
He stains spears ruddy with blood,
Most valiant bulwark in battle,
Before Mynyddawg Mwynfawr's war-band.

Men went to Catraeth at dawn:
Their mettle shortened their lives.
They drank mead, yellow, sweet, ensnaring;
Many a singer for a year was merry.
Crimson their swords, let their blades stay uncleansed,
    Lime-white shields and four-sided spearpoints,
Before Mynyddawg Mwynfawr's war-band.

.   .   .   .

Men went to Catraeth, they were far-famed:
Wine and mead from gold cups was their drink
For a year, according to noble custom,
Three men and three score and three hundred, gold-torqued.
Of those who went forth after lavish drink
But three won free through battle prowess:
Aeron's two war-hounds and Cynon came back,
And I, soaked in blood, for my praise-song's sake.

Translated from the Welsh by Joseph P. Clancy

RIHAKU

8th century

9   *Lament of the Frontier Guard*

By the North Gate, the wind blows full of sand,
Lonely from the beginning of time until now!
Trees fall, the grass goes yellow with autumn.
I climb the towers and towers
        to watch out the barbarous land:
Desolate castle, the sky, the wide desert.
There is no wall left to this village.
Bones white with a thousand frosts,
High heaps, covered with trees and grass;
Who brought this to pass?
Who has brought the flaming imperial anger?

Who has brought the army with drums and with kettle-drums?
Barbarous kings.
A gracious spring, turned to blood-ravenous autumn,
A turmoil of wars-men, spread over the middle kingdom,
Three hundred and sixty thousand,
And sorrow, sorrow like rain.
Sorrow to go, and sorrow, sorrow returning.
Desolate, desolate fields,
And no children of warfare upon them,
      No longer the men for offence and defence.
Ah, how shall you know the dreary sorrow at the North Gate,
With Rihaku's name forgotten,
And we guardsmen fed to the tigers.

Translated from the Chinese by Ezra Pound

ANONYMOUS

8th century

10   *The Finnesburh Fragment**

        '...the gables are not burning.'
Then the young king spoke, a novice in battle:
'This light is not the light of dawn; no fiery dragon flies overhead;
The gables of this hall are not lit up with licking flames;
But men draw near with shining weapons. The birds of battle screech,
The grey wolf howls, the spear rattles,
Shield answers shaft. The pale moon wanders
On her way below the clouds, gleaming; evil deeds will now be done
Provoking pitched battle.
Wake up now, my warriors!
Grasp your shields, steel yourselves,
Step forward and be brave!'
So many a thane, ornamented in gold, buckled his sword-belt.

---

* The Finnesburh fragment recounts a portion of the tale of Finn and Hildeburh sung by the minstrel in the Old English epic *Beowulf*.

Then the stout warriors, Sigeferth and Eaha
Strode to one door and unsheathed their swords;
Ordlaf and Guthlaf went to guard the other,
And Hengest himself followed in their footsteps.
When he saw this, Guthere said to Garulf
That he would be unwise to go to the hall doors
In the first fury of the onslaught, risking his precious life,
For Sigeferth the strong was set upon his death.
But Garulf, a hero of great heart,
Shouted out, 'Who holds the door?'
'I am Sigeferth, a warrior of the Secgan
And a well-known campaigner; I've lived through many conflicts,
Many stern trials. Here, in strife with me,
You'll discover your fate, victory or defeat.'
Then the din of battle broke out in the hall;
The hollow shield, defender of the body, was doomed to disintegrate
In the hero's hand; the hall floor boomed.
Then Garulf, the son of Guthlaf, gave his life
In the fight, first of all the warriors
Living in that land, and many heroes lay prostrate beside him.
A crowd of pale faces fell to the earth. The raven wheeled,
Dusky, dark brown. The gleaming swords so shone
It seemed as if all Finnesburh were in flames.
I have never heard, before or since, of sixty triumphant warriors
Who bore themselves more bravely in the thick of battle.
And never did retainers repay their prince more handsomely
For his gift of glowing mead than did those men repay Hnæf.
They fought five days and not one of the followers
Fell, but they held the doors firmly.
Then Guthere retired, worn out and wounded;
He said that his armour was almost useless,
His corselet broken, his helmet burst open.
The guardian of those people asked him at once
How well the warriors had survived their wounds
Or which of the young men....

Translated from the Anglo-Saxon by Kevin Crossley-Holland

ANONYMOUS

10th century

*The Battle of Brunanburh**

I

Athelstan King,
Lord among Earls,
Bracelet-bestower and
Baron of Barons,
He with his brother,
Edmund Atheling,
Gaining a lifelong
Glory in battle,
Slew with the sword-edge
There by Brunanburh,
Brake the shield-wall,
Hewed the lindenwood,
Hacked the battleshield,
Sons of Edward with hammered brands.

II

Theirs was a greatness
Got from their Grandsires—
Theirs that so often in
Strife with their enemies
Struck for their hoards and their hearths and their homes.

III

Bowed the spoiler,
Bent the Scotsman,
Fell the shipcrews
Doomed to the death.
All the field with blood of the fighters
Flowed, from when first the great
Sun-star of morningtide,

* At the Battle of Brunanburh in 937, King Athelstan's English army defeated the Vikings, supported by the forces of Scotland and Wales.

Lamp of the Lord God
Lord everlasting,
Glode over earth till the glorious creature
Sank to his setting.

IV

There lay many a man
Marred by the javelin,
Men of the Northland
Shot over shield.
There was the Scotsman
Weary of war.

V

We the West-Saxons,
Long as the daylight
Lasted, in companies
Troubled the track of the host that we hated.
Grimly with swords that were sharp from the grindstone,
Fiercely we hacked at the flyers before us.

VI

Mighty the Mercian,
Hard was his hand-play,
Sparing not any of
Those that with Anlaf,
Warriors over the
Weltering waters
Borne in the bark's-bosom,
Drew to this island:
Doomed to the death.

VII

Five young kings put asleep by the sword-stroke,
Seven strong Earls of the army of Anlaf
Fell on the war-field, numberless numbers,
Shipmen and Scotsmen.

VIII

Then the Norse leader,
Dire was his need of it,
Few were his following,
Fled to his warship:
Fleeted his vessel to sea with the king in it,
Saving his life on the fallow flood.

IX

Also the crafty one,
Constantinus,
Crept to his North again,
Hoar-headed hero!

X

Slender warrant had
He to be proud of
The welcome of war-knives—
He that was reft of his
Folk and his friends that had
Fallen in conflict,
Leaving his son too
Lost in the carnage,
Mangled to morsels,
A youngster in war!

XI

Slender reason had
He to be glad of
The clash of the war-glaive—
Traitor and trickster
And spurner of treaties—
He nor had Anlaf
With armies so broken
A reason for bragging
That they had the better
In perils of battle
On places of slaughter—
The struggle of standards,
The rush of the javelins,

The crash of the charges,
The wielding of weapons—
The play that they played with
The children of Edward.

XII

Then with their nailed prows
Parted the Norsemen, a
Blood-reddened relic of
Javelins over
The jarring breaker, the deep-sea billow,
Shaping their way toward Dyflen again,
Shamed in their souls.

XIII

Also the brethren,
King and Atheling,
Each in his glory,
Went to his own in his own West-Saxonland,
Glad of the war.

XIV

Many a carcase they left to be carrion,
Many a livid one, many a sallow-skin—
Left for the white tailed eagle to tear it, and
Left for the horny-nibbed raven to rend it, and
Gave to the garbaging war-hawk to gorge it, and
That gray beast, the wolf of the weald.

XV

Never had huger
Slaughter of heroes
Slain by the sword-edge—
Such as old writers
Have writ of in histories—
Hapt in this isle, since
Up from the East hither
Saxon and Angle from
Over the broad billow

Broke into Britain with
Haughty war-workers who
Harried the Welshmen, when
Earls that were lured by the
Hunger of glory gat
Hold of the land.

Translated from the Anglo-Saxon by Alfred, Lord Tennyson

ANONYMOUS

11th century

12   *The Battle of Maldon**

                    . . . it was shattered.
Then Byrhtnoth ordered every warrior to dismount,
Let loose his horse and go forward into battle
With faith in his own skills and bravery.
Thus Offa's young son could see for himself
That the earl was no man to suffer slackness.
He sent his best falcon flying from his wrist
To the safety of the forest and strode into the fight;
The boy's behaviour was a testament
That he would not be weak in the turmoil of battle.
Eadric too was firmly resolved to follow his leader
Into the fight. At once he hurried forward
With his spear. He feared no foe
For as long as he could lift his shield
And wield a sword: he kept his word
That he would pierce and parry before his prince.
Then Byrhtnoth began to martial his men.
He rode about, issuing instructions
As to how they should stand firm, not yielding an inch,
And how they should tightly grip their shields
Forgetting their qualms and pangs of fear.

---

* At Maldon in Essex, a small force of East Saxons was cut down by Viking invaders in 991.

And when he had arrayed the warriors' ranks
He dismounted with his escort at a carefully chosen place
Where his finest troops stood prepared for the fight.
Then a spokesman for the Vikings stood on the river bank
And aggressively shouted
A message from the seafarers
To Byrhtnoth, the earl, on the opposite bank.
'The brave seafarers have sent me to say to you
That they will be so good as to let you give gold rings
In return for peace. It is better for you
To buy off our raid with gold
Than that we, renowned for cruelty, should cut you down in battle.
Why destroy one another? If you're good for a certain sum,
We'll settle for peace in exchange for gold.
If you, most powerful over there, agree to this
And wisely decide to disband your men,
Giving gold to the seafarers on their own terms
In return for a truce,
We'll take to the sea with the tribute you pay
And keep our promise of peace.'
Then Byrhtnoth spoke. He grasped his shield
And brandished his slender ashen spear,
Resentful and resolute he shouted his reply:
'Can you hear, you pirate, what these people say?
They will pay you a tribute of whistling spears,
Of deadly darts and proven swords,
Weapons to pay you, pierce, slit and slay you in storming battle.
Listen, messenger! Take back this reply:
Tell your people the unpleasant tidings
That over here there stands a noble earl with his troop—
Guardians of the people and of the country,
The home of Ethelred, my prince—who'll defend this land
To the last ditch. We'll sever the heathens' heads
From their shoulders. It would be much to our shame
If you took our tribute and embarked without battle
Since you've intruded so far
And so rudely into this country.
No! You'll not get your treasure so easily.
The spear's point and the sword's edge, savage battle-play,
Must teach us first that we have to yield tribute.'
Then Byrhtnoth gave word that all his warriors should walk
With their shields to the river bank.

The troops on either side could not get at one another,
For there the flood flowed after the turn of the tide;
The water streams ran together. Waiting seemed like passing years,
Waiting to cross and clash their spears.
The East-Saxons and the Ship-army
Stood beside the River Panta in proud array.
But no warrior could work harm on another
Except by the flight of a feathered arrow.
The tide ebbed; the pirates stood prepared,
Many bold Vikings ready for battle.
Then Byrhtnoth, brave protector of his men, ordered
A warrior, Wulfstan by name, to defend the ford.
He was Ceola's son, outstanding for his courage amongst courageous men
He struck the first seafarer with his spear
Who stepped intrepidly on to the ford.
Two experienced warriors stood with Wulfstan,
Ælfere and Maccus, both brave men.
Nothing could have made them take flight at the ford.
They would have defended it
For as long as they could wield their weapons.
But as it was, the Danes found the dauntless guardians
Of the ford too fierce for their liking. . . .
The hateful strangers began to use guile
And asked if they could cross,
Leading their warriors over the water.
Then, in foolhardy pride, the earl permitted
Those hateful strangers to have access to the ford.
The son of Byrhthelm began to call out
Across the cold water (the warriors listened):
'Now the way is clear for you. Come over to us quickly,
Come to the slaughter. God alone can say
Who of us that fight today will live to fight again.'

Then the wolvish Vikings, avid for slaughter,
Waded to the west across the River Panta;
The seafarers hoisted their shields on high
And carried them over the gleaming water.
Byrhtnoth and his warriors awaited them,
Ready for battle: he ordered his men
To form a phalanx with their shields, and to stand firm
Against the onslaught of the enemy. Then was the battle,
With its chance of glory, about to begin. The time had come
For all the doomed men to fall in the fight.

The clamour began; the ravens wheeled and the eagle
Circled overhead, craving for carrion; there was shouting on earth.
They hurled their spears, hard as files,
And sent sharp darts flying from their hands.
Bow strings were busy, shield parried point,
Bitter was the battle. Brave men fell
On both sides, youths choking in the dust.
Byrhtnoth's sister's son, Wulfmær, was wounded;
Slashed by the sword, he decided
To sleep on the bed of death.
This was violently requited, the Vikings were repaid in kind.
I was told that Eadweard swung his sword
So savagely—a full-blooded blow—
That a fated warrior fell lifeless at his feet.
Byrhtnoth shouted out his thanks to him,
His chamberlain, as soon as he had a chance to do so.
The brave men stood resolute, rock firm.
Each of them eagerly hunted for a way
To be first in with his spear,
Winning with his weapons the life
Of a doomed warrior; the dead sank down to the earth.
But the rest stood unshaken and Byrhtnoth spurred them on,
Inciting each man to fight ferociously
Who wished to gain glory against the Danes.
Then a brave seafarer raised up his spear,
Gripped his shield and advanced towards Byrhtnoth.
The resolute earl advanced towards the churl;
Each had evil designs on the other.
The Viking was the quicker—he hurled his foreign spear
Wounding the lord of the warriors.
Byrhtnoth broke the shaft with the edge of his shield;
The imbedded spear-head sprang out of his wound.
Then he flung his spear in fury
At the proud Viking who dared inflict such pain.
His aim was skilful. The spear
Slit open the warrior's neck.
Thus Byrhtnoth put paid to his enemy's life.
Then, for safety's sake, he swiftly hurled another
Which burst the Viking's breastplate, cruelly wounding him
In the chest; the deadly spear pierced his heart.
The brave earl, Byrhtnoth, was delighted at this;
He laughed out loud and gave thanks to the Lord
That such good fortune had been granted to him.

But one of the seafarers sent a sharp javelin
Speeding from his hand
That pierced Byrhtnoth's body, the noble thane of Ethelred.
By his side stood a young warrior,
Wulfmær by name, Wulfstan's son,
Who without a moment's hesitation
Drew out the blood-red javelin from Byrhtnoth's side
And hurled it back as hard as he could
At the man who had grievously injured his prince.
The sharp point struck home; the Viking sagged, and sank into the dust.
Another seafarer advanced on the earl, meaning to make
Short work of him and snatch away his treasures—
His armour and his rings and his ornamented sword.

Byrhtnoth drew out his sword from its sheath,
Broad-faced and gleaming, and made to slash at the seafarer's corselet,
But his enemy stopped him all too soon,
Savagely striking Byrhtnoth's arm.
The golden-hilted sword dropped from his hand.
He could hold it no longer
Nor wield a weapon of any kind. Then the old warrior
Raised his men's morale with bold words,
Called on his brave companions to do battle again.
He no longer stood firmly on his feet
But swayed, and raised his eyes to heaven:
'O Guardian of the people, let me praise and thank you
For all the real joys I received in this world.
Now, gracious Lord, as never before,
I need Your grace,
That my soul may set out on its journey to You,
O Prince of Angels, that my soul may depart
Into Your power in peace. I pray
That the devils may never destroy it.'
Then the heathens hewed him down
And the two men who stood there supporting him;
Ælfnoth and Wulfmær fell to the dust,
Both gave their lives in defence of their lord.
Then certain cowards beat a hasty retreat:
The sons of Odda were the first to take flight;
Godric fled from the battle, forsaking Byrhtnoth.
Forgetting that his lord had given him often the gift of a horse,
He leapt into the saddle
Of his lord's own horse, most unlawfully,

And both his brothers, Godwine and Godwig,
Galloped beside him; forgetting their duty
They fled from the fight
And saved their lives in the silent wood.
And more men followed than was at all fitting
Had they remembered the former rewards
That the prince had given them, generous presents.
It was just as Offa once said to Byrhtnoth
At an open council in the meeting place,
That many spoke proudly of their prowess
Who would prove unworthy of their words under battle-stress.

So Ethelred's earl, the prince of those people,
Fell; all his hearth-companions
Could see for themselves that their lord lay low.
Then the proud thanes, with the utmost bravery,
Threw themselves once more into the thick of the battle.
They all, without exception, strove to one of two ends—
To avenge their lord or to leave this world.
Ælfwine the son of Ælfric, still a young man,
Shouted encouragement, urging them on.
He rallied them with valiant words:
'Think of all the times we boasted
At the mead-bench, heroes in the hall
Predicting our own bravery in battle.
Now we shall see who meant what he said.
Let me announce my ancestry to one and all:
I come from a mighty family of Mercian stock;
My grandfather was Ealhelm,
A wise ealdorman, well endowed with worldly riches.
No thane shall ever have reason to reproach me
With any desire to desert this troop
And hurry home, now that my prince has been hewn down
In battle. This is the most bitter sorrow of all.
He was my kinsman and my lord.'
Then he went forward into the fight
And pierced a pirate's body with his spear.
The man keeled over, dead,
Killed by Ælfwine's weapon. Again he urged
His friends and companions
To follow him into the fray.
Then Offa spoke and brandished his ash-spear:
'Ælfwine, you've encouraged all the thanes

At exactly the right time. Now that our prince
Is slain, the earl on the earth,
We must all encourage each other
To fight, for as long as we can wield
Our weapons, pierce with our spears,
And lunge and parry with our swords.
Godric, the cowardly son of Odda, has betrayed us all.
When he hurried off towards the woods on our lord's fine horse
He misled many men into believing it was Byrhtnoth himself;
And so they followed him, and here on the field
The phalanx was broken: may fortune frown on him
Whose cowardice has caused this catastrophe.'
Then Leofsunu spoke. He raised his shield
For protection, and replied to Offa:
'I give you my word that I will not retreat
One inch; I shall forge on
And avenge my lord in battle.
Now that he has fallen in the fight
No loyal warrior living at Sturmere
Need reproach me for returning home lordless
In unworthy retreat, for the weapon shall take me,
The iron sword.' He strode forward angrily,
Fighting furiously; he spurned escape.
Then Dunnere spoke and shook his spear;
A lowly churl, he cried out loud
And asked every man to avenge Byrhtnoth's death:
'Whoever intends to avenge our prince
Must not flinch, nor care for his own life.'
Then they hurried forward, heedless of their lives;
The brave followers, fiercely carrying spears,
Fought with great courage, and prayed to God
That they should be allowed to avenge their lord
By killing all his enemies.
The hostage helped them with all his might—
His name was Æscferth, the son of Ecglaf;
He came from a family renowned in Northumbria.
In the fire of battle he did not flinch,
Notching arrow after arrow as quick as he could.
Sometimes he hit a shield, sometimes he pierced a man,
Again and again he inflicted wounds
For as long as he could hold a bow in his hands.

Eadweard the tall, eager and impetuous,
Did not stray from the line of battle. He boasted that he
Would not shrink so much as a footstep,
Or seek safety by flight, now that his lord lay dead.
He smashed the wall of shields, and attacked the seafarers
Worthily avenging his ring-giver's death.
He sold his life dearly in the storm of battle.
And so too did Ætheric, a stalwart companion....
He grappled aggressively and without delay.
The brother of Sibyrht, both he and many others
Split the hollow shields and warded off the seafarers.
The corner of the shield broke and the corselet sang
A terrible song. Then in the turmoil
Offa struck a seafarer; he fell dead at his feet.
But the kinsman of Gadd was killed there too,
Offa was quickly brought down in the battle.
Yet he had kept his promise to his prince;
He fulfilled his former boast to Byrhtnoth, the ring-giver,
That they should either return unhurt, riding to the stronghold
In victory together, or together surrender their lives,
Bleeding from wounds on the battlefield.
He lay near his lord as befits a thane.
Then shields were shattered; the seafarers surged forward,
Embittered by bloodshed. Often a spear
Sank into the body of a fated warrior. Then Wistan advanced,
The son of Thurstan; he fought with the Vikings,
Slew three in the struggling throng
Before he, Wigelm's brave son, was himself brought down.
That was a savage fight; the warriors stood firm
In the struggle. Strong men fell,
Utterly worn out by wounds; the dead dropped to the earth.
The brothers Oswold and Eadweard
Continuously encouraged the companions;
They urged their kinsmen to use
Their weapons without slackening
And endure the stress to the best of their strength.
Byrhtwold grasped his shield and spoke.
He was an old companion. He brandished his ash-spear
And with wonderful courage exhorted the warriors:
'Mind must be the firmer, heart the more fierce,
Courage the greater, as our strength diminishes.
Here lies our leader, dead,
An heroic man in the dust.

He who now longs to escape will lament for ever.
I am old. I will not go from here,
But I mean to lie by the side of my lord,
Lie in the dust with the man I loved so dearly.'
Godric, too, the son of Æthelgar, gave them courage
To continue the fight. Often he let fly his spear,
His deadly javelin, at the Vikings
As he advanced at the head of the host.
He humbled and hewed down until at last he fell himself. . . .

Translated from the Anglo-Saxon by Kevin Crossley-Holland

ANONYMOUS

12th century

13   from *The Song of Roland**

In wrath and grief away the Paynims fly;
Backward to Spain with headlong haste they hie.
The County Roland cannot pursue their flight,
Veillantif's lost, he has no steed to ride;
Will he or nill he, he must on foot abide,
He's turned to aid Archbishop Turpin's plight,
And from his head the gilded helm untied,
Stripped off the hauberk of subtle rings and bright,
And all to pieces has cut the bliaut fine
Wherewith to bandage his wounds that gape so wide.
Then to his breast he clasps and lifts him light
And gently lays him upon the green hill-side,
With fair soft speech entreating on this wise:
'Ah, noble sir, pray give me leave awhile;
These friends of ours, we loved so well in life,
We must not leave them thus lying where they died.
I will go seek them, find, and identify,
And lay them here together in your sight.'

---

* Together with his comrade Oliver and Archbishop Turpin, Roland commanded
Emperor Charlemagne's retreating rearguard in the Pyrenees in 778. Far outnumbered
by the attacking Saracens, Roland and the valiant Franks were all killed, in a battle at the
mountain pass of Roncesvalles.

'Go and return,' the Bishop makes reply;
'Thanks be to God, this field is yours and mine.'

Roland departs and through the field is gone;
Alone he searches the valleys and high rocks.
[And there he finds Ivor, and there Ivon],
Gerier and Gerin, the good companions,
[And Engelier whom Gascony begot];
And he has found Berenger and Oton,
And after finds Anseïs and Samson,
And finds Gerard the Old, of Roussillon.
He lifts them up, brave baron, one by one,
To the Archbishop he carries them anon,
And by his knees ranges them all along.
The Bishop weeps, he cannot stint thereof;
He lifts his hand and gives them benison,
And after saith: 'Alack, brave champions!
May your souls rest with the all-glorious God
In Paradise, amid the rose-blossoms.
I too am dying and sorrow for my lot,
Who the great Emperor no more may look upon.'

Roland once more unto the field repairs,
And has sought out his comrade Oliver.
Close to his breast he lifts him, and with care
As best he may to the Archbishop bears
And on his shield lays with the others there;
The Bishop signs and shrives them all with prayer.
With tears renewed their sorrow is declared,
And Roland saith: 'Fair fellow Oliver,
You were own son unto Duke Renier
That held the marches of the Vale of Runers.
To shatter shield or break lance anywhere,
And from their seat proud men to overbear,
And cheer the brave with words of counsel fair,
And bring the cruel to ruin and despair,
No knight on earth was valiant as you were.'

Translated from the French by Dorothy L. Sayers

ANONYMOUS

12th century

14   *The Lament of Maev Leith-Dherg*

Raise the Cromlech high!
   MacMoghcorb is slain,
And other men's renown
   Has leave to live again.

Cold at last he lies
   Neath the burial-stone;
All the blood he shed
   Could not save his own.

Stately-strong he went,
   Through his nobles all
When we paced together
   Up the banquet-hall.

Dazzling white as lime
   Was his body fair,
Cherry-red his cheeks,
   Raven-black his hair.

Razor-sharp his spear,
   And the shield he bore,
High as champion's head—
   His arm was like an oar.

Never aught but truth
   Spake my noble king;
Valour all his trust
   In all his warfaring.

As the forkèd pole
   Holds the roof-tree's weight,
So my hero's arm
   Held the battle straight.

Terror went before him,
   Death behind his back;

Well the wolves of Erinn
   Knew his chariot's track.

Seven bloody battles
   He broke upon his foes;
In each a hundred heroes
   Fell beneath his blows.

Once he fought at Fossud
   Thrice at Ath-finn-Fail
'Twas my king that conquered
   At bloody Ath-an-Scail.

At the boundary Stream
   Fought the Royal Hound,
And for Bernas battle
   Stands his name renowned.

Here he fought with Leinster—
   Last of all his frays—
On the Hill of Cucorb's Fate
   High his Cromlech raise.

Translated from the Irish by T. W. Rolleston

MIROSLAV HOLUB

1923–1988

15   *The Fly*

She sat on a willow trunk
watching
part of the battle of Crécy,
the shouts,
the gasps,
the groans,
the tramping and the tumbling.

During the fourteenth charge
of the French cavalry

she mated
with a brown-eyed male fly
from Vadincourt.

She rubbed her legs together
as she sat on a disembowelled horse
meditating
on the immortality of flies.

With relief she alighted
on the blue tongue
of the Duke of Clervaux.

When silence settled
and only the whisper of decay
softly circled the bodies

and only
a few arms and legs
still twitched jerkily under the trees,

she began to lay her eggs
on the single eye
of Johann Uhr,
the Royal Armourer.

And thus it was
that she was eaten by a swift
fleeing
from the fires of Estrées.

1961

Translated from the Czechoslovakian by George Theiner

GEOFFREY CHAUCER

1343–1400

16   from *The Knight's Tale*

But in the dome of mighty Mars the red
With different figures all the sides were spread;

This temple, less in form, with equal grace,
Was imitative of the first in Thrace:
For that cold region was the loved abode
And sovereign mansion of the warrior god.
The landscape was a forest wide and bare,
Where neither beast nor humankind repair;
The fowl that scent afar the borders fly,
And shun the bitter blast, and wheel about the sky.
A cake of scurf lies baking on the ground,
And prickly stubs, instead of trees, are found;
Or woods with knots and knares deformed and old;
Headless the most, and hideous to behold:
A rattling tempest through the branches went,
That stripped 'em bare, and one sole way they bent.
Heaven froze above, severe; the clouds congeal,
And through the crystal vault appeared the standing hail.
Such was the face without: a mountain stood
Threatening from high, and overlooked the wood;
Beneath the lowering brow, and on a bent,
The temple stood of Mars armipotent:
The frame of burnished steel, that cast a glare
From far, and seemed to thaw the freezing air.
A strait, long entry to the temple led,
Blind with high walls, and horror overhead:
Thence issued such a blast and hollow roar,
As threatened from the hinge to heave the door.
In through that door, a northern light there shone;
'Twas all it had, for windows there were none.
The gate was adamant; eternal frame!
Which, hewed by Mars himself, from Indian quarries came,
The labour of a god; and all along
Tough iron plates were clenched to make it strong.
A tun about was every pillar there;
A polished mirror shone not half so clear.
There saw I how the secret felon wrought,
And treason labouring in the traitor's thought,
And midwife Time the ripened plot to murder brought.
There the red Anger dared the pallid Fear;
Next stood Hypocrisy, with holy leer;
Soft smiling, and demurely looking down,
But hid the dagger underneath the gown:
Th' assassinating wife, the household fiend;
And, far the blackest there, the traitor-friend.

On t'other side there stood Destruction bare;
Unpunished Rapine, and a waste of war;
Contest, with sharpened knives, in cloisters drawn,
And all with blood bespread the holy lawn.
Loud menaces were heard, and foul disgrace,
And bawling infamy, in language base;
Till sense was lost in sound, and silence fled the place.
The slayer of himself yet saw I there;
The gore congealed was clottered in his hair:
With eyes half closed and gaping mouth he lay,
And grim, as when he breathed his sullen soul away.
In midst of all the dome Misfortune sat,
And gloomy Discontent, and fell Debate,
And Madness laughing in his ireful mood,
And armed complaint on theft, and cries of blood.
There was the murdered corpse, in covert laid,
And violent death in thousand shapes displayed;
The city to the soldier's rage resigned;
Successless wars, and poverty behind;
Ships burnt in fight, or forced on rocky shores,
And the rash hunter strangled by the boars;
The newborn babe by nurses overlaid;
And the cook caught within the raging fire he made.
All ills of Mars his nature, flame, and steel;
The gasping charioteer, beneath the wheel
Of his own car, the ruined house that falls
And intercepts her lord betwixt the walls;
The whole division that to Mars pertains,
All trades of death that deal in steel for gains,
Were there: the butcher, armourer, and smith,
Who forges sharpened fauchions, or the scythe.
The scarlet conquest on a tower was placed,
With shouts and soldiers' acclamations graced;
A pointed sword hung threatening o'er his head,
Sustained but by a slender twine of thread.
There saw I Mars his ides, the Capitol,
The seer in vain foretelling Caesar's fall;
The last triumvirs, and the wars they move,
And Antony, who lost the world for love.
These, and a thousand more, the fane adorn;
Their fates were painted ere the men were born,

GEOFFREY CHAUCER

All copied from the heavens, and ruling force
Of the red star, in his revolving course.

Translated from the Middle English by John Dryden

MICHAEL DRAYTON
1563–1631

17   *To the Cambro-Britons, and their harp,*
        his Ballad of Agincourt*

Fair stood the wind for France,
When we our sails advance,
Nor now to prove our chance,
    Longer will tarry;
But putting to the main,
At Caux, the mouth of Seine,
With all his martial train,
    Landed King Harry.

And taking many a fort,
Furnished in warlike sort,
Marcheth towards Agincourt,
    In happy hour;
Skirmishing day by day,
With those that stopped his way,
Where the French General lay,
    With all his power.

Which in his height of pride,
King Henry to deride,
His ransom to provide
    To the King sending.
Which he neglects the while,
As from a nation vile,
Yet with an angry smile,
    Their fall portending.

* In 1415, Henry V renewed the Hundred Years War with France, laying successful siege to Harfleur. On 25 October 1415, with an army of only 14,000 men, he defeated a French force numbering 50,000 in a famous battle at Agincourt.

39

And turning to his men,
Quoth our brave Henry then,
Though they to one be ten,
  Be not amazed.
Yet have we well begun,
Battles so bravely won,
Have ever to the sun,
  By fame been raised.

And for my self (quoth he,)
This my full rest shall be,
England ne'er mourn for me,
  Nor more esteem me.
Victor I will remain,
Or on this earth lie slain,
Never shall she sustain,
  Loss to redeem me.

Poitiers and Cressy tell,
When most their pride did swell,
Under our swords they fell,
  No less our skill is,
Than when our grandsire great,
Claiming the regal seat,
By many a warlike feat,
  Lopped the French lilies.

The Duke of York so dread,
The eager vaward led;
With the main, Henry sped,
  Amongst his henchmen.
Exeter had the rear,
A braver man not there,
O Lord, how hot they were,
  On the false Frenchmen!

They now to fight are gone,
Armour on armour shone,
Drum now to drum did groan,
  To hear, was wonder;
That with cries they make,
The very earth did shake,

Trumpet to trumpet spake,
  Thunder to thunder.

Well it thine age became,
O noble Erpingham,
Which didst the signal aim,
  To our hid forces;
When from a meadow by,
Like a storm suddenly,
The English archery
  Struck the French horses,

With Spanish yew so strong,
Arrows a cloth-yard long,
That like to serpents stung,
  Piercing the weather;
None from his fellow starts,
But playing manly parts,
And like true English hearts,
  Stuck close together.

When down their bows they threw,
And forth their bilboes drew,
And on the French they flew,
  Not one was tardy;
Arms were from shoulders sent,
Scalps to the teeth were rent,
Down the French peasants went,
  Our men were hardy.

This while our noble King,
His broad sword brandishing,
Down the French host did ding,
  As to o'erwhelm it;
And many a deep wound lent,
His arms with blood besprent,
And many a cruel dent
  Bruisèd his helmet.

Gloucester, that Duke so good,
Next of the royal blood,
For famous England stood,
  With his brave brother;

Clarence, in steel so bright,
Though but a maiden knight,
Yet in that furious fight,
    Scarce such another.

Warwick in blood did wade,
Oxford the foe invade,
And cruel slaughter made,
    Still as they ran up;
Suffolk his axe did ply,
Beaumont and Willoughby
Bare them right doughtily,
    Ferrers and Fanhope.

Upon Saint Crispin's day
Fought was this noble fray,
Which fame did not delay,
    To England to carry;
O, when shall English men
With such acts fill a pen,
Or England breed again,
    Such a King Harry?

1606

EDMUND SPENSER
1552–1599

18   from *Astrophel*
                    A Pastorall Elegie

Upon the Death of the Most Noble and Valorous Knight,
*Sir Philip Sidney**

Such skill, matcht with such courage as he had,
Did prick him foorth with proud desire of praise
To seek abroad, of daunger nought ydrad,

* In 1586, the Earl of Leicester unsuccessfully attempted to wrest the city of
Zutphen in the Netherlands from the Spanish. Sir Philip Sidney, his thirty-two-
year-old nephew, was killed in the skirmish.

His mistresse name, and his owne fame, to raise.
What needeth perill to be sought abroad,
Since, round about us, it doth make aboad!

It fortunèd as he that perilous game
In forreine soyle pursuèd far away;
Into a forest wide and waste he came,
Where store he heard to be of salvage pray.
So wide a forest and so waste as this,
Nor famous Ardeyn, nor fowle Arlo, is.

There his welwoven toyles, and subtil traines,
He laid the brutish nation to enwrap:
So well he wrought with practice and with paines,
That he of them great troups did soone entrap.
Full happie man (misweening much) was hee,
So rich a spoile within his power to see.

Eftsoones, all heedlesse of his dearest hale,
Full greedily into the heard he thrust,
To slaughter them, and worke their finall balc,
Least that his toyle should of their troups be brust.
Wide wounds emongst them many one he made,
Now with his sharp borespear, now with his blade.

His care was all how he them all might kill,
That none might scape, (so partiall unto none:)
Ill mynd so much to mynd anothers ill,
As to become unmyndfull of his owne.
But pardon that unto the cruell skies,
That from himselfe to them withdrew his eies.

So as he rag'd emongst that beastly rout,
A cruell beast of most accursèd brood
Upon him turnd, (despeyre makes cowards stout,)
And, with fell tooth accustomèd to blood,
Launchèd his thigh with so mischievous might,
That it both bone and muscles ryvèd quight.

So deadly was the dint and deep the wound,
And so huge streames of blood thereout did flow,
That he endurèd not the direfull stound,
But on the cold deare earth himselfe did throw;

43

The whiles the captive heard his nets did rend,
And, having none to let, to wood did wend.

Ah! where were ye this while his shepheard peares,
To whom alive was nought so deare as hee:
And ye faire Mayds, the matches of his yeares,
Which in his grace did boast you most to bee!
Ah! where were ye, when he of you had need,
To stop his wound that wondrously did bleed!

Ah! wretched boy, the shape of dreryhead,
And sad ensample of mans suddein end:
Full litle faileth but thou shalt be dead,
Unpitièd, unplaynd, of foe or frend!
Whilest none is nigh, thine eyelids up to close,
And kisse thy lips like faded leaves of rose.

1595

SAMUEL DANIEL
1562–1619

19   from *The Civil Wars between the Two Houses of Lancaster and York**

It was upon the twilight of that day
(That peaceful day) when the religious bear
The olive-branches as they go to pray,
(And we, in lieu, the blooming palm use here)
When both the armies, ready in array
For th'early sacrifice of blood, appear
Prepared for mischief, ere they had full light
To see to do it, and to do it right.

Th'advantage of the time, and of the wind
(Which, both, with York seem as retained in pay)

---

* In 1461, Edward IV was proclaimed King in London, and went on to defeat the Lancastrians and Henry VI at Towton Field in Yorkshire. 'In this battle of Towton, on King Henry's side were slain Henry Percy Earl of Northumberland, the Earls of Shrewsbury and Devonshire ... The whole number slain were accounted, by some, 33,000; by others, 35,091.' [SD]

Brave Falconbridge takes hold-on, and assigned
The archers their flight-shafts to shoot away:
Which, th'adverse side (with sleet and dimness, blind,
Mistaken in the distance of the way)
Answer with their sheaf-arrows; that come short
Of their intended aim, and did no hurt;

But, gathered by th'on-marching enemy,
Returnèd were, like clouds of steel; which pour
Destruction down, and did new-night the sky:
As if the day had failed to keep his hour.
Whereat, the rangèd horse break-out, deny
Obedience to the riders, scorn their power,
Disrank the troops, set all in disarray,
To make th'assailant owner of the day.

Thus, thou peculiar engine of our land
(Weapon of conquest, master of the field)
Renownèd Bow (that mad'st this Crown command
The towers of France, and all their powers to yield)
Art made at home to have th'especial hand
In our dissensions, by thy work upheld:
Thou first didst conquer us; then raised our skill
To vanquish others; here ourselves to spill.

And now how com'st thou to be out of date,
And all neglected leav'st us, and art gone?
And with thee, th'ancient strength, the manly state
Of valour, and of worth, that glory won?
Or else stay'st thou, till new prized shot abate?
(That never shall effect what thou hast done)
And only but attend'st some blessèd Reign,
When thou and Virtue shalt be graced again.

But this sharp tempest drave Northumberland,
(Who led the vanguard of King Henry's side)
With eager heat join battle, out of hand;
And this disorder, with their swords to hide.
Where, twice five hours, these furious armies stand;
And Fortune's Balance weighed on neither side;
Nor either did but equal bloodshed gain,
Till Henry's chiefest leaders all were slain.

45

Then, lo, those spirits, which from these heads derive
Their motions gave off working; and, in haste,
Turn all their backs to Death, and mainly strive
Who from themselves shall run away most fast.
The after-flyers on the former drive:
And they again, by the pursuers chased
Make bridges of their fellows' backs, to pass
The brooks and rivers, where-as danger was.

Witness O clear-streamed Cock: within whose banks,
So many thousand, crawling, helpless lay,
With wounds and weariness; who in their ranks
Had valiantly behaved themselves that day:
And might have had more honour, and more thanks
By standing to their work, and by their stay,
'But men, at once, life seem to love and loath;
Running to lose it, and to save it both.'

Unhappy Henry, from a little hill,
Placed not far off (whence he might view the fight)
Had all th'entire full prospect of this ill,
With all the scattered slaughter, in his sight:
Saw how the victor raged, and spoiled at will,
And left not off when all was in his might:
Saw, with how great ado himself was won;
And with what store of blood kings are undone.

1601

HENRY HOWARD, EARL OF SURREY*

1517–1547

20   Norfolk sprang thee, Lambeth holds thee dead,
     Clere of the County of Cleremont though hight;

* Henry Howard, Earl of Surrey, and Thomas Clere, his squire and companion, fought together in expeditions to Kelsal in Scotland, Landrecy in the Netherlands, and Boulogne in France. At the siege of Montreuil, on 19 September 1544, Clere received wounds while protecting Surrey, from which he died the following spring. He was buried at Lambeth, in the chapel assigned to the Howards.

Within the womb of Ormond's race thou bred,
And saw'st thy cousin crownèd in thy sight.
Shelton for love, Surrey for Lord thou chase:
Ay me, while life did last that league was tender;
Tracing whose steps thou saw'st Kelsal blaze,
Laundersey burnt, and battered Bullen render.
At Muttrell gates, hopeless of all recure,
Thine Earl half dead gave in thy hand his Will;
Which cause did thee this pining death procure,
Ere summers four times seven thou could'st fulfil.
    Ah Clere, if love had booted, care, or cost,
    Heaven had not won, nor Earth so timely lost.

1557

GEORGE GASCOIGNE

?1525–1577

21   from *The Fruits of War*

A conference among ourselves we called,
Of officers and captains all yfere,
For truth (to tell) the soldiers were appalled,
And when we asked, 'Now mates, what merry cheer?'
Their answer was: 'It is no biding here.'
So that perforce we must from thence be gone,
Unless we meant to keep the place alone.

Herewith we thought that if in time we went,
Before all straits were stopped and taken up,
We might perhaps our enemies prevent,
And teach them eke to taste of sorrow's cup:
At Maesland Sluyse, we hopèd for to sup,
A place whereas we might good service do,
To keep them out which took it after too.

Whiles thus we talk, a messenger behold,
From Alphen came, and told us heavy news.

'Captains,' quoth he, 'Hereof you may be bold,
Not one poor soul of all your fellows' crews
Can scape alive, they have no choice to choose:
They sent me thus to bid you shift in time,
Else look like them to stick in Spanish lime.'

This tale once told, none other speech prevailed,
But pack and trudge, all leisure was too long,
To mend the mart, our watch (which never failed)
Descried our foes which marchèd all along,
And towards us began in haste to throng,
So that before our last could pass the port,
The foremost foes were now within the Fort.

I promised once and did perform it too,
To bide therein as long as any would,
What booted that? or what could captains do,
When common sort would tarry for no good?
To speak a truth, the good did what they could,
To keep the bad in ranks and good array,
But labour lost to hold that will away.

It needless were to tell what deeds were done,
Nor who did best, nor who did worst that day,
Nor who made head, nor who began to run,
Nor in retreat what chief was last alway,
But soldier-like we held our enemies' play:
And every captain strove to do his best,
To stay his own and so to stay the rest.

In this retire three English miles we trod,
With face to foes and shot as thick as hail,
Of whose choice men full fifty souls and odd,
We laid on ground, this is withouten fail,
Yet of our own, we lost but three by tale:
Our foes themselves confessed they bought full dear
The hot pursuit which they attempted there.

Thus came we late at last to Leyden walls,
Too late, too soon, and so may we well say,
For notwithstanding all our cries and calls,
They shut their gates and turned their ears away:
In fine they did forsake us every way,

And bade us shift to save ourselves apace,
For unto them were fond to trust for grace.

They neither gave us meat to feed upon,
Nor drink, nor powder, pickaxe, tool, nor spade,
So might we starve, like misers woebegone,
And fend our foes, with blows of English blade,
For shot was shrunk, and shift could none be made:
Yea more than this, we stood in open field,
Without defence from shot ourselves to shield.

This thus well weighed, when weary night was past,
And day gan peep, we heard the Spanish drums,
Which struck a march about us round to cast,
And forth withall their ensigns quickly comes,
At sight whereof, our soldiers bit their thumbs:
For well they wist it was no boot to fly,
And biding there, there was no boot but die.

So that we sent a drum to summon talk,
And came to parley middle way between.
Monsieur de Licques and Mario did walk
From foemen's side, and from our side were seen
Myself, that match for Mario might been,
And Captain Sheffield born of noble race,
To match de Licques, which there was chief in place.

Thus met we talked, and stood upon our toes,
With great demands whom little might content,
We craved not only freedom from our foes,
But shipping eke with sails and all full bent,
To come again from whence we first were went:
I mean to come, into our English coast,
Which soil was sure, and might content us most.

An old-said saw, and oft seen, that whereas
Thou comest to crave, and doubts for to obtain,
Iniquum pete (then) *ut æquum feras*,
This had I heard, and sure I was full fain
To prove what profit we thereby might gain:
But at the last when time was stolen away,
We were full glad to play another play.

We rendered then with safety for our lives,
Our ensigns 'splayed, and managing our arms,
With further faith, that from all kinds of gives,
Our soldiers should remain withouten harms:
And sooth to say, these were no false alarms,
For why? they were within twelve days discharged,
And sent away from prison quite enlarged.

They were sent home, and we remainèd still,
In prison pent, but yet right gently used,
To take our lives, it was not Licques' will,
(That noble blood, which never man abused,)
Nor ever yet was for his faith accused.
Would God I had the skill to write his praise,
Which lent me comfort in my doleful days.

We bode behind, four months or little less,
But whereupon that God he knows not I,
Yet if I might be bold to give a guess,
Then would I say it was for to espy
What ransom we would pay contentedly;
Or else to know how much we were esteemed,
In England here, and for what men ydeemed.

Howso it were, at last we were despatched,
And home we came as children come from school,
As glad as fish which were but lately catched,
And straight again were cast into the pool;
For by my fay I count him but a fool,
Which would not rather poorly live at large,
Than rest in prison fed with costly charge.

Now I have told a tedious tale in rhyme,
Of my mishaps, and what ill luck I had,
Yet some may say, that all too loud I chime,
Since that in wars my fortune was not bad,
And many a man in prison would be glad
To fare no worse, and lodge no worse than we,
And eke at last to scape and go so free.

1575

GEORGE PEELE
?1558–1596

22   *Farewell to Arms*
      To Queen Elizabeth

His golden locks time hath to silver turned;
 O time too swift, O swiftness never ceasing!
His youth 'gainst time and age hath ever spurned,
 But spurned in vain; youth waneth by increasing:
Beauty, strength, youth, are flowers but fading seen;
Duty, faith, love, are roots, and ever green.

His helmet now shall make a hive for bees;
 And, lovers' sonnets turned to holy psalms,
A man-at-arms must now serve on his knees,
 And feed on prayers, which are age's alms:
But though from court to cottage he depart,
His saint is sure of his unspotted heart.

And when he saddest sits in homely cell,
 He'll teach his swains this carol for a song:
'Blest be the hearts that wish my sovereign well,
 Curst be the souls that think her any wrong.'
Goddess, allow this agèd man his right,
To be your beadsman now, that was your knight.

1589

JOHN DONNE
1572–1631

23   *A Burnt Ship**

Out of a fired ship, which, by no way
But drowning, could be rescued from the flame,

---

* John Donne took part in the naval expeditions against Cadiz in June to August 1596 (under the Earl of Essex and Sir Walter Raleigh) and against the Azores in July to October 1597.

Some men leaped forth, and ever as they came
Near the foe's ships, did by their shot decay;
So all were lost, which in the ship were found,
    They in the sea being burnt, they in the burnt ship drowned.

1633

SIR WILLIAM DAVENANT
1606–1668

24   *The Soldier Going to the Field*

Preserve thy sighs, unthrifty girl,
   To purify the air;
Thy tears to thread instead of pearl
   On bracelets of thy hair.

The trumpet makes the echo hoarse
   And wakes the louder drum;
Expense of grief gains no remorse
   When sorrow should be dumb.

For I must go where lazy Peace
   Will hide her drowsy head,
And, for the sport of Kings, increase
   The number of the dead.

But first I'll chide thy cruel theft:
   Can I in war delight,
Who being of my heart bereft
   Can have no heart to fight?

Thou know'st the sacred Laws of old
   Ordained a thief should pay,
To quit him of his theft, sevenfold
   What he had stolen away.

Thy payment shall but double be;
   O then with speed resign

My own seducèd heart to me,
  Accompanied with thine.

1672

RICHARD LOVELACE
1618–1658

25   *To Lucasta, Going to the Wars*

Tell me not, sweet, I am unkind,
  That from the nunnery
Of thy chaste breast and quiet mind
  To war and arms I fly.

True, a new mistress now I chase,
  The first foe in the field;
And with a stronger faith embrace
  A sword, a horse, a shield.

Yet this inconstancy is such
  As you too shall adore;
I could not love thee, dear, so much,
  Loved I not honour more.

1649

ANDREW MARVELL
1621–1678

26   *An Horatian Ode upon Cromwell's
          Return from Ireland*

The forward youth that would appear
Must now forsake his Muses dear,

ANDREW MARVELL

Nor in the shadows sing
His numbers languishing.

'Tis time to leave the books in dust.
And oil the unusèd armour's rust,
   Removing from the wall
   The corslet of the hall.

So restless Cromwell could not cease
In the inglorious arts of peace,
   But through adventurous war
   Urgèd his active star:

And like the three-forked lightning, first
Breaking the clouds where it was nurst,
   Did thorough his own side
   His fiery way divide:

For 'tis all one to courage high,
The emulous, or enemy;
   And with such, to enclose
   Is more than to oppose.

Then burning through the air he went
And palaces and temples rent;
   And Caesar's head at last
   Did through his laurels blast.

'Tis madness to resist or blame
The force of angry Heaven's flame;
   And if we would speak true,
   Much to the man is due,

Who, from his private gardens, where
He lived reservèd and austere
   (As if his highest plot
   To plant the bergamot),

Could by industrious valour climb
To ruin the great work of time,
   And cast the Kingdom old
   Into another mould.

Though Justice against Fate complain,
And plead the ancient rights in vain—
   But those do hold or break
   As men are strong or weak—

Nature, that hateth emptiness,
Allows of penetration less,
   And therefore must make room
   Where greater spirits come.

What field of all the civil wars
Where his were not the deepest scars?
   And Hampton shows what part
   He had of wiser art;

Where, twining subtle fears with hope,
He wove a net of such a scope
   That Charles himself might chase
   To Car'sbrook's narrow case;

That thence the Royal Actor borne
The tragic scaffold might adorn:
   While round the armèd bands
   Did clap their bloody hands.

He nothing common did or mean
Upon that memorable scene,
   But with his keener eye
   The axe's edge did try;

Nor called the Gods, with vulgar spite,
To vindicate his helpless right;
   But bowed his comely head
   Down, as upon a bed.

This was that memorable hour
Which first assured the forcèd power:
   So when they did design
   The Capitol's first line,

A bleeding head, where they begun,
Did fright the architects to run;

And yet in that the State
Foresaw its happy fate!

And now the Irish are ashamed
To see themselves in one year tamed:
    So much one man can do
    That does both act and know.

They can affirm his praises best,
And have, though overcome, confest
    How good he is, how just
    And fit for highest trust;

Nor yet grown stiffer with command,
But still in the Republic's hand—
    How fit he is to sway
    That can so well obey!

He to the Commons' feet presents
A Kingdom for his first year's rents,
    And, what he may, forbears
    His fame, to make it theirs:

And has his sword and spoils ungirt
To lay them at the public's skirt.
    So when the falcon high
    Falls heavy from the sky,

She, having killed, no more does search
But on the next green bough to perch,
    Where, when he first does lure,
    The falconer has her sure.

What may not then our Isle presume
While victory his crest does plume?
    What may not others fear,
    If thus he crown each year?

As Caesar he, ere long, to Gaul,
To Italy an Hannibal,
    And to all States not free
    Shall climacteric be.

The Pict no shelter now shall find
Within his particoloured mind,
    But from this valour sad
    Shrinks underneath the plaid,

Happy, if in the tufted brake
The English hunter him mistake,
    Nor lay his hounds in near
    The Caledonian deer.

But thou, the War's and Fortune's son,
March indefatigably on;
    And for the last effect,
    Still keep thy sword erect:

Besides the force it has to fright
The spirits of the shady night,
    The same arts that did gain
    A power, must it maintain.

1650

JOHN MILTON
1608–1674

27   *On the Late Massacre in Piedmont**

Avenge, O Lord, thy slaughtered saints, whose bones
    Lie scattered on the Alpine mountains cold,
    Even them who kept thy truth so pure of old
    When all our fathers worshipped stocks and stones,
Forget not; in thy book record their groans
    Who were thy sheep and in their ancient fold
    Slain by the bloody Piedmontese that rolled
    Mother with infant down the rocks. Their moans

---

* The heretical Waldensian sect, which inhabited northern Italy (Piedmont) and southern France, held beliefs compatible with Protestant doctrine. Their massacre by Catholics in 1655 was widely protested by Protestant powers, including Oliver Cromwell and his Latin secretary, John Milton.

The vales redoubled to the hills, and they
To Heaven. Their martyred blood and ashes sow
O'er all th' Italian fields where still doth sway
The triple tyrant, that from these may grow
    A hundredfold, who having learnt thy way,
    Early may fly the Babylonian woe.

1673

28   from *Paradise Lost*, book 6

They ended parle, and both addressed for fight
Unspeakable; for who, though with the tongue
Of angels, can relate, or to what things
Liken on earth conspicuous, that may lift
Human imagination to such heighth
Of godlike power: for likest gods they seemed,
Stood they or moved, in stature, motion, arms
Fit to decide the Empire of great Heaven.
Now waved their fiery swords, and in the air
Made horrid circles; two broad suns their shields
Blazed opposite, while expectation stood
In horror; from each hand with speed retired
Where erst was thickest fight, th' angelic throng,
And left large field, unsafe within the wind
Of such commotion, such as to set forth
Great things by small, if Nature's concord broke,
Among the constellations war were sprung,
Two planets rushing from aspect malign
Of fiercest opposition in mid sky,
Should combat, and their jarring spheres confound.
Together both with next to almighty arm,
Uplifted imminent one stroke they aimed
That might determine, and not need repeat,
As not of power, at once; nor odds appeared
In might or swift prevention; but the sword
Of Michael from the armoury of God
Was given him tempered so, that neither keen
Nor solid might resist that edge: it met
The sword of Satan with steep force to smite
Descending, and in half cut sheer, nor stayed
But with swift wheel reverse, deep entering sheared

All his right side; then Satan first knew pain,
And writhed him to and fro convolved; so sore
The griding sword with discontinuous wound
Passed through him, but th' ethereal substance closed
Not long divisible, and from the gash
A stream of nectarous humour issuing flowed
Sanguine, such as celestial spirits may bleed,
And all his armour stained ere while so bright.
Forthwith on all sides to his aid was run
By angels many and strong, who interposed
Defence, while others bore him on their shields
Back to his chariot, where it stood retired
From off the files of war; there they him laid
Gnashing for anguish and despite and shame
To find himself not matchless, and his pride
Humbled by such rebuke, so far beneath
His confidence to equal God in power.
Yet soon he healed; for spirits that live throughout
Vital in every part, not as frail man
In entrails, heart or head, liver or reins,
Cannot but by annihilating die;
Nor in their liquid texture mortal wound
Receive, no more than can the fluid air:
All heart they live, all head, all eye, all ear,
All intellect, all sense, and as they please,
They limb themselves, and colour, shape or size
Assume, as likes them best, condense or rare.

1667

CHARLES SACKVILLE, EARL OF DORSET

1638–1706

29   *Song*
Written at Sea in the First Dutch War,
the night before an Engagement

To all you ladies now at land
   We men at sea indite;
But first would have you understand
   How hard it is to write:

The Muses now, and Neptune too,
We must implore to write to you—
   With a fa, la, la, la, la.

For though the Muses should prove kind,
   And fill our empty brain,
Yet if rough Neptune rouse the wind
   To wave the azure main,
Our paper, pen, and ink and we,
Roll up and down our ships at sea—
   With a fa, la, la, la, la.

Then if we write not by each post,
   Think not we are unkind;
Nor yet conclude our ships are lost
   By Dutchmen or by wind:
Our tears we'll send a speedier way,
The tide shall bring them twice a day—
   With a fa, la, la, la, la.

The King with wonder and surprise
   Will swear the seas grow bold,
Because the tides will higher rise
   Than e'er they did of old:
But let him know it is our tears
Bring floods of grief to Whitehall stairs—
   With a fa, la, la, la, la.

Should foggy Opdam chance to know
   Our sad and dismal story,
The Dutch would scorn so weak a foe,
   And quit their fort at Goree:
For what resistance can they find
From men who've left their hearts behind?—
   With a fa, la, la, la, la.

Let wind and weather do its worst,
   Be you to us but kind;
Let Dutchmen vapour, Spaniards curse,
   No sorrow we shall find:
'Tis then no matter how things go,
Or who's our friend, or who's our foe—
   With a fa, la, la, la, la.

To pass our tedious hours away
    We throw a merry main,
Or else at serious ombre play;
    But why should we in vain
Each other's ruin thus pursue?
We were undone when we left you—
    With a fa, la, la, la, la.

But now our fears tempestuous grow
    And cast our hopes away;
Whilst you, regardless of our woe,
    Sit careless at a play:
Perhaps permit some happier man
To kiss your hand, or flirt your fan—
    With a fa, la, la, la, la.

When any mournful tune you hear,
    That dies in every note
As if it sighed with each man's care
    For being so remote,
Think then how often love we've made
To you, when all those tunes were played—
    With a fa, la, la, la, la.

In justice you cannot refuse
    To think of our distress,
When we for hopes of honour lose
    Our certain happiness:
All those designs are but to prove
Ourselves more worthy of your love—
    With a fa, la, la, la, la.

And now we've told you all our loves,
    And likewise all our fears,
In hopes this declaration moves
    Some pity for our tears:
Let's hear of no inconstancy—
We have too much of that at sea—
    With a fa, la, la, la, la.

1665

JOHN DRYDEN

1631–1700

30   from *Annus Mirabilis**

Now van to van the foremost squadrons meet,
    The midmost battles hasting up behind,
Who view, far off, the storm of falling sleet,
    And hear their thunder rattling in the wind.

At length the adverse admirals appear:
    (The two bold champions of each country's right)
Their eyes describe the lists as they come near,
    And draw the lines of death before they fight.

The distance judged for shot of every size,
    The linstocks touch, the pond'rous ball expires:
The vig'rous seaman every port-hole plies,
    And adds his heart to every gun he fires.

Fierce was the fight on the proud Belgians' side,
    For honour, which they seldom sought before:
But now they by their own vain boasts were tied,
    And forced, at least in show, to prize it more.

But sharp remembrance on the English part,
    And shame of being matched by such a foe:
Rouse conscious virtue up in every heart,
    And seeming to be stronger makes them so.

Nor long the Belgians could that fleet sustain,
    Which did two gen'rals' fates, and Caesar's bear.
Each several ship a victory did gain,
    As Rupert or as Albemarl were there.

Their battered admiral too soon withdrew,
    Unthanked by ours for his unfinished fight:

---

* The second of the Dutch Wars erupted in 1664; in March 1665, Charles II
officially declared war on the Netherlands. The English victory at sea described here
took place off the coast of Holland at North Foreland on 25 July 1666.

But he the minds of his Dutch masters knew,
   Who called that providence which we called flight.

Never did men more joyfully obey,
   Or sooner understand the sign to fly:
With such alacrity they bore away,
   As if to praise them all the states stood by.

O famous Leader of the Belgian fleet,
   Thy monument inscribed such praise shall wear
As Varro, timely flying, once did meet,
   Because he did not of his Rome despair.

Behold that navy which a while before
   Provoked the tardy English to the fight,
Now draw their beaten vessels close to shore,
   As larks die dared to shun the hobbies' flight.

Who ere would English monuments survey,
   In other records may our courage know:
But let them hide the story of this day,
   Whose fame was blemished by too base a foe.

Or if too busily they will enquire
   Into a victory which we disdain:
Then let them know, the Belgians did retire
   Before the Patron Saint of injured Spain.

Repenting England this revengeful day
   To Philip's manes did an off'ring bring:
England, which first, by leading them astray,
   Hatched up rebellion to destroy her King.

Our fathers bent their baneful industry
   To check a monarchy that slowly grew:
But did not France or Holland's fate foresee,
   Whose rising power to swift dominion flew.

In fortune's empire blindly thus we go,
   And wander after pathless destiny:
Whose dark resorts since prudence cannot know,
   In vain it would provide for what shall be.

But what ere English to the blessed shall go,
   And the fourth Harry or first Orange meet:
Find him disowning of a Bourbon foe,
   And him detesting a Batavian fleet.

Now on their coasts our conquering navy rides,
   Waylays their merchants, and their land besets:
Each day new wealth without their care provides,
   They lie asleep with prizes in their nets.

1666

DANIEL DEFOE

1660–1731

31   from *The Spanish Descent**

The word's gone out, and now they spread the main
With swelling sails, and swelling hopes, for Spain:
To double vengeance pressed where'er they come,
Resolved to pay the haughty Spaniard home:
Resolved by future conduct to atone
For all our past mistakes, and all their own.
New life springs up in every English face,
And fits them all for glorious things apace:
The booty some excites, and some the cause;
But more the hope to gain their lost applause.
Eager their sullied honour to restore,
Some anger whets, some pride and vengeance more.
      The lazy minutes now pass on too slow,
Fancy flies faster than the winds can blow:
Impatient wishes lengthen out the day;
They chide the loitering winds for their delay.

* In 1702, during the War of the Spanish Succession, an unsuccessful expedition to
Cadiz by the British and the Dutch was followed by a dramatic victory in the Bay of
Vigo, where, without losing a single ship themselves, they were able to capture an entire
fleet, including 12 Spanish galleons and 15 French men-of-war.

But time is nature's faithful messenger,
And brings up all we wish, as well as all we fear.
    The mists clear up, and now the scout decries
The subject of their hopes and victories:
The wished for fleets embayed, in harbour lie,
Unfit to fight, and more unfit to fly.
Triumphant joy throughout the navy flies,
Echoed from shore with terror and surprise.
Strange power of noise! which at one simple sound
At once shall some encourage, some confound.
    In vain the lion tangled in the snare
With anguish roars, and rends the trembling air:
'Tis vain to struggle with Almighty Fate;
Vain and impossible the weak debate.
The mighty boom, the forts, resist in vain.
The guns with fruitless force in noise complain.
See how the troops intrepidly fall on!
Wish for more foes, and think they fly too soon.
With eager fury to their forts pursue,
And think the odds of four to one too few.
The land's first conquered and the prize attends;
Fate beckons in the fleet to back their friends:
Despair succeeds, they struggle now too late,
And soon submit to their prevailing fate:
Courage is madness when occasion's past,
Death's the securest refuge, and the last.
    And now the rolling flames come threat'ning on,
And mighty streams of melted gold run down.
The flaming ore down to its centre makes,
To form new mines beneath the oozy lakes.
    Here a galleon with spicy drugs inflamed,
In odoriferous folds of sulphur streamed.
The gods of old no such oblations knew,
Their spices weak, and their perfumes but few.
The frighted Spaniards from their treasure fly,
Loath to forsake their wealth, but loath to die.
    Here a vast carrack flies while none pursue,
Bulged on the shore by her distracted crew:
There like a mighty mountain she appears,
And groans beneath the golden weight she bears.
Conquest perverts the property of friend,
And makes men ruin what they can't defend:

Some blow their treasures up into the air
With all the wild excesses of despair.
Strange fate! that war such odd events should have;
Friends would destroy, and enemies would save:
Others their safety to their wealth prefer,
And mix some small discretion with their fear.
Life's the best gift that nature can bestow;
The first that we receive, the last which we forgo:
And he that's vainly prodigal of blood,
Forfeits his sense to do his cause no good.
All desperation's the effect of fear;
Courage is temper, valour can't despair.
    And now the victory's completely gained;
No ships to conquer now, no foes remained.
The mighty spoils exceed whate'er was known
That vanquished ever lost, or victor won:
So great, if Fame shall future times remind,
They'll think she lies, and libels all mankind.

1702

JOSEPH ADDISON
1672–1719

32   from *The Campaign**
     A Poem to His Grace the Duke of Marlborough

But, O my muse, what numbers wilt thou find
To sing the furious troops in battle joined!
Methinks I hear the drum's tumultuous sound
The victor's shouts and dying groans confound,
The dreadful burst of cannon rend the skies,
And all the thunder of the battle rise.
'Twas then great Marlborough's mighty soul was proved
That, in the shock of charging hosts unmoved,

---

* At the Battle of Blenheim, on 13 August 1704, the Duke of Marlborough and
Prince Eugene of Savoy won one of the most important victories of the War of the
Spanish Succession, defeating the French and Bavarians and capturing the French
Marshal Tallard.

Amidst confusion, horror, and despair,
Examined all the dreadful scenes of war;
In peaceful thought the field of death surveyed,
To fainting squadrons sent the timely aid,
Inspired repulsed battalions to engage,
And taught the doubtful battle where to rage.
So when an angel by divine command
With rising tempests shakes a guilty land,
Such as of late o'er pale Britannia past,
Calm and serene he drives the furious blast;
And, pleased the Almighty's orders to perform,
Rides in the whirlwind, and directs the storm.

1705

ROBERT SOUTHEY
1774–1843

33   *The Battle of Blenheim*

I

It was a summer evening,
    Old Kaspar's work was done,
And he before his cottage door
    Was sitting in the sun,
And by him sported on the green
His little grandchild Wilhelmine.

II

She saw her brother Peterkin
    Roll something large and round,
Which he beside the rivulet
    In playing there had found;
He came to ask what he had found,
That was so large, and smooth, and round.

III

Old Kaspar took it from the boy,
    Who stood expectant by;

And then the old man shook his head,
   And, with a natural sigh,
''Tis some poor fellow's skull,' said he,
'Who fell in the great victory.

IV

'I find them in the garden,
   For there's many here about;
And often when I go to plough,
   The ploughshare turns them out!
For many thousand men,' said he,
'Were slain in that great victory.'

V

'Now tell us what 'twas all about,'
   Young Peterkin, he cries;
And little Wilhelmine looks up
   With wonder-waiting eyes;
'Now tell us all about the war,
And what they fought each other for.'

VI

'It was the English,' Kaspar cried,
   'Who put the French to rout;
But what they fought each other for,
   I could not well make out;
But everybody said,' quoth he,
'That 'twas a famous victory.

VII

'My father lived at Blenheim then,
   Yon little stream hard by;
They burnt his dwelling to the ground,
   And he was forced to fly;
So with his wife and child he fled,
Nor had he where to rest his head.

VIII

'With fire and sword the country round
   Was wasted far and wide,

68

And many a childing mother then,
    And new-born baby died;
But things like that, you know, must be
At every famous victory.

IX

'They say it was a shocking sight
    After the field was won;
For many thousand bodies here
    Lay rotting in the sun;
But things like that, you know, must be
After a famous victory.

X

'Great praise the Duke of Marlbro' won,
    And our good Prince Eugene.'
'Why 'twas a very wicked thing!'
    Said little Wilhelmine.
'Nay . . . nay . . . my little girl,' quoth he,
'It was a famous victory.

XI

'And everybody praised the Duke
    Who this great fight did win.'
'But what good came of it at last?'
    Quoth little Peterkin.
'Why that I cannot tell,' said he
'But 'twas a famous victory.'

1798

JAMES THOMSON
1700–1748

34   *Rule, Britannia!*

When Britain first, at Heaven's command,
    Arose from out the azure main,

69

This was the charter of the land,
  And guardian angels sung this strain.
    'Rule, Britannia, rule the waves;
    Britons never will be slaves.'

The nations, not so blest as thee,
  Must, in their turns, to tyrants fall;
While thou shalt flourish great and free,
  The dread and envy of them all.
    'Rule,' &c.

Still more majestic shalt thou rise,
  More dreadful from each foreign stroke;
As the loud blast that tears the skies
  Serves but to root thy native oak.
    'Rule,' &c.

Thee haughty tyrants ne'er shall tame;
  All their attempts to bend thee down
Will but arouse thy generous flame,
  But work their woe, and thy renown.
    'Rule,' &c.

To thee belongs the rural reign;
  Thy cities shall with commerce shine;
All thine shall be the subject main;
  And every shore it circles, thine.
    'Rule,' &c.

The Muses, still with freedom found,
  Shall to thy happy coast repair:
Blest isle! with matchless beauty crowned,
  And manly hearts to guard the fair:
    'Rule, Britannia, rule the waves,
    Britons never will be slaves.'

1740

SAMUEL JOHNSON
1709–1784

35   from *The Vanity of Human Wishes**

On what foundation stands the warrior's pride,
How just his hopes, let Swedish Charles decide;
A frame of adamant, a soul of fire,
No dangers fright him, and no labours tire;
O'er love, o'er fear, extends his wide domain,
Unconquered lord of pleasure and of pain;
No joys to him pacific sceptres yield,
War sounds the trump, he rushes to the field;
Behold surrounding kings their powers combine,
And one capitulate, and one resign;
Peace courts his hand, but spreads her charms in vain;
'Think nothing gained,' he cries, 'till naught remain,
On Moscow's walls till Gothic standards fly,
And all be mine beneath the polar sky.'
The march begins in military state,
And nations on his eye suspended wait;
Stern Famine guards the solitary coast,
And Winter barricades the realms of Frost;
He comes, nor want nor cold his course delay—
Hide, blushing Glory, hide Pultowa's day:
The vanquished hero leaves his broken bands,
And shows his miseries in distant lands;
Condemned a needy supplicant to wait,
While ladies interpose, and slaves debate.
But did not Chance at length her error mend?
Did no subverted empire mark his end?
Did rival monarchs give the fatal wound?
Or hostile millions press him to the ground?
His fall was destined to a barren strand,

* King Charles XII of Sweden invaded Russia in 1708, where he was disastrously defeated at Pultowa in 1709. Unsuccessful in his efforts to forge a lasting alliance against Russia with Turkey, he invaded Norway; in 1816 he was killed in the attack on Fredrikshald.

A petty fortress, and a dubious hand;
He left the name at which the world grew pale,
To point a moral, or adorn a tale.

1748

JOHN SCOTT OF AMWELL
1730–1783

36 *The Drum*

I hate that drum's discordant sound,
Parading round, and round, and round:
To thoughtless youth it pleasure yields,
And lures from cities and from fields,
To sell their liberty for charms
Of tawdry lace, and glittering arms;
And when Ambition's voice commands,
To march, and fight, and fall, in foreign lands.

I hate that drum's discordant sound,
Parading round, and round, and round:
To me it talks of ravaged plains,
And burning towns, and ruined swains,
And mangled limbs, and dying groans,
And widows' tears, and orphans' moans;
And all that Misery's hand bestows,
To fill the catalogue of human woes.

1782

THOMAS CAMPBELL
1777–1844

37 *Ye Mariners of England*

Ye Mariners of England
That guard our native seas!
Whose flag has braved a thousand years
The battle and the breeze!

Your glorious standard launch again
　To match another foe;
And sweep through the deep,
　While the stormy winds do blow!
While the battle rages loud and long
　And the stormy winds do blow.

The spirits of your fathers
　Shall start from every wave—
For the deck it was their field of fame,
　And Ocean was their grave:
Where Blake and mighty Nelson fell
　Your manly hearts shall glow,
As ye sweep through the deep,
　While the stormy winds do blow!
While the battle rages loud and long
　And the stormy winds do blow.

Britannia needs no bulwarks,
　No towers along the steep;
Her march is o'er the mountain-waves,
　Her home is on the deep.
With thunders from her native oak
　She quells the floods below,
As they roar on the shore,
　When the stormy winds do blow!
When the battle rages loud and long,
　And the stormy winds do blow.

The meteor flag of England
　Shall yet terrific burn;
Till danger's troubled night depart
　And the star of peace return.
Then, then, ye ocean-warriors!
　Our song and feast shall flow
To the fame of your name,
　When the storm has ceased to blow!
When the fiery fight is heard no more,
　And the storm has ceased to blow.

1801

38 *Hohenlinden**

On Linden, when the sun was low,
All bloodless lay the untrodden snow,
And dark as winter was the flow
    Of Iser, rolling rapidly.

But Linden saw another sight,
When the drum beat, at dead of night,
Commanding fires of death to light
    The darkness of her scenery.

By torch and trumpet fast arrayed,
Each horseman drew his battle blade,
And furious every charger neighed
    To join the dreadful revelry.

Then shook the hills, with thunder riven;
Then rushed the steed, to battle driven;
And, louder than the bolts of heaven,
    Far flashed the red artillery.

But redder yet that light shall glow,
On Linden's hills of stainèd snow;
And bloodier yet, the torrent flow
    Of Iser, rolling rapidly.

'Tis morn; but scarce yon level sun
Can pierce the war-clouds, rolling dun,
Where furious Frank, and fiery Hun,
    Shout in their sulphurous canopy.

The combat deepens. On, ye brave,
Who rush to glory, or the grave!
Wave, Munich, all thy banners wave,
    And charge with all thy chivalry!

* On 3 December 1800, the French General Jean Victor Moreau crossed the Rhine with his troops, decisively defeating the Austrian and allied forces in the Bavarian village of Hohenlinden. The battle marked a turning point in the French Revolutionary Wars.

THOMAS CAMPBELL

Few, few shall part, where many meet!
The snow shall be their winding sheet,
And every turf, beneath their feet,
    Shall be a soldier's sepulchre.

1800–01

SAMUEL TAYLOR COLERIDGE
1772–1834

39   *Fears in Solitude*
Written in April 1798, during the alarm of an invasion

A green and silent spot, amid the hills,
A small and silent dell! O'er stiller place
No singing sky-lark ever poised himself.
The hills are heathy, save that swelling slope,
Which hath a gay and gorgeous covering on,
All golden with the never-bloomless furze,
Which now blooms most profusely: but the dell,
Bathed by the mist, is fresh and delicate
As vernal corn-field, or the unripe flax,
When, through its half-transparent stalks, at eve,
The level sunshine glimmers with green light.
Oh! 'tis a quiet spirit-healing nook!
Which all, methinks, would love; but chiefly he,
The humble man, who, in his youthful years,
Knew just so much of folly, as had made
His early manhood more securely wise!
Here he might lie on fern or withered heath,
While from the singing lark (that sings unseen
The minstrelsy that solitude loves best),
And from the sun, and from the breezy air,
Sweet influences trembled o'er his frame;
And he, with many feelings, many thoughts,
Made up a meditative joy, and found
Religious meanings in the forms of Nature!
And so, his senses gradually wrapt
In a half sleep, he dreams of better worlds,
And dreaming hears thee still, O singing lark,
That singest like an angel in the clouds!

75

My God! it is a melancholy thing
For such a man, who would full fain preserve
His soul in calmness, yet perforce must feel
For all his human brethren—O my God!
It weighs upon the heart, that he must think
What uproar and what strife may now be stirring
This way or that way o'er these silent hills—
Invasion, and the thunder and the shout,
And all the crash of onset; fear and rage,
And undetermined conflict—even now,
Even now, perchance, and in his native isle:
Carnage and groans beneath this blessed sun!
We have offended, Oh! my countrymen!
We have offended very grievously,
And been most tyrannous. From east to west
A groan of accusation pierces Heaven!
The wretched plead against us; multitudes
Countless and vehement, the sons of God,
Our brethren! Like a cloud that travels on,
Steamed up from Cairo's swamps of pestilence,
Even so, my countrymen! have we gone forth
And borne to distant tribes slavery and pangs,
And, deadlier far, our vices, whose deep taint
With slow perdition murders the whole man,
His body and his soul! Meanwhile, at home,
All individual dignity and power
Engulfed in Courts, Committees, Institutions,
Associations and Societies,
A vain, speech-mouthing, speech-reporting Guild,
One Benefit-Club for mutual flattery,
We have drunk up, demure as at a grace,
Pollutions from the brimming cup of wealth;
Contemptuous of all honourable rule,
Yet bartering freedom and the poor man's life
For gold, as at a market! The sweet words
Of Christian promise, words that even yet
Might stem destruction, were they wisely preached,
Are muttered o'er by men, whose tones proclaim
How flat and wearisome they feel their trade:
Rank scoffers some, but most too indolent
To deem them falsehoods or to know their truth.
Oh! blasphemous! the Book of Life is made
A superstitious instrument, on which

We gabble o'er the oaths we mean to break;
For all must swear—all and in every place,
College and wharf, council and justice-court;
All, all must swear, the briber and the bribed,
Merchant and lawyer, senator and priest,
The rich, the poor, the old man and the young;
All, all make up one scheme of perjury,
That faith doth reel; the very name of God
Sounds like a juggler's charm; and, bold with joy,
Forth from his dark and lonely hiding-place,
(Portentous sight!) the owlet Atheism,
Sailing on obscene wings athwart the noon,
Drops his blue-fringèd lids, and holds them close,
And hooting at the glorious sun in Heaven,
Cries out, 'Where is it?'
                              Thankless too for peace,
(Peace long preserved by fleets and perilous seas)
Secure from actual warfare, we have loved
To swell the war-whoop, passionate for war!
Alas! for ages ignorant of all
Its ghastlier workings, (famine or blue plague,
Battle, or siege, or flight through wintry snows,)
We, this whole people, have been clamorous
For war and bloodshed; animating sports,
The which we pay for as a thing to talk of,
Spectators and not combatants! No guess
Anticipative of a wrong unfelt,
No speculation on contingency,
However dim and vague, too vague and dim
To yield a justifying cause; and forth,
(Stuffed out with big preamble, holy names,
And adjurations of the God in Heaven,)
We send our mandates for the certain death
Of thousands and ten thousands! Boys and girls,
And women, that would groan to see a child
Pull off an insect's leg, all read of war,
The best amusement for our morning meal!
The poor wretch, who has learnt his only prayers
From curses, who knows scarcely words enough
To ask a blessing from his Heavenly Father,
Becomes a fluent phraseman, absolute
And technical in victories and defeats,
And all our dainty terms for fratricide;

Terms which we trundle smoothly o'er our tongues
Like mere abstractions, empty sounds to which
We join no feeling and attach no form!
As if the soldier died without a wound;
As if the fibres of this godlike frame
Were gored without a pang; as if the wretch,
Who fell in battle, doing bloody deeds,
Passed off to Heaven, translated and not killed;
As though he had no wife to pine for him,
No God to judge him! Therefore, evil days
Are coming on us, O my countrymen!
And what if all-avenging Providence,
Strong and retributive, should make us know
The meaning of our words, force us to feel
The desolation and the agony
Of our fierce doings?
                    Spare us yet awhile,
Father and God! O! spare us yet awhile!
Oh! let not English women drag their flight
Fainting beneath the burthen of their babes,
Of the sweet infants, that but yesterday
Laughed at the breast! Sons, brothers, husbands, all
Who ever gazed with fondness on the forms
Which grew up with you round the same fire-side,
And all who ever heard the sabbath-bells
Without the infidel's scorn, make yourselves pure!
Stand forth! be men! repel an impious foe,
Impious and false, a light yet cruel race,
Who laugh away all virtue, mingling mirth
With deeds of murder; and still promising
Freedom, themselves too sensual to be free,
Poison life's amities, and cheat the heart
Of faith and quiet hope, and all that soothes,
And all that lifts the spirit! Stand we forth;
Render them back upon the insulted ocean,
And let them toss as idly on its waves
As the vile seaweed, which some mountain-blast
Swept from our shores! And oh! may we return
Not with a drunken triumph, but with fear,
Repenting of the wrongs with which we stung
So fierce a foe to frenzy!
                    I have told,
O Britons! O my brethren! I have told

Most bitter truth, but without bitterness.
Nor deem my zeal or factious or mistimed;
For never can true courage dwell with them,
Who, playing tricks with conscience, dare not look
At their own vices. We have been too long
Dupes of a deep delusion! Some, belike,
Groaning with restless enmity, expect
All change from change of constituted power;
As if a Government had been a robe,
On which our vice and wretchedness were tagged
Like fancy-points and fringes, with the robe
Pulled off at pleasure. Fondly these attach
A radical causation to a few
Poor drudges of chastising Providence,
Who borrow all their hues and qualities
From our own folly and rank wickedness,
Which gave them birth and nursed them. Others, meanwhile,
Dote with a mad idolatry; and all
Who will not fall before their images,
And yield them worship, they are enemies
Even of their country!
                  Such have I been deemed.—
But, O dear Britain! O my Mother Isle!
Needs must thou prove a name most dear and holy
To me, a son, a brother, and a friend,
A husband, and a father! who revere
All bonds of natural love, and find them all
Within the limits of thy rocky shores.
O native Britain! O my Mother Isle!
How shouldst thou prove aught else but dear and holy
To me, who from thy lakes and mountain-hills,
Thy clouds, thy quiet dales, thy rocks and seas,
Have drunk in all my intellectual life,
All sweet sensations, all ennobling thoughts,
All adoration of the God in nature,
All lovely and all honourable things,
Whatever makes this mortal spirit feel
The joy and greatness of its future being?
There lives nor form nor feeling in my soul
Unborrowed from my country! O divine
And beauteous island! thou hast been my sole
And most magnificent temple, in the which
I walk with awe, and sing my stately songs,

Loving the God that made me!—
                              May my fears,
My filial fears, be vain! and may the vaunts
And menace of the vengeful enemy
Pass like the gust, that roared and died away
In the distant tree: which heard, and only heard
In this low dell, bowed not the delicate grass.

   But now the gentle dew-fall sends abroad
The fruit-like perfume of the golden furze:
The light has left the summit of the hill,
Though still a sunny gleam lies beautiful,
Aslant the ivied beacon. Now farewell,
Farewell, awhile, O soft and silent spot!
On the green sheep-track, up the heathy hill,
Homeward I wind my way; and lo! recalled
From bodings that have well-nigh wearied me,
I find myself upon the brow, and pause
Startled! And after lonely sojourning
In such a quiet and surrounded nook,
This burst of prospect, here the shadowy main,
Dim-tinted, there the mighty majesty
Of that huge amphitheatre of rich
And elmy fields, seems like society—
Conversing with the mind, and giving it
A livelier impulse and a dance of thought!
And now, belovèd Stowey! I behold
Thy church-tower, and, methinks, the four huge elms
Clustering, which mark the mansion of my friend;
And close behind them, hidden from my view,
Is my own lowly cottage, where my babe
And my babe's mother dwell in peace! With light
And quickened footsteps thitherward I tend,
Remembering thee, O green and silent dell!
And grateful, that by nature's quietness
And solitary musings, all my heart
Is softened, and made worthy to indulge
Love, and the thoughts that yearn for human kind.

Nether Stowey, 20 April 1798

WILLIAM WORDSWORTH
1770–1850

40   *Old Man Travelling*

                    The little hedgerow birds,
That peck along the road, regard him not.
He travels on, and in his face, his step,
His gait, is one expression; every limb,
His look and bending figure, all bespeak
A man who does not move with pain, but moves
With thought—He is insensibly subdued
To settled quiet; he is one by whom
All effort seems forgotten, one to whom
Long patience has such mild composure given,
That patience now doth seem a thing, of which
He hath no need. He is by nature led
To peace so perfect, that the young behold
With envy, what the old man hardly feels.
—I asked him whither he was bound, and what
The object of his journey; he replied
'Sir! I am going many miles to take
A last leave of my son, a mariner,
Who from a sea-fight has been brought to Falmouth,
And there is dying in an hospital.'

                                          1797

41   It is not to be thought of that the flood
Of British freedom, which to the open sea
Of the world's praise from dark antiquity
Hath flowed, 'with pomp of waters, unwithstood,'
Road by which all might come and go that would,
And bear out freights of worth to foreign lands;
That this most famous stream in bogs and sands
Should perish: and to evil and to good
Be lost for ever. In our halls is hung
Armoury of the invincible knights of old:
We must be free or die, who speak the tongue
That Shakespeare spake; the faith and morals hold

Which Milton held. In everything we are sprung
Of earth's first blood, have titles manifold.

1803

42   *To the Men of Kent*

Vanguard of liberty, ye Men of Kent,
Ye children of a soil that doth advance
Its haughty brow against the coast of France,
Now is the time to prove your hardiment!
To France be words of invitation sent!
They from their fields can see the countenance
Of your fierce war, may ken the glittering lance,
And hear you shouting forth your brave intent.
Left single, in bold parley, ye, of yore,
Did from the Norman win a gallant wreath;
Confirmed the charters that were yours before;
No parleying now! In Britain is one breath;
We all are with you now from shore to shore;
Ye Men of Kent, 'tis victory or death!

October 1803

43   *November, 1806**

Another year!—another deadly blow!
Another mighty empire overthrown!
And we are left, or shall be left alone;
The last that dare to struggle with the foe.
'Tis well! from this day forward we shall know
That in ourselves our safety must be sought;
That by our own right hands it must be wrought;
That we must stand unpropped, or be laid low.
O dastard whom such foretaste doth not cheer!
We shall exult, if they who rule the land
Be men who hold its many blessings dear,

* The Battle of Jena, on 14 October 1806, resulted in the complete overthrow of Prussia by the French under Napoleon.

Wise, upright, valiant; not a servile band,
Who are to judge of danger which they fear,
And honour which they do not understand.

November 1806

PERCY BYSSHE SHELLEY
1792–1822

44   from *The Revolt of Islam*

Over the utmost hill at length I sped,
    A snowy-steep:—the moon was hanging low
Over the Asian mountains, and outspread
    The plain, the city, and the camp below,
    Skirted the midnight ocean's glimmering flow;
The city's moonlit spires and myriad lamps,
    Like stars in a sublunar sky did glow,
And fires blazed far amid the scattered camps,
Like springs of flame, which burst where'er swift earthquake stamps.

All slept but those in watchful arms who stood,
    And those who sate tending the beacon's light,
And the few sounds from that vast multitude
    Made silence more profound.—Oh, what a might
    Of human thought was cradled in that night!
How many hearts impenetrably veiled
    Beat underneath its shade, what secret fight
Evil and good, in woven passions mailed,
Waged through that silent throng; a war that never failed!

And now the Power of Good held victory,
    So, through the labyrinth of many a tent,
Among the silent millions who did lie
    In innocent sleep, exultingly I went;
    The moon had left Heaven desert now, but lent
From eastern morn the first faint lustre showed
    An armèd youth—over his spear he bent
His downward face.—'A friend!' I cried aloud,
And quickly common hopes made freemen understood.

I sate beside him while the morning beam
    Crept slowly over Heaven, and talked with him
Of those immortal hopes, a glorious theme!
    Which led us forth, until the stars grew dim:
    And all the while, methought, his voice did swim
As if it drownèd in remembrance were
    Of thoughts which make the moist eyes overbrim:
At last, when daylight 'gan to fill the air,
He looked on me, and cried in wonder—'Thou art here!'

Then, suddenly, I knew it was the youth
    In whom its earliest hopes my spirit found;
But envious tongues had stained his spotless truth,
    And thoughtless pride his love in silence bound,
    And shame and sorrow mine in toils had wound,
Whilst he was innocent, and I deluded;
    The truth now came upon me, on the ground
Tears of repenting joy, which fast intruded,
Fell fast, and o'er its peace our mingling spirits brooded.

Thus, while with rapid lips and earnest eyes
    We talked, a sound of sweeping conflict spread
As from the earth did suddenly arise;
    From every tent roused by that clamour dread,
    Our bands outsprung and seized their arms—we sped
Towards the sound: our tribes were gathering far.
    Those sanguine slaves amid ten thousand dead
Stabbed in their sleep, trampled in treacherous war
The gentle hearts whose power their lives had sought to spare.

Like rabid snakes, that sting some gentle child
    Who brings them food, when winter false and fair
Allures them forth with its cold smiles, so wild
    They rage among the camp;—they overbear
    The patriot hosts—confusion, then despair
Descends like night—when 'Laon!' one did cry:
    Like a bright ghost from Heaven that shout did scare
The slaves, and widening through the vaulted sky,
Seemed sent from Earth to Heaven in sign of victory.

In sudden panic those false murderers fled,
    Like insect tribes before the northern gale:
But swifter still, our hosts encompassèd

Their shattered ranks, and in a craggy vale,
    Where even their fierce despair might nought avail,
Hemmed them around!—and then revenge and fear
    Made the high virtue of the patriots fail:
One pointed on his foe the mortal spear—
I rushed before its point, and cried, 'Forbear, forbear!'

The spear transfixed my arm that was uplifted
    In swift expostulation, and the blood
Gushed round its point: I smiled, and—'Oh! thou gifted
    With eloquence which shall not be withstood,
    Flow thus!'—I cried in joy, 'thou vital flood,
Until my heart be dry, ere thus the cause
    For which thou wert aught worthy be subdued—
Ah, ye are pale,—ye weep,—your passions pause,—
'Tis well! ye feel the truth of love's benignant laws.

'Soldiers, our brethren and our friends are slain.
    Ye murdered them, I think, as they did sleep!
Alas, what have ye done? the slightest pain
    Which ye might suffer, there were eyes to weep,
    But ye have quenched them—there were smiles to steep
Your hearts in balm, but they are lost in woe;
    And those whom love did set his watch to keep
Around your tents, truth's freedom to bestow,
Ye stabbed as they did sleep—but they forgive ye now.

'Oh wherefore should ill ever flow from ill,
    And pain still keener pain for ever breed?
We all are brethren—even the slaves who kill
    For hire, are men; and to avenge misdeed
    On the misdoer, doth but Misery feed
With her own broken heart! O Earth, O Heaven!
    And thou, dread Nature, which to every deed
And all that lives or is, to be hath given,
Even as to thee have these done ill, and are forgiven!

'Join then your hands and hearts, and let the past
    Be as a grave which gives not up its dead
To evil thoughts.'—A film then overcast
    My sense with dimness, for the wound, which bled
    Freshly, swift shadows o'er mine eyes had shed.
When I awoke, I lay mid friends and foes,

And earnest countenances on me shed
The light of questioning looks, whilst one did close
My wound with balmiest herbs, and soothed me to repose;

And one whose spear had pierced me, leaned beside,
    With quivering lips and humid eyes;—and all
Seemed like some brothers on a journey wide
    Gone forth, whom now strange meeting did befall
    In a strange land, round one whom they might call
Their friend, their chief, their father, for assay
    Of peril, which had saved them from the thrall
Of death, now suffering. Thus the vast array
Of those fraternal bands were reconciled that day.

1817

CHARLES WOLFE

1791–1823

45   *The Burial of Sir John Moore after Corunna**

Not a drum was heard, not a funeral note,
    As his corse to the rampart we hurried;
Not a soldier discharged his farewell shot
    O'er the grave where our hero we buried.

We buried him darkly at dead of night,
    The sods with our bayonets turning,
By the struggling moonbeam's misty light
    And the lanthorn dimly burning.

No useless coffin enclosed his breast,
    Not in sheet or in shroud we wound him;
But he lay like a warrior taking his rest
    With his martial cloak around him.

---

* Sir John Moore commanded British troops supporting the Spanish Army against Napoleon in the Peninsular War (1808–14). Forced into a 250-mile retreat by a French defeat of the Spanish, he fought valiantly at Corunna, Spain, where he won the battle against the French, but lost his own life (1809).

Few and short were the prayers we said,
    And we spoke not a word of sorrow;
But we steadfastly gazed on the face that was dead,
    And we bitterly thought of the morrow.

We thought, as we hollowed his narrow bed
    And smoothed down his lonely pillow,
That the foe and the stranger would tread o'er his head,
    And we far away on the billow!

Lightly they'll talk of the spirit that's gone,
    And o'er his cold ashes upbraid him—
But little he'll reck, if they let him sleep on
    In the grave where a Briton has laid him.

But half of our heavy task was done
    When the clock struck the hour for retiring;
And we heard the distant and random gun
    That the foe was sullenly firing.

Slowly and sadly we laid him down,
    From the field of his fame fresh and gory;
We carved not a line, and we raised not a stone,
    But we left him alone with his glory.

1816

JOEL BARLOW
1754–1812

46   *Advice to a Raven in Russia*

Black fool, why winter here? These frozen skies,
Worn by your wings and deafened by your cries,
Should warn you hence, where milder suns invite,
And day alternates with his mother night.
    You fear perhaps your food will fail you there,
Your human carnage, that delicious fare
That lured you hither, following still your friend
The great Napoleon to the world's bleak end.
You fear, because the southern climes poured forth
Their clustering nations to infest the north,

Bavarians, Austrians, those who drink the Po
And those who skirt the Tuscan seas below,
With all Germania, Neustria, Belgia, Gaul,
Doomed here to wade through slaughter to their fall,
You fear he left behind no wars, to feed
His feathered cannibals and nurse the breed.

    Fear not, my screamer, call your greedy train,
Sweep over Europe, hurry back to Spain,
You'll find his legions there; the valiant crew
Please best their master when they toil for you.
Abundant there they spread the country o'er
And taint the breeze with every nation's gore,
Iberian, Lusian, British widely strown,
But still more wide and copious flows their own.

    Go where you will; Calabria, Malta, Greece,
Egypt and Syria still his fame increase,
Domingo's fattened isle and India's plains
Glow deep with purple drawn from Gallic veins.
No raven's wing can stretch the flight so far
As the torn bandrols of Napoleon's war.
Choose then your climate, fix your best abode,
He'll make you deserts and he'll bring you blood.

    How could you fear a dearth? have not mankind,
Though slain by millions, millions left behind?
Has not Conscription still the power to wield
Her annual faulchion o'er the human field?
A faithful harvester! or if a man
Escape that gleaner, shall he scape the Ban?
The triple Ban, that like the hound of hell
Gripes with three jowls, to hold his victim well.

    Fear nothing then, hatch fast your ravenous brood,
Teach them to cry to Bonaparte for food;
They'll be like you, of all his suppliant train,
The only class that never cries in vain.
For see what mutual benefits you lend!
(The surest way to fix the mutual friend)
While on his slaughtered troops your tribe are fed,
You cleanse his camp and carry off his dead.
Imperial scavenger! but now you know
Your work is vain amid these hills of snow.
His tentless troops are marbled through with frost
And change to crystal when the breath is lost.
Mere trunks of ice, though limbed like human frames

And lately warmed with life's endearing flames,
They cannot taint the air, the world impest,
Nor can you tear one fibre from their breast.
No! from their visual sockets, as they lie,
With beak and claws you cannot pluck an eye.
The frozen orb, preserving still its form,
Defies your talons as it braves the storm,
But stands and stares to God, as if to know
In what cursed hands he leaves his world below.
    Fly then, or starve; though all the dreadful road
From Minsk to Moscow with their bodies strowed
May count some myriads, yet they can't suffice
To feed you more beneath these dreary skies.
Go back, and winter in the wilds of Spain;
Feast there awhile, and in the next campaign
Rejoin your master; for you'll find him then,
With his new million of the race of men,
Clothed in his thunders, all his flags unfurled,
Raging and storming o'er the prostrate world.
    War after war his hungry soul requires,
State after state shall sink beneath his fires,
Yet other Spains in victim smoke shall rise
And other Moscows suffocate the skies,
Each land lie reeking with its people's slain
And not a stream run bloodless to the main.
Till men resume their souls, and dare to shed
Earth's total vengeance on the monster's head,
Hurl from his blood-built throne this king of woes,
Dash him to dust, and let the world repose.

December 1812

ADAM MICKIEWICZ

1798–1855

47   *The Year 1812*

Year well remembered! Happy who beheld thee!
The commons knew thee as the year of yield,
But as the year of war, the soldiery.

Rumours and skyward prodigies revealed
The poet's dream, the tale on old men's lips,
The spring when kine preferred the barren field.

Short of the acres green with growing tips
They halted lowing, chewed the winter's cud;
The men awaited an apocalypse.

Languid the farmer sought his livelihood
And checked his team and gazed, as if enquiring
What marvels gathered westward while he stood.

He asked the stork, whose white returning wing
Already spread above its native pine
Had raised the early standard of the Spring.

From swallows gathering frozen mud to line
Their tiny homes, or in loud regiments
Ranged over water, he implored a sign.

The thickets hear each night as dusk descends
The woodcock's call. The forests hear the geese
Honk, and go down. The crane's voice never ends.

What storms have whirled them from what shaken seas,
The watchers ask, that they should come so soon?
Or in the feathered world, what mutinies?

For now fresh migrants of a brighter plume
Than finch or plover gleam above the hills,
Impend, descend, and on our meadows loom.

Cavalry! Troop after troop it spills
With strange insignia, strangely armed,
As snow in a spring thaw fills

The valley roads. From the forests long
Bright bayonets issue, as brigades of foot
Debouch like ants, form up, and densely throng;

All heading north as if the bird, the scout,
Had led men here from halcyon lands, impelled
By instincts too imperative to doubt.

War! the war!—a meaning that transpires
To the remotest corner. In the wood
Beyond whose bounds no rustic mind enquires,

Where in the sky the peasant understood
Only the wind's cry, and on earth the brute's
(And all his visitors the neighbourhood),

A sudden glare! A crash! A ball that shoots
Far from the field, makes its impeded way,
Rips through the branches and lays bare the roots.

The bearded bison trembles, and at bay
Heaves to his forelegs, ruffs his mane, and glares
At sudden sparks that glitter on the spray.

The stray bomb spins and hisses; as he stares,
Bursts. And the beast that never knew alarm
Blunders in panic to profounder lairs.

'Whither the battle?'—and the young men arm.
The women pray, 'God is Napoleon's shield,
Napoleon ours', as to the outcome calm.

Spring well remembered! Happy who saw thee then,
Spring of the war, Spring of the mighty yield,
That promised corn but ripened into men.

1834

Translated from the Polish by Donald Davie via the prose version of George Rapall Noyes

VICTOR HUGO
1802–1885

48   *Russia 1812*

The snow fell, and its power was multiplied.
For the first time the Eagle bowed its head—

dark days! Slowly the Emperor returned—
behind him Moscow! Its onion domes still burned.
The snow rained down in blizzards—rained and froze.
Past each white waste a further white waste rose.
None recognized the captains or the flags.
Yesterday the Grand Army, today its dregs!
No one could tell the vanguard from the flanks.
The snow! The hurt men struggled from the ranks,
hid in the bellies of dead horse, in stacks
of shattered caissons. By the bivouacs,
one saw the picket dying at his post,
still standing in his saddle, white with frost,
the stone lips frozen to the bugle's mouth!
Bullets and grapeshot mingled with the snow,
that hailed . . . The Guard, surprised at shivering, march
in a dream now; ice rimes the grey moustache.
The snow falls, always snow! The driving mire
submerges; men, trapped in that white empire,
have no more bread and march on barefoot—gaps!
They were no longer living men and troops,
but a dream drifting in a fog, a mystery,
mourners parading under the black sky.
The solitude, vast, terrible to the eye,
was like a mute avenger everywhere,
as snowfall, floating through the quiet air,
buried the huge army in a huge shroud.
Could anyone leave this kingdom? A crowd—
each man, obsessed with dying, was alone.
Men slept—and died! The beaten mob sludged on,
ditching the guns to burn their carriages.
Two foes. The North, the Czar. The North was worse.
In hollows where the snow was piling up,
one saw whole regiments fallen asleep.
Attila's dawn, Cannaes of Hannibal!
The army marching to its funeral!
Litters, wounded, the dead, deserters—swarm,
crushing the bridges down to cross a stream.
They went to sleep ten thousand, woke up four.
Ney, bringing up the former army's rear,
hacked his horse loose from three disputing Cossacks . . .
All night, the *qui vive?* The alert! Attacks;

retreats! White ghosts would wrench away our guns,
or we would see dim, terrible squadrons,
circles of steel, whirlpools of savages,
rush sabring through the camp like dervishes.
And in this way, whole armies died at night.

The Emperor was there, standing—he saw.
This oak already trembling from the axe,
watched his glories drop from him branch by branch:
chiefs, soldiers. Each one had his turn and chance—
they died! Some lived. These still believed his star,
and kept their watch. They loved the man of war,
this small man with his hands behind his back,
whose shadow, moving to and fro, was black
behind the lighted tent. Still believing, they
accused their destiny of *lèse-majesté*.
His misfortune had mounted on their back.
The man of glory shook. Cold stupefied
him, then suddenly he felt terrified.
Being without belief, he turned to God:
'God of armies, is this the end?' he cried.
And then at last the expiation came,
as he heard someone call him by his name,
someone half-lost in shadow, who said, 'No,
Napoleon.' Napoleon understood,
restless, bareheaded, leaden, as he stood
before his butchered legions in the snow.

1852

Translated from the French by Robert Lowell

FYODOR TYUTCHEV
1803–1873

49　　　　　　*At Vshchizh*

After the tumult and the blood
Had died, had dried,

Silence unmade its history:
A group of mounds; on them
A group of oaks. They spread
Their broad unmindful glories
Over the unheard rumour of those dead
And rustle there, rooted on ruin.
All nature's knowledge
Is to stay unknowing—
Ours, to confess confusion:
Dreamt-out by her,
Our years are apparitions in their coming-going.
Her random seed
Spread to their fruitless feat, she then
Regathers them
Into that peace all history must feed.

17 August 1871

Translated from the Russian by Charles Tomlinson

ROBERT BROWNING
1812–1889

50   *Incident of the French Camp*

I

You know, we French stormed Ratisbon:
    A mile or so away,
On a little mound, Napoleon
    Stood on our storming-day;
With neck out-thrust, you fancy how,
    Legs wide, arms locked behind,
As if to balance the prone brow
    Oppressive with its mind.

II

Just as perhaps he mused 'My plans
    That soar, to earth may fall,

Let once my army-leader Lannes
    Waver at yonder wall,'—
Out 'twixt the battery-smokes there flew
    A rider, bound on bound
Full-galloping; nor bridle drew
    Until he reached the mound.

III

Then off there flung in smiling joy,
    And held himself erect
By just his horse's mane, a boy:
    You hardly could suspect—
(So tight he kept his lips compressed,
    Scarce any blood came through)
You looked twice ere you saw his breast
    Was all but shot in two.

IV

'Well,' cried he, 'Emperor, by God's grace
    We've got you Ratisbon!
The Marshal's in the market-place,
    And you'll be there anon
To see your flag-bird flap his vans
    Where I, to heart's desire,
Perched him!' The chief's eye flashed; his plans
    Soared up again like fire.

V

The chief's eye flashed; but presently
    Softened itself, as sheathes
A film the mother-eagle's eye
    When her bruised eaglet breathes;
'You're wounded!' 'Nay,' the soldier's pride
    Touched to the quick, he said:
'I'm killed, Sire!' And his chief beside,
    Smiling the boy fell dead.

1842

THOMAS HARDY
1840–1928

51

from *The Dynasts*
[*The Eve of Waterloo*]*

(Chorus of Phantoms)

The eyelids of eve fall together at last,
And the forms so foreign to field and tree
Lie down as though native, and slumber fast!

Sore are the thrills of misgiving we see
In the artless champaign at this harlequinade,
Distracting a vigil where calm should be!

The green seems opprest, and the Plain afraid
Of a Something to come, whereof these are the proofs,—
Neither earthquake, nor storm, nor eclipse's shade!

Yea, the coneys are scared by the thud of hoofs,
And their white scuts flash at their vanishing heels,
And swallows abandon the hamlet-roofs.

The mole's tunnelled chambers are crushed by wheels,
The lark's eggs scattered, their owners fled;
And the hedgehog's household the sapper unseals.

The snail draws in at the terrible tread,
But in vain; he is crushed by the felloe-rim;
The worm asks what can be overhead,

And wriggles deep from a scene so grim,
And guesses him safe; for he does not know
What a foul red flood will be soaking him!

---

* The French defeat at the Battle of Waterloo, on 18 June 1815, concluded the
Napoleonic Wars. British and Prussian forces under the Duke of Wellington and Field
Marshal Blücher routed Napoleon's army; on 22 June Napoleon left the field and
signed his abdication. French casualties totalled over 32,000, British and Prussian
23,000.

Beaten about by the heel and toe
Are butterflies, sick of the day's long rheum,
To die of a worse than the weather-foe.

Trodden and bruised to a miry tomb
Are ears that have greened but will never be gold,
And flowers in the bud that will never bloom.

So the season's intent, ere its fruit unfold,
Is frustrate, and mangled, and made succumb,
Like a youth of promise struck stark and cold! . . .

And what of these who tonight have come?
—The young sleep sound; but the weather awakes
In the veterans, pains from the past that numb;

Old stabs of Ind, old Peninsular aches,
Old Friedland chills, haunt their moist mud bed,
Cramps from Austerlitz; till their slumber breaks.

And each soul shivers as sinks his head
On the loam he's to lease with the other dead
From tomorrow's mist-fall till Time be sped!

1908

GEORGE GORDON NOEL, LORD BYRON
1788–1824

52   *The Destruction of Sennacherib**

I

The Assyrian came down like the wolf on the fold,
And his cohorts were gleaming in purple and gold;

---

* Sennacherib, King of Assyria from 709 BC to his death in 681 BC, demolished a series of Judaean cities and besieged Jerusalem. In the account in 2 Chronicles 32, upon which Byron based his poem, the Assyrian army was destroyed by an angel, and Sennacherib retreated in defeat.

And the sheen of their spears was like stars on the sea,
When the blue wave rolls nightly on deep Galilee.

II

Like the leaves of the forest when Summer is green,
That host with their banners at sunset were seen:
Like the leaves of the forest when Autumn hath blown,
That host on the morrow lay withered and strown.

III

For the Angel of Death spread his wings on the blast,
And breathed in the face of the foe as he passed;
And the eyes of the sleepers waxed deadly and chill,
And their hearts but once heaved, and for ever grew still!

IV

And there lay the steed with his nostril all wide,
But through it there rolled not the breath of his pride:
And the foam of his gasping lay white on the turf,
And cold as the spray of the rock-beating surf.

V

And there lay the rider distorted and pale,
With the dew on his brow, and the rust on his mail;
And the tents were all silent, the banners alone,
The lances unlifted, the trumpet unblown.

VI

And the widows of Ashur are loud in their wail,
And the idols are broke in the temple of Baal;
And the might of the Gentile, unsmote by the sword,
Hath melted like snow in the glance of the Lord!

1815

53   from *Childe Harold's Pilgrimage**

There was a sound of revelry by night,
  And Belgium's Capital had gathered then
  Her Beauty and her Chivalry, and bright
  The lamps shone o'er fair women and brave men;
  A thousand hearts beat happily; and when
  Music arose with its voluptuous swell,
  Soft eyes looked love to eyes which spake again,
  And all went merry as a marriage bell;
But hush! hark! a deep sound strikes like a rising knell!

Did ye not hear it?—No; 'twas but the wind,
  Or the car rattling o'er the stony street;
  On with the dance! let joy be unconfined;
  No sleep till morn, when Youth and Pleasure meet
  To chase the glowing Hours with flying feet—
  But hark!—that heavy sound breaks in once more,
  As if the clouds its echo would repeat;
  And nearer, clearer, deadlier than before!
Arm! Arm! it is—it is the cannon's opening roar!

Within a windowed niche of that high hall
  Sate Brunswick's fated chieftain; he did hear
  That sound the first amidst the festival,
  And caught its tone with Death's prophetic ear;
  And when they smiled because he deemed it near,
  His heart more truly knew that peal too well
  Which stretched his father on a bloody bier,
  And roused the vengeance blood alone could quell;
He rushed into the field, and, foremost fighting, fell.

Ah! then and there was hurrying to and fro,
  And gathering tears, and tremblings of distress,
  And cheeks all pale, which but an hour ago
  Blushed at the praise of their own loveliness;
  And there were sudden partings, such as press
  The life from out young hearts, and choking sighs
  Which ne'er might be repeated; who could guess

* The Duchess of Richmond gave a famous ball in Brussels, Wellington's head-quarters, on the evening before the Battle of Waterloo. The Duke of Wellington and most of his officers were present.

If ever more should meet those mutual eyes,
Since upon night so sweet such awful morn could rise!

And there was mounting in hot haste: the steed,
   The mustering squadron, and the clattering car,
   Went pouring forward with impetuous speed,
   And swiftly forming in the ranks of war;
   And the deep thunder peal on peal afar;
   And near, the beat of the alarming drum
   Roused up the soldier ere the morning star;
   While thronged the citizens with terror dumb,
Or whispering, with white lips—'The foe! They come! they come!'

And wild and high the 'Cameron's Gathering' rose!
   The war-note of Lochiel, which Albyn's hills
   Have heard, and heard, too, have her Saxon foes:—
   How in the noon of night that pibroch thrills,
   Savage and shrill! But with the breath which fills
   Their mountain-pipe, so fill the mountaineers
   With the fierce native daring which instils
   The stirring memory of a thousand years,
And Evan's, Donald's fame rings in each clansman's ears!

And Ardennes waves above them her green leaves,
   Dewy with nature's tear-drops, as they pass,
   Grieving, if aught inanimate e'er grieves,
   Over the unreturning brave,—alas!
   Ere evening to be trodden like the grass
   Which now beneath them, but above shall grow
   In its next verdure, when this fiery mass
   Of living valour, rolling on the foe
And burning with high hope, shall moulder cold and low.

Last noon beheld them full of lusty life,
   Last eve in Beauty's circle proudly gay,
   The midnight brought the signal-sound of strife,
   The morn the marshalling in arms,—the day
   Battle's magnificently-stern array!
   The thunder-clouds close o'er it, which when rent
   The earth is covered thick with other clay
   Which her own clay shall cover, heaped and pent,
Rider and horse,—friend, foe,—in one red burial blent!

1816

54   from *Don Juan*

'Let there be light!' said God, and there was light!
   'Let there be blood!' says man, and there's a sea!
The fiat of this spoiled child of the Night
   (For Day ne'er saw his merits) could decree
More evil in an hour, than thirty bright
   Summers could renovate, though they should be
Lovely as those which ripened Eden's fruit;
For war cuts up not only branch, but root.

    .   .   .   .

Oh, thou eternal Homer! who couldst charm
   All ears, though long; all ages, though so short,
By merely wielding with poetic arm
   Arms to which men will never more resort,
Unless gunpowder should be found to harm
   Much less than is the hope of every court,
Which now is leagued young Freedom to annoy;
But they will not find Liberty a Troy:—

Oh, thou eternal Homer! I have now
   To paint a siege, wherein more men were slain,
With deadlier engines and a speedier blow,
   Than in thy Greek gazette of that campaign;
And yet, like all men else, I must allow,
   To vie with thee would be about as vain
As for a brook to cope with ocean's flood;
But still we moderns equal you in blood;

If not in poetry, at least in fact;
   And fact is truth, the grand desideratum!
Of which, howe'er the Muse describes each act,
   There should be ne'ertheless a slight substratum.
But now the town is going to be attacked;
   Great deeds are doing—how shall I relate 'em?
Souls of immortal generals! Phœbus watches
To colour up his rays from your despatches.

Oh, ye great bulletins of Bonaparte!
   Oh, ye less grand long lists of killed and wounded!
Shade of Leonidas, who fought so hearty,

When my poor Greece was once, as now, surrounded!
Oh, Cæsar's Commentaries! now impart, ye
   Shadows of glory! (lest I be confounded)
A portion of your fading twilight hues,
So beautiful, so fleeting, to the Muse.

When I call 'fading' martial immortality,
   I mean, that every age and every year,
And almost every day, in sad reality,
   Some sucking hero is compelled to rear,
Who, when we come to sum up the totality
   Of deeds to human happiness most dear,
Turns out to be a butcher in great business,
Afflicting young folks with a sort of dizziness.

Medals, rank, ribands, lace, embroidery, scarlet,
   Are things immortal to immortal man,
As purple to the Babylonian harlot:
   An uniform to boys is like a fan
To women; there is scarce a crimson varlet
   But deems himself the first in Glory's van.
But Glory's glory; and if you would find
What that is—ask the pig who sees the wind!

At least *he feels it*, and some say he *sees*,
   Because he runs before it like a pig;
Or, if that simple sentence should displease,
   Say, that he scuds before it like a brig,
A schooner, or—but it is time to ease
   This Canto, ere my Muse perceives fatigue.
The next shall ring a peal to shake all people,
Like a bob-major from a village steeple.

Hark! through the silence of the cold, dull night,
   The hum of armies gathering rank on rank!
Lo! dusky masses steal in dubious sight
   Along the leaguered wall and bristling bank
Of the armed river, while with straggling light
   The stars peep through the vapours dim and dank,
Which curl in curious wreaths:—how soon the smoke
Of Hell shall pall them in a deeper cloak!

Here pause we for the present—as even then
   That awful pause, dividing life from death,
Struck for an instant on the hearts of men,
   Thousands of whom were drawing their last breath!
A moment—and all will be life again!
   The march! the charge! the shouts of either faith!
Hurra! and Allah! and—one moment more,
The death-cry drowning in the battle's roar.

1823

55   *On This Day I Complete My Thirty-Sixth Year*

I

'Tis time this heart should be unmoved,
   Since others it hath ceased to move:
Yet, though I cannot be beloved,
     Still let me love!

II

My days are in the yellow leaf;
   The flowers and fruits of Love are gone;
The worm, the canker, and the grief
     Are mine alone!

III

The fire that on my bosom preys
   Is lone as some volcanic isle;
No torch is kindled at its blaze—
     A funeral pile.

IV

The hope, the fear, the jealous care,
   The exalted portion of the pain
And power of love, I cannot share,
     But wear the chain.

V

But 'tis not *thus*—and 'tis not *here*—
   Such thoughts should shake my soul, nor *now*

103

Where Glory decks the hero's bier,
        Or binds his brow.

VI

The Sword, the Banner, and the Field,
    Glory and Greece, around me see!
The Spartan, borne upon his shield,
        Was not more free.

VII

Awake! (not Greece—she *is* awake!)
    Awake, my spirit! Think through *whom*
Thy life-blood tracks its parent lake,
        And then strike home!

VIII

Tread those reviving passions down,
    Unworthy manhood!—unto thee
Indifferent should the smile or frown
        Of Beauty be.

IX

If thou regret'st thy youth, *why live?*
    The land of honourable death
Is here:—up to the Field, and give
        Away thy breath!

X

Seek out—less often sought than found—
    A soldier's grave, for thee the best;
Then look around, and choose thy ground,
        And take thy Rest.

                                        1824

THOMAS BABINGTON MACAULAY,
LORD MACAULAY

1800–1859

56   from *Horatius*
A Lay Made about the Year of the City CCCLX

But hark! the cry is Astur:
    And lo! the ranks divide;
And the great Lord of Luna
    Comes with his stately stride.
Upon his ample shoulders
    Clangs loud the four-fold shield,
And in his hand he shakes the brand
    Which none but he can wield.

He smiled on those bold Romans
    A smile serene and high;
He eyed the flinching Tuscans,
    And scorn was in his eye.
Quoth he, 'The she-wolf's litter
    Stand savagely at bay:
But will ye dare to follow,
    If Astur clears the way?'

Then, whirling up his broadsword
    With both hands to the height,
He rushed against Horatius,
    And smote with all his might.
With shield and blade Horatius
    Right deftly turned the blow.
The blow, though turned, came yet too nigh;
It missed his helm, but gashed his thigh:
The Tuscans raised a joyful cry
    To see the red blood flow.

He reeled, and on Herminius
    He leaned one breathing-space;
Then, like a wild cat mad with wounds,
    Sprang right at Astur's face.

Through teeth, and skull, and helmet
   So fierce a thrust he sped,
The good sword stood a hand-breadth out
   Behind the Tuscan's head.

And the great Lord of Luna
   Fell at that deadly stroke,
As falls on Mount Alvernus
   A thunder-smitten oak.
Far o'er the crashing forest
   The giant arms lie spread;
And the pale augurs, muttering low,
   Gaze on the blasted head.

On Astur's throat Horatius
   Right firmly pressed his heel,
And thrice and four times tugged amain,
   Ere he wrenched out the steel.
'And see,' he cried, 'the welcome,
   Fair guests, that waits you here!
What noble Lucumo comes next
   To taste our Roman cheer?'

But at his haughty challenge
   A sullen murmur ran,
Mingled of wrath, and shame, and dread,
   Along that glittering van.
There lacked not men of prowess,
   Nor men of lordly race;
For all Etruria's noblest
   Were round the fatal place.

But all Etruria's noblest
   Felt their hearts sink to see
On the earth the bloody corpses,
   In the path the dauntless Three:
And, from the ghastly entrance
   Where those bold Romans stood,
All shrank, like boys who unaware,
Ranging the woods to start a hare,
Come to the mouth of the dark lair
Where, growling low, a fierce old bear
   Lies amidst bones and blood.

Was none who would be foremost
  To lead such dire attack:
But those behind cried 'Forward!'
  And those before cried 'Back!'
And backward now and forward
  Wavers the deep array;
And on the tossing sea of steel,
To and fro the standards reel;
And the victorious trumpet-peal
  Dies fitfully away.

Yet one man for one moment
  Strode out before the crowd;
Well known was he to all the Three,
  And they gave him greeting loud.
'Now welcome, welcome, Sextus!
  Now welcome to thy home!
Why dost thou stay, and turn away?
  Here lies the road to Rome.'

Thrice looked he at the city;
  Thrice looked he at the dead;
And thrice came on in fury,
  And thrice turned back in dread:
And, white with fear and hatred,
  Scowled at the narrow way
Where, wallowing in a pool of blood,
  The bravest Tuscans lay.

But meanwhile axe and lever
  Have manfully been plied;
And now the bridge hangs tottering
  Above the boiling tide.
'Come back, come back, Horatius!'
  Loud cried the Fathers all.
'Back, Lartius! back, Herminius!
  Back, ere the ruin fall!'

Back darted Spurius Lartius;
  Herminius darted back:
And, as they passed, beneath their feet
  They felt the timbers crack.

But when they turned their faces,
    And on the farther shore
Saw brave Horatius stand alone,
    They would have crossed once more.

But with a crash like thunder
    Fell every loosened beam,
And, like a dam, the mighty wreck
    Lay right athwart the stream:
And a long shout of triumph
    Rose from the walls of Rome,
As to the highest turret-tops
    Was splashed the yellow foam.

And, like a horse unbroken
    When first he feels the rein,
The furious river struggled hard,
    And tossed his tawny mane,
And burst the curb and bounded,
    Rejoicing to be free,
And whirling down, in fierce career,
Battlement, and plank, and pier,
    Rushed headlong to the sea.

Alone stood brave Horatius,
    But constant still in mind;
Thrice thirty thousand foes before,
    And the broad flood behind.
'Down with him!' cried false Sextus,
    With a smile on his pale face.
'Now yield thee,' cried Lars Porsena,
    'Now yield thee to our grace.'

Round turned he, as not deigning
    Those craven ranks to see;
Nought spake he to Lars Porsena,
    To Sextus nought spake he;
But he saw on Palatinus
    The white porch of his home;
And he spake to the noble river
    That rolls by the towers of Rome.

'Oh, Tiber! father Tiber!
  To whom the Romans pray,
A Roman's life, a Roman's arms,
  Take thou in charge this day!'
So he spake, and speaking sheathed
  The good sword by his side,
And with his harness on his back,
  Plunged headlong in the tide.

No sound of joy or sorrow
  Was heard from either bank;
But friends and foes in dumb surprise,
With parted lips and straining eyes,
  Stood gazing where he sank;
And when above the surges
  They saw his crest appear,
All Rome sent forth a rapturous cry,
And even the ranks of Tuscany
  Could scarce forbear to cheer.

But fiercely ran the current,
  Swollen high by months of rain:
And fast his blood was flowing,
  And he was sore in pain,
And heavy with his armour,
  And spent with changing blows:
And oft they thought him sinking,
  But still again he rose.

Never, I ween, did swimmer,
  In such an evil case,
Struggle through such a raging flood
  Safe to the landing place:
But his limbs were borne up bravely
  By the brave heart within,
And our good father Tiber
  Bare bravely up his chin.

'Curse on him!' quoth false Sextus;
  'Will not the villain drown?
But for this stay, ere close of day
  We should have sacked the town!'
'Heaven help him!' quoth Lars Porsena,

    'And bring him safe to shore;
For such a gallant feat of arms
    Was never seen before.'

And now he feels the bottom;
    Now on dry earth he stands;
Now round him throng the Fathers;
    To press his gory hands;
And now, with shouts and clapping,
    And noise of weeping loud,
He enters through the River-Gate,
    Borne by the joyous crowd.

1842

WILLIAM EDMONSTOUNE AYTOUN
1813–1865

57   from *Edinburgh after Flodden**

Then the Provost he uprose,
    And his lip was ashen white;
But a flush was on his brow,
    And his eye was full of light.
'Thou hast spoken, Randolph Murray,
    Like a soldier stout and true;
Thou hast done a deed of daring
    Had been perilled but by few.
For thou hast not shamed to face us,
    Nor to speak thy ghastly tale,
Standing—thou a knight and captain—
    Here, alive within thy mail!
Now, as my God shall judge me,
    I hold it braver done,
Than hadst thou tarried in thy place,
    And died above my son!
Thou needst not tell it: he is dead.

* In an unsuccessful invasion of England in 1513, King James IV of Scotland was killed in battle at Flodden Field, Northumberland, just over the Scottish border.

God help us all this day!
But speak—how fought the citizens
    Within the furious fray?
For by the might of Mary!
    'Twere something still to tell
That no Scottish foot went backward
    When the Royal Lion fell!'

'No one failed him! He is keeping
    Royal state and semblance still;
Knight and noble lie around him,
    Cold on Flodden's fatal hill.
Of the brave and gallant-hearted,
    Whom ye sent with prayers away,
Not a single man departed
    From his Monarch yesterday.
Had you seen them, O my masters!
    When the night began to fall,
And the English spearmen gathered
    Round a grim and ghastly wall!
As the wolves in winter circle
    Round the leaguer on the heath,
So the greedy foe glared upward,
    Panting still for blood and death.
But a rampart rose before them,
    Which the boldest dared not scale;
Every stone a Scottish body,
    Every step a corpse in mail!
And behind it lay our Monarch,
    Clenching still his shivered sword;
By his side Montrose and Athole,
    At his feet a Southron lord.
All so thick they lay together,
    When the stars lit up the sky,
That I knew not who were stricken,
    Or who yet remained to die.
Few there were when Surrey halted,
    And his wearied host withdrew;
None but dying men around me,
    When the English trumpet blew.
Then I stooped, and took the banner,
    As you see it, from his breast,
And I closed our hero's eyelids,

And I left him to his rest.
In the mountains growled the thunder,
    As I leaped the woeful wall,
And the heavy clouds were settling
    Over Flodden, like a pall.'

1849

MATTHEW ARNOLD
1822–1888

58   from *Sohrab and Rustum*

Then Sohrab with his sword smote Rustum's helm,
Nor clove its steel quite through; but all the crest
He shore away, and that proud horsehair plume,
Never till now defiled, sank to the dust;
And Rustum bowed his head; but then the gloom
Grew blacker, thunder rumbled in the air,
And lightnings rent the cloud; and Ruksh, the horse,
Who stood at hand, uttered a dreadful cry;
No horse's cry was that, most like the roar
Of some pained desert-lion, who all day
Hath trailed the hunter's javelin in his side,
And comes at night to die upon the sand.
The two hosts heard that cry, and quaked for fear,
And Oxus curdled as it crossed his stream.
But Sohrab heard, and quailed not, but rushed on,
And struck again; and again Rustum bowed
His head; but this time all the blade, like glass,
Sprang in a thousand shivers on the helm,
And in the hand the hilt remained alone.
Then Rustum raised his head; his dreadful eyes
Glared, and he shook on high his menacing spear,
And shouted: *Rustum!*—Sohrab heard that shout,
And shrank amazed; back he recoiled one step,
And scanned with blinking eyes the advancing form;
And then he stood bewildered; and he dropped
His covering shield, and the spear pierced his side.
He reeled, and staggering back, sank to the ground;
And then the gloom dispersed, and the wind fell,

And the bright sun broke forth, and melted all
The cloud; and the two armies saw the pair—
Saw Rustum standing, safe upon his feet,
And Sohrab, wounded, on the bloody sand.
    Then, with a bitter smile, Rustum began:—
'Sohrab, thou thoughtest in thy mind to kill
A Persian lord this day, and strip his corpse,
And bear thy trophies to Afrasiab's tent.
Or else that the great Rustum would come down
Himself to fight, and that thy wiles would move
His heart to take a gift, and let thee go.
And then that all the Tartar host would praise
Thy courage or thy craft, and spread thy fame,
To glad thy father in his weak old age.
Fool, thou art slain, and by an unknown man!
Dearer to the red jackals shalt thou be
Than to thy friends, and to thy father old.'

          .   .   .   .   .   .

    Then, at the point of death, Sohrab replied:—
'A life of blood indeed, thou dreadful man!
But thou shalt yet have peace; only not now,
Not yet! but thou shalt have it on that day,
When thou shalt sail in a high-masted ship,
Thou and the other peers of Kai Khosroo,
Returning home over the salt blue sea,
From laying thy dear master in his grave.'
    And Rustum gazed in Sohrab's face, and said:—
'Soon be that day, my son, and deep that sea!
Till then, if fate so wills, let me endure.'
    He spoke; and Sohrab smiled on him, and took
The spear, and drew it from his side, and eased
His wound's imperious anguish; but the blood
Came welling from the open gash, and life
Flowed with the stream; all down his cold white side
The crimson torrent ran, dim now and soiled,
Like the soiled tissue of white violets
Left, freshly gathered, on their native bank,
By children whom their nurses call with haste
Indoors from the sun's eye; his head drooped low,
His limbs grew slack; motionless, white, he lay—
White, with eyes closed; only when heavy gasps,
Deep heavy gasps quivering through all his frame,

Convulsed him back to life, he opened them,
And fixed them feebly on his father's face;
Till now all strength was ebbed, and from his limbs
Unwillingly the spirit fled away,
Regretting the warm mansion which it left,
And youth, and bloom, and this delightful world.
  So, on the bloody sand, Sohrab lay dead;
And the great Rustum drew his horseman's cloak
Down o'er his face, and sate by his dead son.
As those black granite pillars, once high-reared
By Jemshid in Persepolis, to bear
His house, now 'mid their broken flights of steps
Lie prone, enormous, down the mountain side—
So in the sand lay Rustum by his son.
  And night came down over the solemn waste,
And the two gazing hosts, and that sole pair,
And darkened all; and a cold fog, with night,
Crept from the Oxus. Soon a hum arose,
As of a great assembly loosed, and fires
Began to twinkle through the fog; for now
Both armies moved to camp, and took their meal;
The Persians took it on the open sands
Southward, the Tartars by the river marge;
And Rustum and his son were left alone.
  But the majestic river floated on,
Out of the mist and hum of that low land,
Into the frosty starlight, and there moved,
Rejoicing, through the hushed Chorasmian waste,
Under the solitary moon; he flowed
Right for the polar star, past Orgunjè,
Brimming, and bright, and large; then sands begin
To hem his watery march, and dam his streams,
And split his currents; that for many a league
The shorn and parcelled Oxus strains along
Through beds of sand and matted rushy isles—
Oxus, forgetting the bright speed he had
In his high mountain-cradle in Pamere,
A foiled circuitous wanderer—till at last
The longed-for dash of waves is heard, and wide
His luminous home of waters opens, bright

And tranquil, from whose floor the new-bathed stars
Emerge, and shine upon the Aral Sea.

1853

ALFRED, LORD TENNYSON
1809–1892

59   *The Revenge*
A Ballad of the Fleet

I

At Flores in the Azores Sir Richard Grenville lay,
And a pinnace, like a fluttered bird, came flying from far away:
'Spanish ships of war at sea! we have sighted fifty-three!'
Then sware Lord Thomas Howard: ''Fore God I am no coward;
But I cannot meet them here, for my ships are out of gear,
And the half my men are sick. I must fly, but follow quick.
We are six ships of the line; can we fight with fifty-three?'

II

Then spake Sir Richard Grenville: 'I know you are no coward;
You fly them for a moment to fight with them again.
But I've ninety men and more that are lying sick ashore.
I should count myself the coward if I left them, my Lord Howard,
To these Inquisition dogs and the devildoms of Spain.'

III

So Lord Howard past away with five ships of war that day,
Till he melted like a cloud in the silent summer heaven;
But Sir Richard bore in hand all his sick men from the land
Very carefully and slow,
Men of Bideford in Devon,
And we laid them on the ballast down below;
For we brought them all aboard,
And they blest him in their pain, that they were not left to Spain,
To the thumbscrew and the stake, for the glory of the Lord.

IV

He had only a hundred seamen to work the ship and to fight,
And he sailed away from Flores till the Spaniard came in sight,
With his huge sea-castles heaving upon the weather bow.
'Shall we fight or shall we fly?
Good Sir Richard, tell us now,
For to fight is but to die!
There'll be little of us left by the time this sun be set.'
And Sir Richard said again: 'We be all good English men.
Let us bang these dogs of Seville, the children of the devil,
For I never turned my back upon Don or devil yet.'

V

Sir Richard spoke and he laughed, and we roared a hurrah, and so
The little *Revenge* ran on sheer into the heart of the foe,
With her hundred fighters on deck, and her ninety sick below;
For half of their fleet to the right and half to the left were seen,
And the little *Revenge* ran on through the long sea-lane between.

VI

Thousands of their soldiers looked down from their decks and laughed,
Thousands of their seamen made mock at the mad little craft
Running on and on, till delayed
By their mountain-like San Philip that, of fifteen hundred tons,
And up-shadowing high above us with her yawning tiers of guns,
Took the breath from our sails, and we stayed.

VII

And while now the great San Philip hung above us like a cloud
Whence the thunderbolt will fall
Long and loud,
Four galleons drew away
From the Spanish fleet that day,
And two upon the larboard and two upon the starboard lay,
And the battle-thunder broke from them all.

VIII

But anon the great San Philip, she bethought herself and went
Having that within her womb that had left her ill content;
And the rest they came aboard us, and they fought us hand to hand,

For a dozen times they came with their pikes and musqueteers,
And a dozen times we shook 'em off as a dog that shakes his ears
When he leaps from the water to the land.

IX

And the sun went down, and the stars came out far over the summer sea,
But never a moment ceased the fight of the one and the fifty-three.
Ship after ship, the whole night long, their high-built galleons came,
Ship after ship, the whole night long, with her battle-thunder and flame;
Ship after ship, the whole night long, drew back with her dead and her
    shame.
For some were sunk and many were shattered, and so could fight us no
    more—
God of battles, was ever a battle like this in the world before?

X

For he said 'Fight on! fight on!'
Though his vessel was all but a wreck;
And it chanced that, when half of the short summer night was gone,
With a grisly wound to be dressed he had left the deck,
But a bullet struck him that was dressing it suddenly dead,
And himself he was wounded again in the side and the head,
And he said 'Fight on! fight on!'

XI

And the night went down, and the sun smiled out far over the summer
    sea,
And the Spanish fleet with broken sides lay round us all in a ring;
But they dared not touch us again, for they feared that we still could
    sting,
So they watched what the end would be.
And we had not fought them in vain,
But in perilous plight were we,
Seeing forty of our poor hundred were slain,
And half of the rest of us maimed for life
In the crash of the cannonades and the desperate strife;
And the sick men down in the hold were most of them stark and cold,
And the pikes were all broken or bent, and the powder was all of it spent;
And the masts and the rigging were lying over the side;
But Sir Richard cried in his English pride,
'We have fought such a fight for a day and a night
As may never be fought again!

We have won great glory, my men!
And a day less or more
At sea or ashore,
We die—does it matter when?
Sink me the ship, Master Gunner—sink her, split her in twain!
Fall into the hands of God, not into the hands of Spain!'

XII

And the gunner said 'Ay, ay,' but the seamen made reply:
'We have children, we have wives,
And the Lord hath spared our lives.
We will make the Spaniard promise, if we yield, to let us go;
We shall live to fight again and to strike another blow.'
And the lion there lay dying, and they yielded to the foe.

XIII

And the stately Spanish men to their flagship bore him then,
Where they laid him by the mast, old Sir Richard caught at last,
And they praised him to his face with their courtly foreign grace;
But he rose upon their decks, and he cried:
'I have fought for Queen and Faith like a valiant man and true;
I have only done my duty as a man is bound to do:
With a joyful spirit I Sir Richard Grenville die!'
And he fell upon their decks, and he died.

XIV

And they stared at the dead that had been so valiant and true,
And had holden the power and glory of Spain so cheap
That he dared her with one little ship and his English few;
Was he devil or man? He was devil for aught they knew,
But they sank his body with honour down into the deep,
And they manned the *Revenge* with a swarthier alien crew,
And away she sailed with her loss and longed for her own;
When a wind from the lands they had ruined awoke from sleep,
And the water began to heave and the weather to moan,
And or ever that evening ended a great gale blew,
And a wave like the wave that is raised by an earthquake grew,
Till it smote on their hulls and their sails and their masts and their
    flags,

And the whole sea plunged and fell on the shot-sha
   Spain,
And the little *Revenge* herself went down by the islar
To be lost evermore in the main.

1880

60 | *The Charge of the Light Brigade**

I

Half a league, half a league,
   Half a league onward,
All in the valley of Death
   Rode the six hundred.
'Forward, the Light Brigade!
Charge for the guns!' he said:
Into the valley of Death
   Rode the six hundred.

II

'Forward, the Light Brigade!'
Was there a man dismayed?
Not though the soldier knew
   Some one had blundered:
Their's not to make reply,
Their's not to reason why,
Their's but to do and die:
Into the valley of Death
   Rode the six hundred.

III

Cannon to right of them,
Cannon to left of them,
Cannon in front of them
   Volleyed and thundered;
Stormed at with shot and shell,

---

* In 1854, during the Crimean War, an English light-cavalry brigade of over 600 men was led into a hopeless charge against well-protected batteries of Russian artillery at Balaklava. The blunder resulted in the deaths of well over two-thirds of the British soldiers.

Boldly they rode and well,
Into the jaws of Death,
Into the mouth of Hell
   Rode the six hundred.

IV

Flashed all their sabres bare,
Flashed as they turned in air
Sabring the gunners there,
Charging an army, while
   All the world wondered:
Plunged in the battery-smoke
Right through the line they broke;
Cossack and Russian
Reeled from the sabre-stroke
   Shattered and sundered.
Then they rode back, but not
   Not the six hundred.

V

Cannon to right of them,
Cannon to left of them,
Cannon behind them
   Volleyed and thundered;
Stormed at with shot and shell,
While horse and hero fell,
They that had fought so well
Came through the jaws of Death,
Back from the mouth of Hell,
All that was left of them,
   Left of six hundred.

VI

When can their glory fade?
O the wild charge they made!
   All the world wondered.
Honour the charge they made!
Honour the Light Brigade,
   Noble six hundred!

2 December 1854

61   from *Maud*

I

My life has crept so long on a broken wing
Through cells of madness, haunts of horror and fear,
That I come to be grateful at last for a little thing:
My mood is changed, for it fell at a time of year
When the face of night is fair on the dewy downs,
And the shining daffodil dies, and the Charioteer
And starry Gemini hang like glorious crowns
Over Orion's grave low down in the west,
That like a silent lightning under the stars
She seemed to divide in a dream from a band of the blest,
And spoke of a hope for the world in the coming wars—
'And in that hope, dear soul, let trouble have rest,
Knowing I tarry for thee,' and pointed to Mars
As he glowed like a ruddy shield on the Lion's breast.

II

And it was but a dream, yet it yielded a dear delight
To have looked, though but in a dream, upon eyes so fair,
That had been in a weary world my one thing bright;
And it was but a dream, yet it lightened my despair
When I thought that a war would arise in defence of the right,
That an iron tyranny now should bend or cease,
The glory of manhood stand on his ancient height,
Nor Britain's one sole God be the millionaire:
No more shall commerce be all in all, and Peace
Pipe on her pastoral hillock a languid note,
And watch her harvest ripen, her herd increase,
Nor the cannon-bullet rust on a slothful shore,
And the cobweb woven across the cannon's throat
Shall shake its threaded tears in the wind no more.

III

And as months ran on and rumour of battle grew,
'It is time, it is time, O passionate heart,' said I
(For I cleaved to a cause that I felt to be pure and true),
'It is time, O passionate heart and morbid eye,

That old hysterical mock-disease should die.'
And I stood on a giant deck and mixed my breath
With a loyal people shouting a battle cry,
Till I saw the dreary phantom arise and fly
Far into the North, and battle, and seas of death.

IV

Let it go or stay, so I wake to the higher aims
Of a land that has lost for a little her lust of gold,
And love of a peace that was full of wrongs and shames,
Horrible, hateful, monstrous, not to be told;
And hail once more to the banner of battle unrolled!
Though many a light shall darken, and many shall weep
For those that are crushed in the clash of jarring claims,
Yet God's just wrath shall be wreaked on a giant liar;
And many a darkness into the light shall leap,
And shine in the sudden making of splendid names,
And noble thought be freer under the sun,
And the heart of a people beat with one desire;
For the peace, that I deemed no peace, is over and done,
And now by the side of the Black and the Baltic deep,
And deathful-grinning mouths of the fortress, flames
The blood-red blossom of war with a heart of fire.

V

Let it flame or fade, and the war roll down like a wind,
We have proved we have hearts in a cause, we are noble still,
And myself have awaked, as it seems, to the better mind;
It is better to fight for the good than to rail at the ill;
I have felt with my native land, I am one with my kind,
I embrace the purpose of God, and the doom assigned.

1855

WILLIAM MAKEPEACE THACKERAY

1811–1863

62   *The Due of the Dead**

I sit beside my peaceful hearth,
   With curtains drawn and lamp trimmed bright
I watch my children's noisy mirth;
   I drink in home, and its delight.

I sip my tea, and criticise
   The war, from flying rumours caught;
Trace on the map, to curious eyes,
   How here they marched, and there they fought.

In intervals of household chat,
   I lay down strategetic laws;
Why this manœuvre, and why that;
   Shape the event, or show the cause.

Or, in smooth dinner-table phrase,
   'Twixt soup and fish, discuss the fight;
Give to each chief his blame or praise;
   Say who was wrong and who was right.

Meanwhile o'er Alma's bloody plain
   The scathe of battle has rolled by—
The wounded writhe and groan—the slain
   Lie naked staring to the sky.

The out-worn surgeon plies his knife,
   Nor pauses with the closing day;
While those who have escaped with life
   Find food and fuel as they may.

And when their eyes in sleep they close,
   After scant rations duly shared,

---

* Allied British and French forces entered the Crimea in September 1854, engaging in a year-long series of debilitating battles in the area of the Alma River before finally capturing Sevastopol.

Plague picks his victims out, from those
　　Whom chance of battle may have spared.

Still when the bugle sounds the march,
　　He tracks his prey through steppe and dell;
Hangs fruit to tempt the throats that parch,
　　And poisons every stream and well.

All this with gallant hearts is done;
　　All this with patient hearts is borne:
And they by whom the laurel's won
　　Are seldom they by whom 'tis worn.

No deed, no suffering of the war,
　　But wins us fame, or spares us ill;
Those noble swords, though drawn afar,
　　Are guarding English homesteads still.

Owe we a debt to these brave men,
　　Unpaid by aught that's said or sung;
By leaders from a ready pen,
　　Or phrases from a flippant tongue.

The living, England's hand may crown
　　With recognition, frank and free;
With titles, medals, and renown;
　　The wounded shall our pensioners be.

But they, who meet a soldier's doom—
　　Think you, it is enough, good friend,
To plant the laurel at their tomb,
　　And carve their names—and there an end?

No. They are gone: but there are left
　　Those they loved best while they were here—
Parents made childless, babes bereft,
　　Desolate widows, sisters dear.

All these let grateful England take;
　　And, with a large and liberal heart,
Cherish, for her slain soldiers' sake,
　　And of her fullness give them part.

Fold them within her sheltering breast;
    Their parent, husband, brother, prove.
That so the dead may be at rest,
    Knowing those cared for whom they love.

1854

RALPH WALDO EMERSON
1803–1882

63   *Concord Hymn**

Sung at the completion of the Battle Monument,
19 April 1836

By the rude bridge that arched the flood,
    Their flag to April's breeze unfurled,
Here once the embattled farmers stood,
    And fired the shot heard round the world.

The foe long since in silence slept;
    Alike the conqueror silent sleeps;
And Time the ruined bridge has swept
    Down the dark stream which seaward creeps.

On this green bank, by this soft stream,
    We set today a votive stone;
That memory may their deed redeem,
    When, like our sires, our sons are gone.

Spirit, that made those heroes dare
    To die, and leave their children free,
Bid Time and Nature gently spare
    The shaft we raise to them and thee.

1836

* On the night of 18–19 April 1775, Paul Revere and other riders gathered a band of minute men from the Massachusetts countryside to confront advancing British troops. Battles with the British in Lexington and Concord the following day marked the beginning of the American War of Independence.

WALT WHITMAN
1819–1892

64 *Beat! Beat! Drums!*

Beat! beat! drums!—blow! bugles! blow!
Through the windows—through doors—burst like a ruthless force,
Into the solemn church, and scatter the congregation,
Into the school where the scholar is studying;
Leave not the bridegroom quiet—no happiness must he have now with
his bride,
Nor the peaceful farmer any peace, ploughing his field or gathering his
grain,
So fierce you whirr and pound you drums—so shrill you bugles blow.

Beat! beat! drums!—blow! bugles! blow!
Over the traffic of cities—over the rumble of wheels in the streets;
Are beds prepared for sleepers at night in the houses? no sleepers must
sleep in those beds,
No bargainers' bargains by day—no brokers or speculators—would
they continue?
Would the talkers be talking? would the singer attempt to sing?
Would the lawyer rise in the court to state his case before the judge?
Then rattle quicker, heavier drums—you bugles wilder blow.

Beat! beat! drums!—blow! bugles! blow!
Make no parley—stop for no expostulation,
Mind not the timid—mind not the weeper or prayer,
Mind not the old man beseeching the young man,
Let not the child's voice be heard, nor the mother's entreaties,
Make even the trestles to shake the dead where they lie awaiting the
hearses,
So strong you thump O terrible drums—so loud you bugles blow.

1861

65 *Come up from the Fields Father*

Come up from the fields father, here's a letter from our Pete,
And come to the front door mother, here's a letter from thy dear son.

126

Lo, 'tis autumn,
Lo, where the trees, deeper green, yellower and redder,
Cool and sweeten Ohio's villages with leaves fluttering in the moderate
 wind,
Where apples ripe in the orchards hang and grapes on the trellised
 vines,
(Smell you the smell of the grapes on the vines?
Smell you the buckwheat where the bees were lately buzzing?)
Above all, lo, the sky so calm, so transparent after the rain, and with
 wondrous clouds,
Below too, all calm, all vital and beautiful, and the farm prospers well.
Down in the fields all prospers well,
But now from the fields come father, come at the daughter's call,
And come to the entry mother, to the front door come right away.

Fast as she can she hurries, something ominous, her steps trembling,
She does not tarry to smooth her hair nor adjust her cap.

Open the envelope quickly,
O this is not our son's writing, yet his name is signed,
O a strange hand writes for our dear son, O stricken mother's soul!

All swims before her eyes, flashes with black, she catches the main
 words only,
Sentences broken, *gunshot wound in the breast, cavalry skirmish, taken to
 hospital,*
At present low, but will soon be better.

Ah now the single figure to me,
Amid all teeming and wealthy Ohio with all its cities and farms,
Sickly white in the face and dull in the head, very faint,
By the jamb of a door leans.

Grieve not so, dear mother, (the just–grown daughter speaks through her
 sobs,
The little sisters huddle around speechless and dismayed,)
See, dearest mother, the letter says Pete will soon be better.

Alas poor boy, he will never be better, (nor may-be needs to be better,
 that brave and simple soul,)
While they stand at home at the door he is dead already,
The only son is dead.

But the mother needs to be better,
She with thin form presently dressed in black,
By day her meals untouched, then at night fitfully sleeping, often
  waking,
In the midnight waking, weeping, longing with one deep longing,
O that she might withdraw unnoticed, silent from life escape and
  withdraw,
To follow, to seek, to be with her dear dead son.

1865

66   *Vigil Strange I Kept on the Field one Night*

Vigil strange I kept on the field one night;
When you my son and my comrade dropped at my side that day,
One look I but gave which your dear eyes returned with a look I shall
  never forget,
One touch of your hand to mine O boy, reached up as you lay on the
  ground,
Then onward I sped in the battle, the even-contested battle,
Till late in the night relieved to the place at last again I made my way,
Found you in death so cold dear comrade, found your body son of
  responding kisses, (never again on earth responding,)
Bared your face in the starlight, curious the scene, cool blew the
  moderate night-wind,
Long there and then in vigil I stood, dimly around me the battlefield
  spreading,
Vigil wondrous and vigil sweet there in the fragrant silent night,
But not a tear fell, not even a long-drawn sigh, long, long I gazed,
Then on the earth partially reclining sat by your side leaning my chin
  in my hands,
Passing sweet hours, immortal and mystic hours with you dearest
  comrade—not a tear, not a word,
Vigil of silence, love and death, vigil for you my son and my soldier,
As onward silently stars aloft, eastward new ones upward stole,
Vigil final for you brave boy, (I could not save you, swift was your death,
I faithfully loved you and cared for you living, I think we shall surely
  meet again,)
Till at latest lingering of the night, indeed just as the dawn appeared,
My comrade I wrapped in his blanket, enveloped well his form,
Folded the blanket well tucking it carefully over head and carefully
  under feet,

And there and then and bathed by the rising sun, my son in his grave,
    in his rude-dug grave I deposited,
Ending my vigil strange with that, vigil of night and battlefield dim,
Vigil for boy of responding kisses, (never again on earth responding,)
Vigil for comrade swiftly slain, vigil I never forget, how as day
    brightened,
I rose from the chill ground and folded my soldier well in his blanket,
And buried him where he fell.

1865

67   *The Wound-Dresser*

An old man bending I come among new faces,
Years looking backward resuming in answer to children,
Come tell us old man, as from young men and maidens that love me,
(Aroused and angry, I'd thought to beat the alarum, and urge relentless
    war,
But soon my fingers failed me, my face drooped and I resigned myself,
To sit by the wounded and soothe them, or silently watch the dead;)
Years hence of these scenes, of these furious passions, these chances,
Of unsurpassed heroes, (was one side so brave? the other was equally
    brave;)
Now be witness again, paint the mightiest armies of earth,
Of those armies so rapid so wondrous what saw you to tell us?
What stays with you latest and deepest? of curious panics,
Of hard-fought engagements or sieges tremendous what deepest
    remains?

*

O maidens and young men I love and that love me,
What you ask of my days those the strangest and sudden your talking
    recalls,
Soldier alert I arrive after a long march covered with sweat and dust,
In the nick of time I come, plunge in the fight, loudly shout in the rush
    of successful charge,
Enter the captured works—yet lo, like a swift-running river they fade,
Pass and are gone they fade—I dwell not on soldiers' perils or soldiers'
    joys,
(Both I remember well—many the hardships, few the joys, yet
    I was content.)

But in silence, in dreams' projections,
While the world of gain and appearance and mirth goes on,
So soon what is over forgotten, and waves wash the imprints off the
    sand,
With hinged knees returning I enter the doors, (while for you up there,
Whoever you are, follow without noise and be of strong heart.)

Bearing the bandages, water and sponge,
Straight and swift to my wounded I go,
Where they lie on the ground after the battle brought in,
Where their priceless blood reddens the grass the ground,

Or to the rows of the hospital tent, or under the roofed hospital,
To the long rows of cots up and down each side I return,
To each and all one after another I draw near, not one do I miss,
An attendant follows holding a tray, he carries a refuse pail,
Soon to be filled with clotted rags and blood, emptied, and filled again.

I onward go, I stop,
With hinged knees and steady hand to dress wounds,
I am firm with each, the pangs are sharp yet unavoidable,
One turns to me his appealing eyes—poor boy! I never knew you,
Yet I think I could not refuse this moment to die for you, if that would
    save you.

*

On, on I go, (open doors of time! open hospital doors!)
The crushed head I dress, (poor crazed hand tear not the bandage
    away,)
The neck of the cavalry-man with the bullet through and through
    I examine,
Hard the breathing rattles, quite glazed already the eye, yet life
    struggles hard,
(Come sweet death! be persuaded O beautiful death!
In mercy come quickly.)

From the stump of the arm, the amputated hand,
I undo the clotted lint, remove the slough, wash off the matter and
    blood,
Back on his pillow the soldier bends with curved neck and side-falling
    head,

His eyes are closed, his face is pale, he dares not look on the bloody
stump,
And has not yet looked on it.

I dress a wound in the side, deep, deep,
But a day or two more, for see the frame all wasted and sinking,
And the yellow-blue countenance see.

I dress the perforated shoulder, the foot with the bullet-wound,
Cleanse the one with a gnawing and putrid gangrene, so sickening, so
offensive,
While the attendant stands behind aside me holding the tray and pail.

I am faithful, I do not give out,
The fractured thigh, the knee, the wound in the abdomen,
These and more I dress with impassive hand, (yet deep in my breast a
fire, a burning flame.)

*

Thus in silence in dreams' projections,
Returning, resuming, I thread my way through the hospitals,
The hurt and wounded I pacify with soothing hand,
I sit by the restless all the dark night, some are so young,
Some suffer so much, I recall the experience sweet and sad,
(Many a soldier's loving arms about this neck have crossed and rested,
Many a soldier's kiss dwells on these bearded lips.)

1876

68   *Reconciliation*

Word over all, beautiful as the sky,
Beautiful that war and all its deeds of carnage must in time be utterly
lost,
That the hands of the sisters Death and Night incessantly softly wash
again, and ever again, this soiled world;
For my enemy is dead, a man divine as myself is dead,
I look where he lies white-faced and still in the coffin—I draw near,
Bend down, and touch lightly with my lips the white face in the coffin.

1866

HERMAN MELVILLE
1819–1891

69   *The Portent**

Hanging from the beam,
  Slowly swaying (such the law),
Gaunt the shadow on your green,
  Shenandoah!
The cut is on the crown
(Lo, John Brown),
And the stabs shall heal no more.

Hidden in the cap
  Is the anguish none can draw;
So your future veils its face,
  Shenandoah!
But the streaming beard is shown
(Weird John Brown),
The meteor of the war.

1859

70   *Ball's Bluff*†
                     A Reverie

One noonday, at my window in the town,
  I saw a sight—saddest that eyes can see—
Young soldiers marching lustily
    Unto the wars,

---

* On 16 October 1859, the abolitionist John Brown and a troop of eighteen men raided the United States Arsenal at Harper's Ferry, Virginia, near the Shenandoah Valley. He was captured two days later, tried on a charge of treason and inciting a slave uprising, convicted, and in December 1859, hanged.
† On 21 October 1861, four regiments of Union troops packed into boats on the Potomac River faced Confederate attack at Ball's Bluff, where they were pinned against a hundred-foot cliff. More than 1,000 Union soldiers were killed in the massacre that ensued.

With fifes, and flags in mottoed pageantry;
        While all the porches, walks, and doors
Were rich with ladies cheering royally.

They moved like Juny morning on the wave,
        Their hearts were fresh as clover in its prime
        (It was the breezy summer time),
                Life throbbed so strong,
How should they dream that Death in a rosy clime
        Would come to thin their shining throng?
Youth feels immortal, like the gods sublime.

Weeks passed; and at my window, leaving bed,
        By night I mused, of easeful sleep bereft,
        On those brave boys (Ah War! thy theft);
                Some marching feet
Found pause at last by cliffs Potomac cleft;
        Wakeful I mused, while in the street
Far footfalls died away till none were left.

October 1861

71   *Shiloh**
                            A Requiem

            Skimming lightly, wheeling still,
                The swallows fly low
            Over the field in clouded days,
                The forest-field of Shiloh—
            Over the field where April rain
            Solaced the parched ones stretched in pain
            Through the pause of night
            That followed the Sunday fight
                Around the church of Shiloh—
            The church so lone, the log-built one,
            That echoed to many a parting groan

* One of the bloodiest battles of the American Civil War was fought around the
Shiloh Baptist Church in Tennessee on 6 and 7 April 1862. Union losses totalled more
than 13,000 men, Confederate losses more then 10,000.

And natural prayer
Of dying foemen mingled there—
Foemen at morn, but friends at eve—
    Fame or country least their care:
(What like a bullet can undeceive!)
    But now they lie low,
While over them the swallows skim,
    And all is hushed at Shiloh.

April 1862

72   *The College Colonel*

He rides at their head;
    A crutch by his saddle just slants in view,
One slung arm is in splints, you see,
    Yet he guides his strong steed—how coldly too.

He brings his regiment home—
    Not as they filed two years before,
But a remnant half-tattered, and battered, and worn,
Like castaway sailors, who—stunned
        By the surf's loud roar,
    Their mates dragged back and seen no more—
Again and again breast the surge,
    And at last crawl, spent, to shore.

A still rigidity and pale—
    An Indian aloofness lones his brow;
He has lived a thousand years
Compressed in battle's pains and prayers,
    Marches and watches slow.

There are welcoming shouts, and flags;
    Old men off hat to the Boy,
Wreaths from gay balconies fall at his feet,
    But to *him*—there comes alloy.

134

It is not that a leg is lost,
    It is not that an arm is maimed,
It is not that the fever has racked—
    Self he has long disclaimed.

But all through the Seven Days' Fight,
    And deep in the Wilderness grim,
And in the field-hospital tent,
    And Petersburg crater, and dim
Lean brooding in Libby, there came—
    Ah heaven!—what *truth* to him.

1866

EMILY DICKINSON
1830–1886

73

My Portion is Defeat—today—
A paler luck than Victory—
Less Paeans—fewer Bells—
The Drums don't follow Me—with tunes—
Defeat—a somewhat slower—means—
More Arduous than Balls—

'Tis populous with Bone and stain—
And Men too straight to stoop again,
And Piles of solid Moan—
And Chips of Blank—in Boyish Eyes—
And scraps of Prayer—
And Death's surprise,
Stamped visible—in Stone—

There's somewhat prouder, over there—
The Trumpets tell it to the Air—
How different Victory
To Him who has it—and the One
Who to have had it, would have been
Contenteder—to die—

circa 1862

74
My Triumph lasted till the Drums
Had left the Dead alone
And then I dropped my Victory
And chastened stole along
To where the finished Faces
Conclusion turned on me
And then I hated Glory
And wished myself were They.

What is to be is best descried
When it has also been—
Could Prospect taste of Retrospect
The tyrannies of Men
Were Tenderer—diviner
The Transitive toward.
A Bayonet's contrition
Is nothing to the Dead.

circa 1872

STEPHEN CRANE
1871–1900

75
Do not weep, maiden, for war is kind.
Because your lover threw wild hands toward the sky
And the affrighted steed ran on alone,
Do not weep.
War is kind.

Hoarse, booming drums of the regiment,
Little souls who thirst for fight,
These men were born to drill and die.
The unexplained glory flies above them,
Great is the Battle-God, great, and his Kingdom—
A field where a thousand corpses lie.

Do not weep, babe, for war is kind.
Because your father tumbled in the yellow trenches,

Raged at his breast, gulped and died,
Do not weep.
War is kind.

Swift blazing flag of the regiment,
Eagle with crest of red and gold,
These men were born to drill and die.
Point for them the virtue of slaughter,
Make plain to them the excellence of killing
And a field where a thousand corpses lie.

Mother whose heart hung humble as a button
On the bright splendid shroud of your son,
Do not weep.
War is kind.

1899

JAMES RUSSELL LOWELL
1819–1891

76   from *Ode Recited at the Harvard Commemoration*

I

Weak-winged is song,
Nor aims at that clear-ethered height
Whither the brave deed climbs for light:
    We seem to do them wrong,
Bringing our robin's-leaf to deck their hearse
Who in warm life-blood wrote their nobler verse,
Our trivial song to honor those who come
With ears attuned to strenuous trump and drum,
And shaped in squadron-strophes their desire,
Live battle-odes whose lines were steel and fire:
    Yet sometimes feathered words are strong,
A gracious memory to buoy up and save
From Lethe's dreamless ooze, the common grave
    Of the unventurous throng.

X

Who now shall sneer?
Who dare again to say we trace
Our lines to a plebeian race?
Roundhead and Cavalier!
Dumb are those names erewhile in battle loud;
Dream-footed as the shadow of a cloud,
They flit across the ear:
That is best blood that hath most iron in't.
To edge resolve with, pouring without stint
For what makes manhood dear.
Tell us not of Plantagenets,
Hapsburgs, and Guelfs, whose thin bloods crawl
Down from some victor in a border-brawl!
How poor their outworn coronets,
Matched with one leaf of that plain civic wreath
Our brave for honor's blazon shall bequeath,
Through whose desert a rescued Nation sets
Her heel on treason, and the trumpet hears
Shout victory, tingling Europe's sullen ears
With vain resentments and more vain regrets!

XI

Not in anger, not in pride,
Pure from passion's mixture rude
Ever to base earth allied,
But with far-heard gratitude,
Still with heart and voice renewed,
To heroes living and dear martyrs dead,
The strain should close that consecrates our brave.
Lift the heart and lift the head!
Lofty be its mood and grave,
Not without a martial ring,
Not without a prouder tread
And a peal of exultation:
Little right has he to sing
Through whose heart in such an hour
Beats no march of conscious power,
Sweeps no tumult of elation!
'Tis no Man we celebrate,
By his country's victories great,

A hero half, and half the whim of Fate,
    But the pith and marrow of a Nation
Drawing force from all her men,
Highest, humblest, weakest, all,
For her time of need, and then
Pulsing it again through them,
Till the basest can no longer cower,
Feeling his soul spring up divinely tall,
Touched but in passing by her mantle-hem.
Come back, then, noble pride, for 'tis her dower!
    How could poet ever tower,
    If his passions, hopes, and fears,
    If his triumphs and his tears,
    Kept not measure with his people?
Boom, cannon, boom to all the winds and waves!
Clash out, glad bells, from every rocking steeple!
Banners, adance with triumph, bend your staves!
    And from every mountain-peak
    Let beacon-fire to answering beacon speak,
    Katahdin tell Monadnock, Whiteface he,
And so leap on in light from sea to sea,
    Till the glad news be sent
    Across a kindling continent,
Making earth feel more firm and air breathe braver:
'Be proud! for she is saved, and all have helped to save her!
    She that lifts up the manhood of the poor,
    She of the open soul and open door,
    With room about her hearth for all mankind!
    The fire is dreadful in her eyes no more;
From her bold front the helm she doth unbind,
Sends all her handmaid armies back to spin,
And bids her navies, that so lately hurled
Their crashing battle, hold their thunders in,
Swimming like birds of calm along the unharmful shore.
No challenge sends she to the elder world,
That looked askance and hated; a light scorn
Plays o'er her mouth, as round her mighty knees
She calls her children back, and waits the morn
Of nobler day, enthroned between her subject seas.'

21 July 1865

JULIA WARD HOWE
1819–1910

77 / *The Battle Hymn of the Republic*

Mine eyes have seen the glory of the coming of the Lord:
He is trampling out the vintage where the grapes of wrath are stored;
He hath loosed the fatal lightning of His terrible swift sword:
   His truth is marching on.

I have seen Him in the watch-fires of a hundred circling camps,
They have builded Him an altar in the evening dews and damps;
I can read His righteous sentence by the dim and flaring lamps:
   His day is marching on.

I have read a fiery gospel writ in burnished rows of steel:
'As ye deal with my contemners, so with you my grace shall deal;
Let the Hero, born of woman, crush the serpent with his heel,
   Since God is marching on.'

He has sounded forth the trumpet that shall never call retreat;
He is sifting out the hearts of men before his judgement seat:
Oh, be swift, my soul, to answer Him! Be jubilant, my feet!
   Our God is marching on.

In the beauty of the lilies Christ was born across the sea,
With a glory in his bosom that transfigures you and me:
As he died to make men holy, let us die to make men free,
   While God is marching on.

19 November 1861

ALLEN TATE
1889–1979

78 / *Ode to the Confederate Dead*

   Row after row with strict impunity
   The headstones yield their names to the element,

ALLEN TATE

The wind whirrs without recollection;
In the riven troughs the splayed leaves
Pile up, of nature the casual sacrament
To the seasonal eternity of death;
Then driven by the fierce scrutiny
Of heaven to their election in the vast breath,
They sough the rumour of mortality.

Autumn is desolation in the plot
Of a thousand acres where these memories grow
From the inexhaustible bodies that are not
Dead, but feed the grass row after rich row.
Think of the autumns that have come and gone!—
Ambitious November with the humors of the year,
With a particular zeal for every slab,
Staining the uncomfortable angels that rot
On the slabs, a wing chipped here, an arm there:
The brute curiosity of an angel's stare
Turns you, like them, to stone,
Transforms the heaving air
Till plunged to a heavier world below
You shift your sea-space blindly
Heaving, turning like the blind crab.

    Dazed by the wind, only the wind
    The leaves flying, plunge

You know who have waited by the wall
The twilight certainty of an animal,
Those midnight restitutions of the blood
You know—the immitigable pines, the smoky frieze
Of the sky, the sudden call: you know the rage,
The cold pool left by the mounting flood,
Of muted Zeno and Parmenides.
You who have waited for the angry resolution
Of those desires that should be yours tomorrow,
You know the unimportant shrift of death
And praise the vision
And praise the arrogant circumstance
Of those who fall
Rank upon rank, hurried beyond decision—
Here by the sagging gate, stopped by the wall.

Seeing, seeing only the leaves
Flying, plunge and expire

Turn your eyes to the immoderate past,
Turn to the inscrutable infantry rising
Demons out of the earth—they will not last.
Stonewall, Stonewall, and the sunken fields of hemp,
Shiloh, Antietam, Malvern Hill, Bull Run.
Lost in that orient of the thick-and-fast
You will curse the setting sun.

Cursing only the leaves crying
Like an old man in a storm

You hear the shout, the crazy hemlock point
With troubled fingers to the silence which
Smothers you, a mummy, in time.

The hound bitch
Toothless and dying, in a musty cellar
Hears the wind only.

Now that the salt of their blood
Stiffens the saltier oblivion of the sea,
Seals the malignant purity of the flood,
What shall we who count our days and bow
Our heads with a commemorial woe
In the ribboned coats of grim felicity,
What shall we say of the bones, unclean,
Whose verdurous anonymity will grow?
The ragged arms, the ragged heads and eyes
Lost in these acres of the insane green?
The gray lean spiders come, they come and go;
In a tangle of willows without light
The singular screech-owl's tight
Invisible lyric seeds the mind
With the furious murmur of their chivalry.

We shall say only the leaves
Flying, plunge and expire

We shall say only the leaves whispering
In the improbable mist of nightfall

That flies on multiple wing;
Night is the beginning and the end
And in between the ends of distraction
Waits mute speculation, the patient curse
That stones the eyes, or like the jaguar leaps
For his own image in a jungle pool, his victim.
What shall we say who have knowledge
Carried to the heart? Shall we take the act
To the grave? Shall we, more hopeful set up the grave
In the house? The ravenous grave?

                          Leave now
The shut gate and the decomposing wall:
The gentle serpent, green in the mulberry bush,
Riots with his tongue through the hush—
Sentinel of the grave who counts us all!

1928

RAINER MARIA RILKE
1875–1926

79   *Last Evening*

And night and distant travel; for the train
of the whole army swept along the park.
He looked up from the harpsichord again
and played and glanced at her without remark,

almost like looking in a mirror's round:
so filled with his young features was that face,
features that bore his sadness with a grace
suing more seductively at every sound.

Then all at once that seemed to disappear:
she stood, as though with a great effort, near
the window-seat, and clasped her beating breast.

His playing stopped. Outside a fresh wind blew.
And on the mirror-table, strange and new,
stood the black shako with the death's head crest.

1907

Translated from the German by J. B. Leishman

ARTHUR RIMBAUD
1854–1891

80   from *Eighteen-Seventy**

I

A POSTER OF OUR DAZZLING VICTORY
AT SAARBRUCKEN

In the centre of the poster, Napoleon
rides in apotheosis, sallow, medalled, a ramrod
perched on a merrygoround horse. He sees life
through rosy glasses, terrible as God,

and sentimental as a bourgeois papa.
Four little conscripts take their nap below
on scarlet guns and drums. One, unbuckling, cheers
Napoleon—he's stunned by the big name!

Another lounges on the butt of his Chassepot,
another feels his hair rise on his neck.
A bearskin shako bounds like a black sun:

VIVE L'EMPEREUR! They're holding back their breath.
And last, some moron, struggling to his knees,
presents a blue and scarlet ass—to what?

---

* After the outbreak of the Franco-Prussian War in July 1870, Emperor Napoleon III greatly exaggerated the significance of the French victory in the battle at Saarbrucken on 2 August. Two days later, the Germans crossed the French border into Alsace; a wave of French defeats followed, culminating in the German capture of Napoleon and 100,000 of his men in September at Sedan.

ARTHUR RIMBAUD

II

NAPOLEON AFTER SEDAN

The man waxy—he jogs along the fields
in flower, black, a cigar between his teeth.
The wax man thinks about the Tuileries
in flower. At times his mossy eye takes fire.

Twenty years of orgy have made him drunk:
he'd said: 'My hand will snuff out Liberty,
politely, gently, as I snuff my stogie.'
Liberty lives; the Emperor is out—

he's captured. Oh what name is shaking on
his lips? What plebiscites? Napoleon
cannot tell you. His shark's eye is dead.

An opera glass on the horses at Compere...
he watches his cigar fume off in smoke...
soirées at Saint Cloud...a bluish vapour.

III

TO THE FRENCH OF THE SECOND EMPIRE

You, dead in '92 and '93,
still pale from the great kiss of Liberty—
when tyrants trampled on humanity,
you broke them underneath your wooden shoes.

You were reborn and great by agony,
your hearts in rage still beat for our salvation—
Oh soldiers, sown by death, your noble lover,
in our old furrows you regenerate!

You, whose life-blood washed our soiled standards red,
the dead of Valmy, Italy, Fleurus,
thousands of Christs, red-bonneted...we

have let you die with our Republic, we
who lick the boots of our bored kings like dogs—
men of the Second Empire, I mean you!

.   .   .   .

145

VII

THE SLEEPER IN THE VALLEY

The swollen river sang through the green hole,
and madly hooked white tatters on the grass.
Light escaladed the hot hills. The whole
valley bubbled with sunbeams like a beer-glass.

The conscript was open-mouthed; his bare head
and neck swam in the bluish water cress.
He slept. The mid-day soothed his heaviness,
sunlight was raining into his green bed,

and baked the bruises from his body, rolled
as a sick child might hug itself asleep . . .
Oh Nature, rock him warmly, he is cold.

The flowers no longer make his hot eyes weep.
The river sucks his hair. His blue eye rolls.
He sleeps. In his right side are two red holes.

VIII

EVIL

All day the red spit of the chain-shot tore
whistling across the infinite blue sky,
while the great captain saw his infantry
flounder in massed battalions into fire.

The criminal injustice that deceives
and rules us, lays our corpses end on end,
then burns us like the summer grass or leaves;
La Patrie is avaricious to this end!

She is a god that laughs at Papal bulls,
the great gold chalice and the thuribles.
She dozes while our grand hosannas drown

the guns and drums, and wakes to hear the grief
of widows or a mother who lays down
her great sou knotted in a handkerchief.

3 September 1870

Translated from the French by Robert Lowell

RUDYARD KIPLING
1865–1936

Arithmetic on the Frontier

A great and glorious thing it is
  To learn, for seven years or so,
The Lord knows what of that and this,
  Ere reckoned fit to face the foe—
The flying bullet down the Pass,
That whistles clear: 'All flesh is grass.'

Three hundred pounds per annum spent
  On making brain and body meeter
For all the murderous intent
  Comprised in 'villainous saltpeter'!
And after?—Ask the Yusufzaies
What comes of all our 'ologies.

A scrimmage in a Border Station—
  A canter down some dark defile—
Two thousand pounds of education
  Drops to a ten-rupee jezail—
The Crammer's boast, the Squadron's pride,
Shot like a rabbit in a ride!

No proposition Euclid wrote
  No formulæ the text-books know,
Will turn the bullet from your coat,
  Or ward the tulwar's downward blow.
Strike hard who cares—shoot straight who can—
The odds are on the cheaper man.

One sword-knot stolen from the camp
  Will pay for all the school expenses
Of any Kurrum Valley scamp
  Who knows no word of moods and tenses,
But, being blessed with perfect sight,
Picks off our messmates left and right.

With home-bred hordes the hillsides teem.
　　The troopships bring us one by one,
At vast expense of time and steam,
　　To slay Afridis where they run.
The 'captives of our bow and spear'
Are cheap, alas! as we are dear.

1886

82　　　　　　　　　　　*Tommy*

I went into a public-'ouse to get a pint o' beer,
The publican 'e up an' sez, 'We serve no red-coats here.'
The girls be'ind the bar they laughed an' giggled fit to die,
I outs into the street again an' to myself sez I:
　　O it's Tommy this, an' Tommy that, an' 'Tommy, go away';
　　But it's 'Thank you, Mister Atkins,' when the band begins to
　　　　play—
　　The band begins to play, my boys, the band begins to play,
　　O it's 'Thank you, Mister Atkins,' when the band begins to play.

I went into a theatre as sober as could be,
They gave a drunk civilian room, but 'adn't none for me;
They sent me to the gallery or round the music-'alls;
But when it comes to fightin', Lord! they'll shove me in the stalls!
　　For it's Tommy this, an' Tommy that, an' 'Tommy wait outside';
　　But it's 'Special train for Atkins' when the trooper's on the tide—
　　The troopship's on the tide, my boys, the troopship's on the tide,
　　O it's 'Special train for Atkins' when the trooper's on the tide.

Yes, makin' mock o' uniforms that guard you while you sleep
Is cheaper than them uniforms, an' they're starvation cheap;
An' hustlin' drunken soldiers when they're goin' large a bit
Is five times better business than paradin' in full kit.
　　Then it's Tommy this, an' Tommy that, an' 'Tommy, 'ow's yer
　　　　soul?'
　　But it's 'Thin red line of 'eroes' when the drums begin to roll—
　　The drums begin to roll, my boys, the drums begin to roll,
　　O it's 'Thin red line of 'eroes' when the drums begin to roll.

We aren't no thin red 'eroes, nor we aren't no blackguards too,
But single men in barricks, most remarkable like you;

An' if sometimes our conduck isn't all your fancy paints,
Why, single men in barricks don't grow into plaster saints;
    While it's Tommy this, an' Tommy that, an' 'Tommy, fall be'ind,'
    But it's 'Please to walk in front, sir,' when there's trouble in the
        wind—
    There's trouble in the wind, my boys, there's trouble in the wind,
    O it's 'Please to walk in front, sir,' when there's trouble in the wind.

You talk o' better food for us, an' schools, an' fires, an' all:
We'll wait for extry rations if you treat us rational.
Don't mess about the cook-room slops, but prove it to our face
The Widow's Uniform is not the soldier-man's disgrace.
    For it's Tommy this, an' Tommy that, an' 'Chuck him out, the
        brute!'
    But it's 'Saviour of 'is country' when the guns begin to shoot;
    An' it's Tommy this, an' Tommy that, an' anything you please;
    An' Tommy ain't a bloomin' fool—you bet that Tommy sees!

1890

SIR HENRY NEWBOLT

1862–1938

83   *He Fell among Thieves*

'Ye have robbed,' said he, 'ye have slaughtered and made an end,
  Take your ill-got plunder, and bury the dead:
What will ye more of your guest and sometime friend?'
  'Blood for our blood,' they said.

He laughed: 'If one may settle the score for five,
  I am ready; but let the reckoning stand till day:
I have loved the sunlight as dearly as any alive.'
  'You shall die at dawn,' said they.

He flung his empty revolver down the slope,
  He climbed alone to the Eastward edge of the trees;

All night long in a dream untroubled of hope
    He brooded, clasping his knees.

He did not hear the monotonous roar that fills
    The ravine where the Yassîn river sullenly flows;
He did not see the starlight on the Laspur hills,
    Or the far Afghan snows.

He saw the April noon on his books aglow,
    The wisteria trailing in at the window wide;
He heard his father's voice from the terrace below
    Calling him down to ride.

He saw the grey little church across the park,
    The mounds that hid the loved and honoured dead;
The Norman arch, the chancel softly dark,
    The brasses black and red.

He saw the School Close, sunny and green,
    The runner beside him, the stand by the parapet wall,
The distant tape, and the crowd roaring between,
    His own name over all.

He saw the dark wainscot and timbered roof,
    The long tables, and the faces merry and keen;
The College Eight and their trainer dining aloof,
    The Dons on the daïs serene.

He watched the liner's stem ploughing the foam,
    He felt her trembling speed and the thrash of her screw;
He heard her passengers' voices talking of home,
    He saw the flag she flew.

And now it was dawn. He rose strong on his feet,
    And strode to his ruined camp below the wood;
He drank the breath of the morning cool and sweet:
    His murderers round him stood.

Light on the Laspur hills was broadening fast,
    The blood-red snow-peaks chilled to a dazzling white:
He turned, and saw the golden circle at last,
    Cut by the Eastern height.

'O glorious Life, Who dwellest in earth and sun,
   I have lived, I praise and adore Thee.'
                      A sword swept.
Over the pass the voices one by one
   Faded, and the hill slept.

1897

84   *Vitaï Lampada*

There's a breathless hush in the Close tonight—
   Ten to make and the match to win—
A bumping pitch and a blinding light,
   An hour to play and the last man in.
And it's not for the sake of a ribboned coat,
   Or the selfish hope of a season's fame,
But his Captain's hand on his shoulder smote—
   'Play up! play up! and play the game!'

The sand of the desert is sodden red,—
   Red with the wreck of a square that broke;—
The Gatling's jammed and the Colonel dead,
   And the regiment blind with dust and smoke.
The river of death has brimmed his banks,
   And England's far, and Honour a name,
But the voice of a schoolboy rallies the ranks:
   'Play up! play up! and play the game!'

This is the word that year by year,
   While in her place the School is set,
Every one of her sons must hear,
   And none that hears it dare forget.
This they all with a joyful mind
   Bear through life like a torch in flame,
And falling fling to the host behind—
   'Play up! play up! and play the game!'

1897

THOMAS HARDY
1840–1928

85   *Embarcation**

Here, where Vespasian's legions struck the sands,
And Cerdic with his Saxons entered in,
And Henry's army leapt afloat to win
Convincing triumphs over neighbour lands,

Vaster battalions press for further strands,
To argue in the selfsame bloody mode
Which this late age of thought, and pact, and code,
Still fails to mend.—Now deckward tramp the bands,

Yellow as autumn leaves, alive as spring;
And as each host draws out upon the sea
Beyond which lies the tragical To-be,
None dubious of the cause, none murmuring,

Wives, sisters, parents, wave white hands and smile,
As if they knew not that they weep the while.

Southampton Docks, October 1899

86   *The Colonel's Soliloquy*

'The quay recedes. Hurrah! Ahead we go! . . .
It's true I've been accustomed now to home,
And joints get rusty, and one's limbs may grow
       More fit to rest than roam.

'But I can stand as yet fair stress and strain;
There's not a little steel beneath the rust;
My years mount somewhat, but here's to't again!
       And if I fall, I must.

* On 12 October 1899, following the dispatch of British troops into their territory,
Dutch settlers (Boers) in the Transvaal and the Orange Free State of South Africa
declared war on Great Britain. Despite ill health, Thomas Hardy bicycled 50 miles and
back to the pier in Southampton to watch the British soldiers embark.

'God knows that for myself I have scanty care;
Past scrimmages have proved as much to all;
In Eastern lands and South I have had my share
    Both of the blade and ball.

'And where those villains ripped me in the flitch
With their old iron in my early time,
I'm apt at change of wind to feel a twitch,
    Or at a change of clime.

'And what my mirror shows me in the morning
Has more of blotch and wrinkle than of bloom;
My eyes, too, heretofore all glasses scorning,
    Have just a touch of rheum....

'Now sounds "The Girl I've left behind me",—Ah,
The years, the ardours, wakened by that tune!
Time was when, with the crowd's farewell "Hurrah!"
    'Twould lift me to the moon.

'But now it's late to leave behind me one
Who if, poor soul, her man goes underground,
Will not recover as she might have done
    In days when hopes abound.

'She's waving from the wharfside, palely grieving,
As down we draw.... Her tears make little show,
Yet now she suffers more than at my leaving
    Some twenty years ago!

'I pray those left at home will care for her;
I shall come back; I have before; though when
The Girl you leave behind you is a grandmother,
    Things may not be as then.'

Southampton Docks, October 1899

87   *A Christmas Ghost-Story*

South of the Line, inland from far Durban,
A mouldering soldier lies—your countryman.

Awry and doubled up are his gray bones,
And on the breeze his puzzled phantom moans
Nightly to clear Canopus: 'I would know
By whom and when the All-Earth-gladdening Law
Of Peace, brought in by that Man Crucified,
Was ruled to be inept, and set aside?
And what of logic or of truth appears
In tacking "Anno Domini" to the years?
Near twenty-hundred liveried thus have hied,
But tarries yet the Cause for which He died.'

Christmas Eve, 1899

88   *Drummer Hodge*

I

They throw in Drummer Hodge, to rest
        Uncoffined—just as found:
His landmark is a kopje-crest
        That breaks the veldt around;
And foreign constellations west
        Each night above his mound.

II

Young Hodge the Drummer never knew—
        Fresh from his Wessex home—
The meaning of the broad Karoo,
        The Bush, the dusty loam,
And why uprose to nightly view
        Strange stars amid the gloam.

III

Yet portion of that unknown plain
        Will Hodge for ever be;
His homely Northern breast and brain
        Grow to some Southern tree,
And strange-eyed constellations reign
        His stars eternally.

1899

89 \ / *A Wife in London*

I

She sits in the tawny vapour
    That the Thames-side lanes have uprolled,
    Behind whose webby fold on fold
Like a waning taper
    The street-lamp glimmers cold.

A messenger's knock cracks smartly,
    Flashed news is in her hand
    Of meaning it dazes to understand
Though shaped so shortly:
    He—has fallen—in the far South Land....

II

'Tis the morrow; the fog hangs thicker,
    The postman nears and goes:
    A letter is brought whose lines disclose
By the firelight flicker
    His hand, whom the worm now knows:

Fresh—firm—penned in highest feather—
    Page-full of his hoped return,
    And of home-planned jaunts by brake and burn
In the summer weather,
    And of new love that they would learn.

December 1899

90 \ *The Man He Killed*

'Had he and I but met
    By some old ancient inn,
We should have sat us down to wet
    Right many a nipperkin!

'But ranged as infantry,
    And staring face to face,

155

I shot at him as he at me,
    And killed him in his place.

'I shot him dead because—
    Because he was my foe,
Just so: my foe of course he was;
    That's clear enough; although

'He thought he'd 'list, perhaps,
    Off-hand like—just as I—
Was out of work—had sold his traps—
    No other reason why.

'Yes; quaint and curious war is!
    You shoot a fellow down
You'd treat if met where any bar is,
    Or help to half-a-crown.'

1902

A. E. HOUSMAN
1859–1936

91

On the idle hill of summer,
Sleepy with the flow of streams,
Far I hear the steady drummer
    Drumming like a noise in dreams.

Far and near and low and louder
    On the roads of earth go by,
Dear to friends and food for powder,
    Soldiers marching, all to die.

East and west on fields forgotten
    Bleach the bones of comrades slain,
Lovely lads and dead and rotten;
    None that go return again.

Far the calling bugles hollo,
    High the screaming fife replies,
Gay the files of scarlet follow:
    Woman bore me, I will rise.

1896

92

Soldier from the wars returning,
    Spoiler of the taken town,
Here is ease that asks not earning;
    Turn you in and sit you down.

Peace is come and wars are over,
    Welcome you and welcome all,
While the charger crops the clover
    And his bridle hangs in stall.

Now no more of winters biting,
    Filth in trench from fall to spring,
Summers full of sweat and fighting
    For the Kesar or the King.

Rest you, charger, rust you, bridle;
    Kings and kesars, keep your pay;
Soldier, sit you down and idle
    At the inn of night for aye.

1922

93

Grenadier

The Queen she sent to look for me,
    The sergeant he did say,
'Young man, a soldier will you be
    For thirteen pence a day?'

For thirteen pence a day did I
    Take off the things I wore,
And I have marched to where I lie,
    And I shall march no more.

My mouth is dry, my shirt is wet,
    My blood runs all away,
So now I shall not die in debt
    For thirteen pence a day.

Tomorrow after new young men
    The sergeant he must see,
For things will all be over then
    Between the Queen and me.

And I shall have to bate my price,
    For in the grave, they say,
Is neither knowledge nor device
    Nor thirteen pence a day.

1922

94   *Lancer*

I 'listed at home for a lancer,
    Oh who would not sleep with the brave?
I 'listed at home for a lancer
    To ride on a horse to my grave.

And over the seas we were bidden
    A country to take and to keep;
And far with the brave I have ridden,
    And now with the brave I shall sleep.

For round me the men will be lying
    That learned me the way to behave,
And showed me my business of dying:
    Oh who would not sleep with the brave?

They ask and there is not an answer;
Says I, I will 'list for a lancer,
    Oh who would not sleep with the brave?

And I with the brave shall be sleeping
    At ease on my mattress of loam,
When back from their taking and keeping
    The squadron is riding at home.

The wind with the plumes will be playing,
    The girls will stand watching them wave,
And eyeing my comrades and saying
    Oh who would not sleep with the brave?

They ask and there is not an answer;
Says you, I will 'list for a lancer,
    Oh who would not sleep with the brave?

1922

95   *Astronomy*

The Wain upon the northern steep
    Descends and lifts away.
Oh I will sit me down and weep
    For bones in Africa.

For pay and medals, name and rank,
    Things that he has not found,
He hove the Cross to heaven and sank
    The pole-star underground.

And now he does not even see
    Signs of the nadir roll
At night over the ground where he
    Is buried with the pole.

1922

T. W. H. CROSLAND
1865–1924

Slain
'Dulce et decorum est pro patria mori'

You who are still and white
   And cold like stone;
For whom the unfailing light
   Is spent and done;

For whom no more the breath
   Of dawn, nor evenfall,
Nor Spring nor love nor death
   Matter at all;

Who were so strong and young,
   And brave and wise,
And on the dark are flung
   With darkened eyes;

Who roystered and caroused
   But yesterday,
And now are dumbly housed
   In stranger clay;

Who valiantly led,
   Who followed valiantly,
Who knew no touch of dread
   Of that which was to be;

Children that were as nought
   Ere ye were tried,
How have ye dared and fought,
   Triumphed and died!

.   .   .

Yea, it is very sweet
   And decorous
The omnipotent Shade to meet
   And flatter thus.

1899

EDGAR WALLACE
1875–1932

War

I

A tent that is pitched at the base:
    A wagon that comes from the night:
A stretcher—and on it a Case:
    A surgeon, who's holding a light.
The Infantry's bearing the brunt—
    O hark to the wind-carried cheer!
A mutter of guns at the front:
    A whimper of sobs at the rear.
And it's *War*! 'Orderly, hold the light.
    You can lay him down on the table: so.
Easily—gently! Thanks—you may go.'
    And it's *War*! but the part that is not for show.

II

A tent, with a table athwart,
    A table that's laid out for one;
A waterproof cover—and nought
    But the limp, mangled work of a gun.
A bottle that's stuck by the pole,
    A guttering dip in its neck;
The flickering light of a soul
    On the wondering eyes of The Wreck,
And it's *War*! 'Orderly, hold his hand.
    I'm not going to hurt you, so don't be afraid.
A richochet! God! what a mess it has made!'
    And it's *War*! and a very unhealthy trade.

III

The clink of a stopper and glass:
    A sigh as the chloroform drips:
A trickle of—what? on the grass,
    And bluer and bluer the lips.
The lashes have hidden the stare...

A rent, and the clothes fall away...
A touch, and the wound is laid bare...
A cut, and the face has turned grey...
And it's *War*! 'Orderly, take It out.
It's hard for his child, and it's rough on his wife,
There might have been—sooner—a chance for his life.
But it's *War*! And—Orderly, clean this knife!'

1900

RUDYARD KIPLING
1865–1936

98   *Bridge-Guard in the Karroo*

'...and will supply details to guard the Blood River Bridge.'
        District Orders: Lines of Communication—
        South African War.

Sudden the desert changes,
   The raw glare softens and clings,
Till the aching Oudtshoorn ranges
   Stand up like the thrones of Kings—

Ramparts of slaughter and peril—
   Blazing, amazing, aglow—
'Twixt the sky-line's belting beryl
   And the wine-dark flats below.

Royal the pageant closes,
   Lit by the last of the sun—
Opal and ash-of-roses,
   Cinnamon, umber, and dun.

The twilight swallows the thicket,
   The starlight reveals the ridge.
The whistle shrills to the picket—
   We are changing guard on the bridge.

(Few, forgotten and lonely,
  Where the empty metals shine—
No, not combatants—only
  Details guarding the line.)

We slip through the broken panel
  Of fence by the ganger's shed;
We drop to the waterless channel
  And the lean track overhead;

We stumble on refuse of rations,
  The beef and the biscuit-tins;
We take our appointed stations,
  And the endless night begins.

We hear the Hottentot herders
  As the sheep click past to the fold—
And the click of the restless girders
  As the steel contracts in the cold—

Voices of jackals calling
  And, loud in the hush between,
A morsel of dry earth falling
  From the flanks of the scarred ravine.

And the solemn firmament marches,
  And the hosts of heaven rise
Framed through the iron arches—
  Banded and barred by the ties,

Till we feel the far track humming,
  And we see her headlight plain,
And we gather and wait her coming—
  The wonderful north-bound train.

(Few, forgotten and lonely,
  Where the white car-windows shine—
No, not combatants—only
  Details guarding the line.)

Quick, ere the gift escape us!
  Out of the darkness we reach

For a handful of week-old papers
   And a mouthful of human speech.

And the monstrous heaven rejoices,
   And the earth allows again
Meetings, greetings, and voices
   Of women talking with men.

So we return to our places,
   As out on the bridge she rolls;
And the darkness covers our faces,
   And the darkness re-enters our souls.

More than a little lonely
   Where the lessening tail-lights shine.
No—not combatants—only
   Details guarding the line!

1901

99   *The Dykes*

We have no heart for the fishing—we have no hand for the oar—
All that our fathers taught us of old pleases us now no more.
All that our own hearts bid us believe we doubt where we do not deny—
There is no proof in the bread we eat nor rest in the toil we ply.

Look you, our foreshore stretches far through sea-gate, dyke, and
   groin—
Made land all, that our fathers made, where the flats and the fairway join.
They forced the sea a sea-league back. They died, and their work stood
   fast.
We were born to peace in the lee of the dykes, but the time of our peace
   is past.

Far off, the full tide clambers and slips, mouthing and testing all,
Nipping the flanks of the water-gates, baying along the wall;
Turning the shingle, returning the shingle, changing the set of the
   sand . . .
We are too far from the beach, men say, to know how the outworks stand.

So we come down, uneasy, to look; uneasily pacing the beach.
These are the dykes our fathers made: we have never known a breach.
Time and again has the gale blown by and we were not afraid;
Now we come only to look at the dykes—at the dykes our fathers made.

O'er the marsh where the homesteads cower apart the harried sunlight
flies,
Shifts and considers, wanes and recovers, scatters and sickens and
dies—
An evil ember bedded in ash—a spark blown west by the wind . . .
We are surrendered to night and the sea—the gale and the tide behind!

At the bridge of the lower saltings the cattle gather and blare,
Roused by the feet of running men, dazed by the lantern-glare.
Unbar and let them away for their lives—the levels drown as they stand,
Where the flood-wash forces the sluices aback and the ditches deliver
inland.

Ninefold deep to the top of the dykes the galloping breakers stride,
And their overcarried spray is a sea—a sea on the landward side.
Coming, like stallions they paw with their hooves, going they snatch with
their teeth,
Till the bents and the furze and the sand are dragged out, and the
old-time hurdles beneath.

Bid men gather fuel for fire, the tar, the oil, and the tow—
Flame we shall need, not smoke, in the dark if the riddled sea-banks go.
Bid the ringers watch in the tower (who knows how the dawn shall
prove?)
Each with his rope between his feet and the trembling bells above.

Now we can only wait till the day, wait and apportion our shame.
These are the dykes our fathers left, but we would not look to the same.
Time and again were we warned of the dykes, time and again we
delayed:
Now, it may fall, we have slain our sons, as our fathers we have betrayed.

.   .   .

Walking along the wreck of the dykes, watching the work of the seas!
These were the dykes our fathers made to our great profit and ease.
But the peace is gone and the profit is gone, with the old sure days
withdrawn . . .
That our own houses show as strange when we come back in the dawn!

1902

HERBERT ASQUITH
1881–1947

100   *The Volunteer*

Here lies a clerk who half his life had spent
Toiling at ledgers in a city grey,
Thinking that so his days would drift away
With no lance broken in life's tournament.
Yet ever 'twixt the books and his bright eyes
The gleaming eagles of the legions came,
And horsemen, charging under phantom skies,
Went thundering past beneath the oriflamme.

And now those waiting dreams are satisfied;
From twilight to the halls of dawn he went;
His lance is broken; but he lies content
With that high hour, in which he lived and died.
And falling thus he wants no recompense,
Who found his battle in the last resort;
Nor need he any hearse to bear him hence,
Who goes to join the men of Agincourt.

1912

THOMAS HARDY
1840–1928

101   *Men Who March Away*
            (*Song of the Soldiers*)

What of the faith and fire within us
        Men who march away
        Ere the barn-cocks say
        Night is growing gray,
Leaving all that here can win us;
What of the faith and fire within us
        Men who march away?

Is it a purblind prank, O think you,
   Friend with the musing eye,
   Who watch us stepping by
   With doubt and dolorous sigh?
Can much pondering so hoodwink you!
Is it a purblind prank, O think you,
   Friend with the musing eye?

Nay. We well see what we are doing,
   Though some may not see—
   Dalliers as they be—
   England's need are we;
Her distress would leave us rueing:
Nay. We well see what we are doing,
   Though some may not see!

In our heart of hearts believing
   Victory crowns the just,
   And that braggarts must
   Surely bite the dust,
Press we to the field ungrieving,
In our heart of hearts believing
   Victory crowns the just.

Hence the faith and fire within us
   Men who march away
   Ere the barn-cocks say
   Night is growing gray,
Leaving all that here can win us;
Hence the faith and fire within us
   Men who march away.

5 September 1914

102   *In Time of 'The Breaking of Nations'*

I

Only a man harrowing clods
   In a slow silent walk
With an old horse that stumbles and nods
   Half asleep as they stalk.

II

Only thin smoke without flame
   From the heaps of couch-grass;
Yet this will go onward the same
   Though Dynasties pass.

III

Yonder a maid and her wight
   Come whispering by:
War's annals will cloud into night
   Ere their story die.

1915

RUPERT BROOKE
1887–1915

103   *Peace*

Now, God be thanked Who has matched us with His hour,
   And caught our youth, and wakened us from sleeping,
With hand made sure, clear eye, and sharpened power,
   To turn, as swimmers into cleanness leaping,
Glad from a world grown old and cold and weary,
   Leave the sick hearts that honour could not move,
And half-men, and their dirty songs and dreary,
   And all the little emptiness of love!

Oh! we, who have known shame, we have found release there,
   Where there's no ill, no grief, but sleep has mending.
     Naught broken save this body, lost but breath;
Nothing to shake the laughing heart's long peace there
   But only agony, and that has ending;
     And the worst friend and enemy is but Death.

1914

104 *The Dead*

Blow out, you bugles, over the rich Dead!
    There's none of these so lonely and poor of old,
    But, dying, has made us rarer gifts than gold.
These laid the world away; poured out the red
Sweet wine of youth; gave up the years to be
    Of work and joy, and that unhoped serene,
    That men call age; and those who would have been,
Their sons, they gave, their immortality.

Blow, bugles, blow! They brought us, for our dearth,
    Holiness, lacked so long, and Love, and Pain.
Honour has come back, as a king, to earth,
    And paid his subjects with a royal wage;
And Noblencss walks in our ways again;
    And we have come into our heritage.

1914

105   /   *The Soldier*

If I should die, think only this of me:
    That there's some corner of a foreign field
That is for ever England. There shall be
    In that rich earth a richer dust concealed;
A dust whom England bore, shaped, made aware,
    Gave, once, her flowers to love, her ways to roam,
A body of England's, breathing English air,
    Washed by the rivers, blest by suns of home.

And think, this heart, all evil shed away,
    A pulse in the eternal mind, no less
        Gives somewhere back the thoughts by England given;
Her sights and sounds; dreams happy as her day;
    And laughter, learnt of friends; and gentleness,
        In hearts at peace, under an English heaven.

1914

WILFRID GIBSON
1878–1962

106 *Breakfast*

We ate our breakfast lying on our backs,
Because the shells were screeching overhead.
I bet a rasher to a loaf of bread
That Hull United would beat Halifax
When Jimmy Stainthorp played full-back instead
Of Billy Bradford. Ginger raised his head
And cursed, and took the bet; and dropt back dead.
We ate our breakfast lying on our backs,
Because the shells were screeching overhead.

1914

PATRICK SHAW-STEWART
1888–1917

107 '*I saw a man this morning*'

I saw a man this morning
    Who did not wish to die:
I ask, and cannot answer,
    If otherwise wish I.

Fair broke the day this morning
    Against the Dardanelles;
The breeze blew soft, the morn's cheeks
    Were cold as cold sea-shells.

But other shells are waiting
    Across the Aegean Sea,
Shrapnel and high explosive,
    Shells and hells for me.

O hell of ships and cities,
  Hell of men like me,
Fatal second Helen,
  Why must I follow thee?

Achilles came to Troyland
  And I to Chersonese:
He turned from wrath to battle,
  And I from three days' peace.

Was it so hard, Achilles,
  So very hard to die?
Thou knowest and I know not—
  So much the happier I.

I will go back this morning
  From Imbros over the sea;
Stand in the trench, Achilles,
  Flame-capped, and shout for me.

1915

JULIAN GRENFELL

1888–1915

108   *Into Battle*

The naked earth is warm with Spring,
  And with green grass and bursting trees
Leans to the sun's gaze glorying,
  And quivers in the sunny breeze;

And life is colour and warmth and light,
  And a striving evermore for these;
And he is dead who will not fight;
  And who dies fighting has increase.

The fighting man shall from the sun
　　Take warmth, and life from the glowing earth;
Speed with the light-foot winds to run,
　　And with the trees to newer birth;
And find, when fighting shall be done,
　　Great rest, and fullness after dearth.

All the bright company of Heaven
　　Hold him in their high comradeship,
The Dog-Star, and the Sisters Seven,
　　Orion's Belt and sworded hip.

The woodland trees that stand together,
　　They stand to him each one a friend;
They gently speak in the windy weather;
　　They guide to valley and ridge's end.

The kestrel hovering by day,
　　And the little owls that call by night,
Bid him be swift and keen as they,
　　As keen of ear, as swift of sight.

The blackbird sings to him, 'Brother, brother,
　　If this be the last song you shall sing,
Sing well, for you may not sing another;
　　Brother, sing.'

In dreary, doubtful waiting hours,
　　Before the brazen frenzy starts,
The horses show him nobler powers;
　　O patient eyes, courageous hearts!

And when the burning moment breaks,
　　And all things else are out of mind,
And only joy of battle takes
　　Him by the throat, and makes him blind,

Through joy and blindness he shall know,
　　Not caring much to know, that still
Nor lead nor steel shall reach him, so
　　That it be not the Destined Will.

The thundering line of battle stands,
    And in the air Death moans and sings;
But Day shall clasp him with strong hands,
    And Night shall fold him in soft wings.

Flanders, April 1915

JOHN McCRAE
1872–1918

109   *In Flanders Fields*

In Flanders fields the poppies blow
Between the crosses, row on row,
    That mark our place; and in the sky
    The larks, still bravely singing, fly
Scarce heard amid the guns below.

We are the Dead. Short days ago
We lived, felt dawn, saw sunset glow,
    Loved and were loved, and now we lie
    In Flanders fields.

Take up our quarrel with the foe:
To you from failing hands we throw
    The torch; be yours to hold it high.
    If ye break faith with us who die
We shall not sleep, though poppies grow
    In Flanders fields.

1915

T. P. CAMERON WILSON
1889–1918

Magpies in Picardy

The magpies in Picardy
Are more than I can tell.
They flicker down the dusty roads
And cast a magic spell
On the men who march through Picardy,
Through Picardy to hell.

(The blackbird flies with panic,
The swallow goes like light,
The finches move like ladies,
The owl floats by at night;
But the great and flashing magpie
He flies as artists might.)

A magpie in Picardy
Told me secret things—
Of the music in white feathers,
And the sunlight that sings
And dances in deep shadows—
He told me with his wings.

(The hawk is cruel and rigid,
He watches from a height;
The rook is slow and sombre,
The robin loves to fight;
But the great and flashing magpie
He flies as lovers might.)

He told me that in Picardy,
An age ago or more,
While all his fathers still were eggs,
These dusty highways bore
Brown singing soldiers marching out
Through Picardy to war.

1916

174

CHARLES SORLEY
1895–1915

All the hills and vales along
Earth is bursting into song,
And the singers are the chaps
Who are going to die perhaps.
⋅ O sing, marching men,
   Till the valleys ring again.
   Give your gladness to earth's keeping,
   So be glad, when you are sleeping.

Cast away regret and rue,
Think what you are marching to.
Little live, great pass.
Jesus Christ and Barabbas
Were found the same day.
This died, that went his way.
   So sing with joyful breath,
   For why, you are going to death.
   Teeming earth will surely store
   All the gladness that you pour.

Earth that never doubts nor fears,
Earth that knows of death, not tears,
Earth that bore with joyful ease
Hemlock for Socrates,
Earth that blossomed and was glad
'Neath the cross that Christ had,
Shall rejoice and blossom too
When the bullet reaches you.
   Wherefore, men marching
   On the road to death, sing!
   Pour your gladness on earth's head,
   So be merry, so be dead.

From the hills and valleys earth
Shouts back the sound of mirth,
Tramp of feet and lilt of song
Ringing all the road along.

All the music of their going,
Ringing swinging glad song-throwing,
Earth will echo still, when foot
Lies numb and voice mute.
   On, marching men, on
   To the gates of death with song.
   Sow your gladness for earth's reaping,
   So you may be glad, though sleeping.
   Strew your gladness on earth's bed,
   So be merry, so be dead.

1915

112   When you see millions of the mouthless dead
Across your dreams in pale battalions go,
Say not soft things as other men have said,
That you'll remember. For you need not so.
Give them not praise. For, deaf, how should they know
It is not curses heaped on each gashed head?
Nor tears. Their blind eyes see not your tears flow.
Nor honour. It is easy to be dead.
Say only this, 'They are dead.' Then add thereto,
'Yet many a better one has died before.'
Then, scanning all the o'ercrowded mass, should you
Perceive one face that you loved heretofore,
It is a spook. None wears the face you knew.
Great death has made all his for evermore.

1915

A. E. HOUSMAN
1859–1936

113   *Epitaph on an Army of Mercenaries*

These, in the day when heaven was falling,
   The hour when earth's foundations fled,

Followed their mercenary calling
And took their wages and are dead.

Their shoulders held the sky suspended;
  They stood, and earth's foundations stay;
What God abandoned, these defended,
  And saved the sum of things for pay.

1917

HUGH MacDIARMID
1892–1978

114   *Another Epitaph on an Army of Mercenaries*

It is a God-damned lie to say that these
Saved, or knew, anything worth any man's pride.
They were professional murderers and they took
Their blood money and impious risks and died.
In spite of all their kind some elements of worth
With difficulty persist here and there on earth.

1935

CARL SANDBURG
1878–1967

115   *Grass*

Pile the bodies high at Austerlitz and Waterloo.
Shovel them under and let me work—
              I am the grass; I cover all.

And pile them high at Gettysburg
And pile them high at Ypres and Verdun.
Shovel them under and let me work.
Two years, ten years, and passengers ask the conductor:
               What place is this?
               Where are we now?

               I am the grass.
               Let me work.

1918

ROBERT FROST
1874–1963

116   *Range-Finding*

The battle rent a cobweb diamond-strung
And cut a flower beside a ground bird's nest
Before it stained a single human breast.
The stricken flower bent double and so hung.
And still the bird revisited her young.
A butterfly its fall had dispossessed
A moment sought in air his flower of rest,
Then lightly stooped to it and fluttering clung.

On the bare upland pasture there had spread
O'ernight 'twixt mullein stalks a wheel of thread
And straining cables wet with silver dew.
A sudden passing bullet shook it dry.
The indwelling spider ran to greet the fly,
But finding nothing, sullenly withdrew.

1916

WALLACE STEVENS
1879–1955

117   *The Death of a Soldier*

Life contracts and death is expected,
As in a season of autumn.
The soldier falls.

He does not become a three-days personage,
Imposing his separation,
Calling for pomp.

Death is absolute and without memorial,
As in a season of autumn,
When the wind stops,

When the wind stops and, over the heavens,
The clouds go, nevertheless,
In their direction.

1918

GUILLAUME APOLLINAIRE
1880–1918

118   *Calligram, 15 May 1915*

The sky's as blue and black as ink
My eyes drown in it and sink

Darkness a shell whines over me
I write this under a willow tree

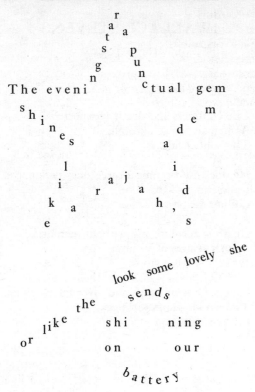

1918

Translated from the French by O. Bernard

BENJAMIN PÉRET
1899–1959

119   *Little Song of the Maimed*

Lend me your arm
to replace my leg
The rats ate it for me

at Verdun
at Verdun
I ate lots of rats
but they didn't give me back my leg
and that's why I was given the CROIX DE GUERRE
and a wooden leg
and a wooden leg

1936

Translated from the French by David Gascoyne

W. B. YEATS
1865–1939

120   *On Being Asked for a War Poem*

I think it better that in times like these
A poet's mouth be silent, for in truth
We have no gift to set a statesman right;
He has had enough of meddling who can please
A young girl in the indolence of her youth,
Or an old man upon a winter's night.

1915

121   *Sixteen Dead Men*

O but we talked at large before
The sixteen men were shot,
But who can talk of give and take,
What should be and what not
While those dead men are loitering there
To stir the boiling pot?

You say that we should still the land
Till Germany's overcome;

But who is there to argue that
Now Pearse is deaf and dumb?
And is their logic to outweigh
MacDonagh's bony thumb?

How could you dream they'd listen
That have an ear alone
For those new comrades they have found,
Lord Edward and Wolfe Tone,
Or meddle with our give and take
That converse bone to bone?

1916–17

122   *An Irish Airman Foresees His Death**

I know that I shall meet my fate
Somewhere among the clouds above;
Those that I fight I do not hate,
Those that I guard I do not love;
My country is Kiltartan Cross,
My countrymen Kiltartan's poor,
No likely end could bring them loss
Or leave them happier than before.
Nor law, nor duty bade me fight,
Nor public men, nor cheering crowds,
A lonely impulse of delight
Drove to this tumult in the clouds;
I balanced all, brought all to mind,
The years to come seemed waste of breath,
A waste of breath the years behind
In balance with this life, this death.

1918

* Major Robert Gregory, recipient of the Military Cross and the Légion d'Honneur, was killed in action when his plane was shot down on the Italian front on 23 January 1918.

123 *Reprisals*

Some nineteen German planes, they say,
You had brought down before you died.
We called it a good death. Today
Can ghost or man be satisfied?
Although your last exciting year
Outweighed all other years, you said,
Though battle joy may be so dear
A memory, even to the dead,
It chases other thought away,
Yet rise from your Italian tomb,
Flit to Kiltartan Cross and stay
Till certain second thoughts have come
Upon the cause you served, that we
Imagined such a fine affair:
Half-drunk or whole-mad soldiery
Are murdering your tenants there.
Men that revere your father yet
Are shot at on the open plain.
Where may new-married women sit
And suckle children now? Armed men
May murder them in passing by
Nor law nor parliament take heed.
Then close your ears with dust and lie
Among the other cheated dead.

1920

124 *The Second Coming*

Turning and turning in the widening gyre
The falcon cannot hear the falconer;
Things fall apart; the centre cannot hold;
Mere anarchy is loosed upon the world,
The blood-dimmed tide is loosed, and everywhere
The ceremony of innocence is drowned;
The best lack all conviction, while the worst
Are full of passionate intensity.

Surely some revelation is at hand;
Surely the Second Coming is at hand.
The Second Coming! Hardly are those words out
When a vast image out of *Spiritus Mundi*
Troubles my sight: somewhere in sands of the desert
A shape with lion body and the head of a man,
A gaze blank and pitiless as the sun,
Is moving its slow thighs, while all about it
Reel shadows of the indignant desert birds.
The darkness drops again; but now I know
That twenty centuries of stony sleep
Were vexed to nightmare by a rocking cradle,
And what rough beast, its hour come round at last,
Slouches towards Bethlehem to be born?

January 1919

ROBERT W. SERVICE
1874–1958

125   *Only a Boche*

We brought him in from between the lines: we'd better
    have let him lie;
For what's the use of risking one's skin for a *type*
    that's going to die?
What's the use of tearing him loose
    under a gruelling fire,
When he's shot in the head, and worse than dead,
    and all messed up on the wire?
However, I say, we brought him in. *Diable!*
    The mud was bad;
The trench was crooked and greasy and high, and oh,
    what a time we had!
And often we slipped, and often we tripped,
    but never he made a moan;
And how we were wet with blood and with sweat!
    But we carried him in like our own.

Now there he lies in the dug-out dim, awaiting
   the ambulance,
And the doctor shrugs his shoulders at him, and remarks:
   "He hasn't a chance."
And we squat and smoke at our game of bridge
   on the glistening, straw-packed floor,
And above our oaths we can hear his breath
   deep drawn in a kind of snore.

For the dressing station is long and low, and
   the candles gutter dim,
And the mean light falls on the cold clay walls
   and our faces bristly and grim;
And we flap our cards on the lousy straw, and we laugh
   and jibe as we play,
And you'd never know that the cursed foe
   was less than a mile away.
As we con our cards in the rancid gloom, oppressed
   by that snoring breath,
You'd never dream that our broad roof-beam
   was swept by the broom of death.

Heigh-ho! My turn for the dummy hand; I rise
   and I stretch a bit;
The fetid air is making me yawn, and my cigarette's
   unlit,
So I go to the nearest candle flame, and the man
   we brought is there,
And his face is white in the shabby light, and I stand
   at his feet and stare.
Stand for awhile, and quietly stare; for strange
   though it seems to be,
The dying Boche on the stretcher there has a queer
   resemblance to me.

It gives one a kind of a turn, you know,
   to come on a thing like that.
It's just as if I were lying there, with a turban of blood
   for a hat,
Lying there in a coat grey-green instead of a coat
   grey-blue,
With one of my eyes all shot away, and my brain
   half tumbling through;

Lying there with a chest that heaves
   like a bellows up and down,
And a cheek as white as snow on a grave,
   and lips that are coffee brown.

And confound him, too! He wears, like me,
   on his finger a wedding ring,
And around his neck, as around my own,
   by a greasy bit of string,
A locket hangs with a woman's face, and I turn it
   about to see;
Just as I thought... on the other side the faces
   of children three;
Clustered together cherub-like, three little
   laughing girls,
With the usual tiny rosebud mouths and the usual
   silken curls.
"Zut!" I say, "he has beaten me; for me,
   I have only two,"
And I push the locket beneath his shirt,
   feeling a little blue.

Oh, it isn't cheerful to see a man, the marvellous
   work of God,
Crushed in the mutilation mill, crushed
   to a smeary clod;
Oh, it isn't cheerful to hear him moan, but it isn't
   that I mind,
It isn't the anguish that goes with him, it's the anguish
   he leaves behind.
For his going opens a tragic door that gives
   on a world of pain,
And the death he dies, those who live and love
   will die again and again.

So here I am at my cards once more, but it's kind
   of spoiling my play,
Thinking of those three brats of his so many a mile
   away.
War is war, and he's only a Boche, and we all of us
   take our chance;
But all the same I'll be mighty glad when I'm hearing
   the ambulance.

One foe the less, but all the same I'm heartily glad
   I'm not
The man who gave him his broken head, the sniper
   who fired the shot....
Not trumps you make it, I think you said?
   You'll pardon me if I err;
For a moment I thought of other things.... *Mon Dieu!*
   Quelle vache de guerre.

1916

126   *Tipperary Days*

Oh, weren't they the fine boys! You never saw
   the beat of them,
Singing all together with their throats bronze-bare;
Fighting-fit and mirth-mad, music in the feet of them,
Swinging on to glory and the wrath out there.
Laughing by and chaffing by, frolic in the smiles of them,
On the road, the white road, all the afternoon;
Strangers in a strange land, miles and miles
   and miles of them,
Battle-bound and heart-high, and singing this tune:

   It's a long way to Tipperary,
   It's a long way to go;
   It's a long way to Tipperary,
   And the sweetest girl I know.
   Good-bye, Piccadilly,
   Farewell, Leicester Square:
   It's a long, long way to Tipperary,
   But my heart's right there.

Come Yvonne and Juliette! Come Mimi and cheer for them!
Throw them flowers and kisses as they pass you by.
Aren't they the lovely lads! Haven't you a tear for them
Going out so gallantly to dare and die?
What is it they're singing so? Some high hymn
   of Motherland?
Some immortal chanson of their Faith and King?

Marseillaise or Brabançon, anthem of that other land,
Dears, let us remember it, that song they sing:

"*C'est un chemin long 'to Tepararee,'*
C'est un chemin long, c'est vrai;
C'est un chemin long 'to Tepararee,'
Et la belle fille qu'je connais;
Bonjour, Peckadeely!
'Au revoir, Lestaire Squaire!
C'est un chemin long 'to Tepararee,'
Mais mon coeur 'ees zaire.'"

The gallant old "Contemptibles"! There isn't much
    remains of them,
So full of fun and fitness, and a-singing in their pride;
For some are cold as clabber and the corby picks
    the brains of them,
And some are back in Blighty, and a-wishing they
    had died.
Ah me! It seems but yesterday, that great, glad
    sight of them,
Swinging on to battle as the sky grew black and
    black;
Yet oh their glee and glory, and the great, grim
    fight of them! —
Just whistle Tipperary and it all comes back;

It's a long way to Tipperary,
(Which means "'ome" anywhere);
It's a long way to Tipperary,
(And the things wot make you care).
Good-bye, Piccadilly,
('Ow I 'opes my folks is well);
It's a long, long way to Tipperary—
('R! Ain't War just 'ell?)

1916

SIEGFRIED SASSOON
1886–1967

The Redeemer

Darkness: the rain sluiced down; the mire was deep;
It was past twelve on a mid-winter night,
When peaceful folk in beds lay snug asleep;
There, with much work to do before the light,
We lugged our clay-sucked boots as best we might
Along the trench; sometimes a bullet sang,
And droning shells burst with a hollow bang;
We were soaked, chilled and wretched, every one;
Darkness; the distant wink of a huge gun.

I turned in the black ditch, loathing the storm;
A rocket fizzed and burned with blanching flare,
And lit the face of what had been a form
Floundering in mirk. He stood before me there;
I say that He was Christ; stiff in the glare;
And leaning forward from His burdening task,
Both arms supporting it; His eyes on mine
Stared from the woeful head that seemed a mask
Of mortal pain in Hell's unholy shine.

No thorny crown, only a woollen cap
He wore—an English soldier, white and strong,
Who loved his time like any simple chap,
Good days of work and sport and homely song;
Now he has learned that nights are very long,
And dawn a watching of the windowed sky.
But to the end, unjudging, he'll endure
Horror and pain, not uncontent to die
That Lancaster on Lune may stand secure.

He faced me, reeling in his weariness,
Shouldering his load of planks, so hard to bear.
I say that He was Christ, who wrought to bless
All groping things with freedom bright as air,
And with His mercy washed and made them fair.
Then the flame sank, and all grew black as pitch,

While we began to struggle along the ditch;
And someone flung his burden in the muck,
Mumbling: "O Christ Almighty, now I'm stuck!"

1915–16

128   *Christ and the Soldier*

I

The straggled soldier halted—stared at Him—
Then clumsily dumped down upon his knees,
Gasping, "O blessed crucifix, I'm beat!"
And Christ, still sentried by the seraphim,
Near the front-line, between two splintered trees,
Spoke him: "My son, behold these hands and feet."

The soldier eyed Him upward, limb by limb,
Paused at the Face; then muttered, "Wounds like these
Would shift a bloke to Blighty just a treat!"
Christ, gazing downward, grieving and ungrim,
Whispered, "I made for you the mysteries,
Beyond all battles moves the Paraclete."

II

The soldier chucked his rifle in the dust,
And slipped his pack, and wiped his neck, and said—
"O Christ Almighty, stop this bleeding fight!"
Above that hill the sky was stained like rust
With smoke. In sullen daybreak flaring red
The guns were thundering bombardment's blight.

The soldier cried, "I was born full of lust,
With hunger, thirst, and wishfulness to wed.
Who cares today if I done wrong or right?"
Christ asked all pitying, "Can you put no trust
In my known word that shrives each faithful head?
Am I not resurrection, life and light?"

III

Machine-guns rattled from below the hill;
High bullets flicked and whistled through the leaves;
And smoke came drifting from exploding shells.
Christ said, "Believe; and I can cleanse your ill.
I have not died in vain between two thieves;
Nor made a fruitless gift of miracles."

The soldier answered, "Heal me if you will,
Maybe there's comfort when a soul believes
In mercy, and we need it in these hells.
But be you for both sides? I'm paid to kill
And if I shoot a man his mother grieves.
Does that come into what your teaching tells?"

A bird lit on the Christ and twittered gay;
Then a breeze passed and shook the ripening corn.
A Red Cross waggon bumped along the track.
Forsaken Jesus dreamed in the desolate day—
Uplifted Jesus, Prince of Peace forsworn—
An observation post for the attack.

"Lord Jesus, ain't you got no more to say?"
Bowed hung that head below the crown of thorns.
The soldier shifted, and picked up his pack,
And slung his gun, and stumbled on his way.
"O God," he groaned, "why ever was I born?" ...
The battle boomed, and no reply came back.

5 August 1916

129   '*They*'

The Bishop tells us: 'When the boys come back
They will not be the same; for they'll have fought

In a just cause: they lead the last attack
On Anti-Christ; their comrades' blood has bought
New right to breed an honourable race,
They have challenged Death and dared him face to face.'

'We're none of us the same!' the boys reply.
'For George lost both his legs; and Bill's stone blind;
Poor Jim's shot through the lungs and like to die;
And Bert's gone syphilitic: you'll not find
A chap who's served that hasn't found *some* change.'
And the Bishop said: 'The ways of God are strange!'

31 August 1916

130   *The Hero*

'Jack fell as he'd have wished,' the Mother said,
And folded up the letter that she'd read.
'The Colonel writes so nicely.' Something broke
In the tired voice that quavered to a choke.
She half looked up. 'We mothers are so proud
Of our dead soldiers.' Then her face was bowed.

Quietly the Brother Officer went out.
He'd told the poor old dear some gallant lies
That she would nourish all her days, no doubt.
For while he coughed and mumbled, her weak eyes
Had shone with gentle triumph, brimmed with joy,
Because he'd been so brave, her glorious boy.

He thought how 'Jack', cold-footed, useless swine,
Had panicked down the trench that night the mine
Went up at Wicked Corner; how he'd tried
To get sent home, and how, at last, he died,
Blown to small bits. And no one seemed to care
Except that lonely woman with white hair.

August 1916

131 *The General*

'Good-morning; good-morning!' the General said
When we met him last week on our way to the line.
Now the soldiers he smiled at are most of 'em dead,
And we're cursing his staff for incompetent swine.
'He's a cheery old card,' grunted Harry to Jack
As they slogged up to Arras with rifle and pack.

.   .   .

But he did for them both by his plan of attack.

April 1917

132 / *Glory of Women*

You love us when we're heroes, home on leave,
Or wounded in a mentionable place.
You worship decorations; you believe
That chivalry redeems the war's disgrace.
You make us shells. You listen with delight,
By tales of dirt and danger fondly thrilled.
You crown our distant ardours while we fight,
And mourn our laurelled memories when we're killed.
You can't believe that British troops 'retire'
When hell's last horror breaks them, and they run,
Trampling the terrible corpses—blind with blood.
　O German mother dreaming by the fire,
　While you are knitting socks to send your son
　His face is trodden deeper in the mud.

Craiglockhart, 1917

133 *Everyone Sang*

Everyone suddenly burst out singing;
And I was filled with such delight
As prisoned birds must find in freedom,
Winging wildly across the white
Orchards and dark-green fields; on—on—and out of sight.

Everyone's voice was suddenly lifted;
And beauty came like the setting sun:
My heart was shaken with tears; and horror
Drifted away . . . O, but Everyone
Was a bird; and the song was wordless; the singing will never be done.

April 1919

EDWARD THOMAS
1878–1917

134   *In Memoriam (Easter 1915)*

The flowers left thick at nightfall in the wood
This Eastertide call into mind the men,
Now far from home, who, with their sweethearts, should
Have gathered them and will do never again.

6 April 1915

135   *The Cherry Trees*

The cherry trees bend over and are shedding
On the old road where all that passed are dead,
Their petals, strewing the grass as for a wedding
This early May morn when there is none to wed.

7, 8 May 1916

136   *Rain*

Rain, midnight rain, nothing but the wild rain
On this bleak hut, and solitude, and me
Remembering again that I shall die

And neither hear the rain nor give it thanks
For washing me cleaner than I have been
Since I was born into this solitude.
Blessed are the dead that the rain rains upon:
But here I pray that none whom once I loved
Is dying tonight or lying still awake
Solitary, listening to the rain,
Either in pain or thus in sympathy
Helpless among the living and the dead,
Like a cold water among broken reeds,
Myriads of broken reeds all still and stiff,
Like me who have no love which this wild rain
Has not dissolved except the love of death,
If love it be towards what is perfect and
Cannot, the tempest tells me, disappoint.

7 January 1916

137   *As the team's head brass*

As the team's head brass flashed out on the turn
The lovers disappeared into the wood.
I sat among the boughs of the fallen elm
That strewed an angle of the fallow, and
Watched the plough narrowing a yellow square
Of charlock. Every time the horses turned
Instead of treading me down, the ploughman leaned
Upon the handles to say or ask a word,
About the weather, next about the war.
Scraping the share he faced towards the wood,
And screwed along the furrow till the brass flashed
Once more.
          The blizzard felled the elm whose crest
I sat in, by a woodpecker's round hole,
The ploughman said. 'When will they take it away?'
'When the war's over.' So the talk began—
One minute and an interval of ten,
A minute more and the same interval.
'Have you been out?' 'No.' 'And don't want to, perhaps?'
'If I could only come back again, I should.

195

I could spare an arm. I shouldn't want to lose
A leg. If I should lose my head, why, so,
I should want nothing more.... Have many gone
From here?' 'Yes.' 'Many lost?' 'Yes, a good few.
Only two teams work on the farm this year.
One of my mates is dead. The second day
In France they killed him. It was back in March,
The very night of the blizzard, too. Now if
He had stayed here we should have moved the tree.'
'And I should not have sat here. Everything
Would have been different. For it would have been
Another world.' 'Ay, and a better, though
If we could see all all might seem good.' Then
The lovers came out of the wood again:
The horses started and for the last time
I watched the clods crumble and topple over
After the ploughshare and the stumbling team.

27 May 1916

IVOR GURNEY

1890–1937

138   *To His Love*

He's gone, and all our plans
    Are useless indeed.
We'll walk no more on Cotswold
    Where the sheep feed
    Quietly and take no heed.

His body that was so quick
    Is not as you
Knew it, on Severn river
    Under the blue
    Driving our small boat through.

You would not know him now...
    But still he died

Nobly, so cover him over
  With violets of pride
  Purple from Severn side.

Cover him, cover him soon!
  And with thick-set
Masses of memoried flowers—
  Hide that red wet
  Thing I must somehow forget.

December 1917

139   *Ballad of the Three Spectres*

As I went up by Ovillers
  In mud and water cold to the knee,
There went three jeering, fleering spectres,
  That walked abreast and talked of me.

The first said, 'Here's a right brave soldier
  That walks the dark unfearingly;
Soon he'll come back on a fine stretcher,
  And laughing for a nice Blighty.'

The second, 'Read his face, old comrade,
  No kind of lucky chance I see;
One day he'll freeze in mud to the marrow,
  Then look his last on Picardie.'

Though bitter the word of these first twain
  Curses the third spat venomously;
'He'll stay untouched till the war's last dawning
  Then live one hour of agony.'

Liars the first two were. Behold me
  At sloping arms by one—two—three;
Waiting the time I shall discover
  Whether the third spake verity.

February 1917

140   *First Time In*

After the dread tales and red yarns of the Line
Anything might have come to us; but the divine
Afterglow brought us up to a Welsh colony
Hiding in sandbag ditches, whispering consolatory
Soft foreign things. Then we were taken in
To low huts candle-lit, shaded close by slitten
Oilsheets, and there but boys gave us kind welcome,
So that we looked out as from the edge of home.
Sang us Welsh things, and changed all former notions
To human hopeful things. And the next day's guns
Nor any Line-pangs ever quite could blot out
That strangely beautiful entry to War's rout;
Candles they gave us, precious and shared over-rations—
Ulysses found little more in his wanderings without doubt.
'David of the White Rock', the 'Slumber Song' so soft, and that
Beautiful tune to which roguish words by Welsh pit boys
Are sung—but never more beautiful than here under the guns' noise.

January 1918

141   *The Silent One*

Who died on the wires, and hung there, one of two—
Who for his hours of life had chattered through
Infinite lovely chatter of Bucks accent:
Yet faced unbroken wires; stepped over, and went
A noble fool, faithful to his stripes—and ended.
But I weak, hungry, and willing only for the chance
Of line—to fight in the line, lay down under unbroken
Wires, and saw the flashes and kept unshaken,
Till the politest voice—a finicking accent, said:
'Do you think you might crawl through there: there's a hole.'
Darkness, shot at: I smiled, as politely replied—
'I'm afraid not, Sir.' There was no hole no way to be seen,
Nothing but chance of death, after tearing of clothes.
Kept flat, and watched the darkness, hearing bullets whizzing—

And thought of music—and swore deep heart's deep oaths
(Polite to God) and retreated and came on again,
Again retreated—and a second time faced the screen.

1925

ISAAC ROSENBERG
1890–1918

142   *On Receiving News of the War*

Snow is a strange white word;
No ice or frost
Have asked of bud or bird
For Winter's cost.

Yet ice and frost and snow
From earth to sky
This Summer land doth know,
No man knows why.

In all men's hearts it is.
Some spirit old
Hath turned with malign kiss
Our lives to mould.

Red fangs have torn His face.
God's blood is shed.
He mourns from His lone place
His children dead.

O! ancient crimson curse!
Corrode, consume.
Give back this universe
Its pristine bloom.

Capetown, 1914–15

143   *August 1914*

What in our lives is burnt
In the fire of this?
The heart's dear granary?
The much we shall miss?

Three lives hath one life—
Iron, honey, gold.
The gold, the honey gone—
Left is the hard and cold.

Iron are our lives
Molten right through our youth.
A burnt space through ripe fields,
A fair mouth's broken tooth.

Summer 1916

144   *Break of Day in the Trenches*

The darkness crumbles away.
It is the same old druid Time as ever,
Only a live thing leaps my hand,
A queer sardonic rat,
As I pull the parapet's poppy
To stick behind my ear.
Droll rat, they would shoot you if they knew
Your cosmopolitan sympathies.
Now you have touched this English hand
You will do the same to a German
Soon, no doubt, if it be your pleasure
To cross the sleeping green between.
It seems you inwardly grin as you pass
Strong eyes, fine limbs, haughty athletes,
Less chanced than you for life,
Bonds to the whims of murder,
Sprawled in the bowels of the earth,
The torn fields of France.
What do you see in our eyes

ISAAC ROSENBERG

At the shrieking iron and flame
Hurled through still heavens?
What quaver—what heart aghast?
Poppies whose roots are in man's veins
Drop, and are ever dropping;
But mine in my ear is safe—
Just a little white with the dust.

June 1916

145   *Dead Man's Dump*

The plunging limbers over the shattered track
Racketed with their rusty freight,
Stuck out like many crowns of thorns,
And the rusty stakes like sceptres old
To stay the flood of brutish men
Upon our brothers dear.

The wheels lurched over sprawled dead
But pained them not, though their bones crunched,
Their shut mouths made no moan,
They lie there huddled, friend and foeman,
Man born of man, and born of woman,
And shells go crying over them
From night till night and now.

Earth has waited for them
All the time of their growth
Fretting for their decay:
Now she has them at last!
In the strength of their strength
Suspended—stopped and held.

What fierce imaginings their dark souls lit?
Earth! have they gone into you?
Somewhere they must have gone,
And flung on your hard back
Is their souls' sack,

Emptied of God–ancestralled essences.
Who hurled them out? Who hurled?

None saw their spirits' shadow shake the grass,
Or stood aside for the half–used life to pass
Out of those doomed nostrils and the doomed mouth,
When the swift iron burning bee
Drained the wild honey of their youth.

What of us, who flung on the shrieking pyre,
Walk, our usual thoughts untouched,
Our lucky limbs as on ichor fed,
Immortal seeming ever?
Perhaps when the flames beat loud on us,
A fear may choke in our veins
And the startled blood may stop.

The air is loud with death,
The dark air spurts with fire
The explosions ceaseless are.
Timelessly now, some minutes past,
These dead strode time with vigorous life,
Till the shrapnel called 'an end!'
But not to all. In bleeding pangs
Some borne on stretchers dreamed of home,
Dear things, war–blotted from their hearts.

A man's brains splattered on
A stretcher–bearer's face;
His shook shoulders slipped their load,
But when they bent to look again
The drowning soul was sunk too deep
For human tenderness.

They left this dead with the older dead,
Stretched at the cross roads.
Burnt black by strange decay,
Their sinister faces lie;
The lid over each eye,
The grass and coloured clay
More motions have then they,
Joined to the great sunk silences.

Here is one not long dead;
His dark hearing caught our far wheels,
And the choked soul stretched weak hands
To reach the living word the far wheels said,
The blood-dazed intelligence beating for light,
Crying through the suspense of the far torturing wheels
Swift for the end to break,
Or the wheels to break,
Cried as the tide of the world broke over his sight.

Will they come? Will they ever come?
Even as the mixed hoofs of the mules,
The quivering-bellied mules,
And the rushing wheels all mixed
With his tortured upturned sight,
So we crashed round the bend,
We heard his weak scream,
We heard his very last sound,
And our wheels grazed his dead face.

1917

146   *Returning, We Hear the Larks*

Sombre the night is.
And though we have our lives, we know
What sinister threat lurks there.

Dragging these anguished limbs, we only know
This poison-blasted track opens on our camp—
On a little safe sleep.

But hark! joy—joy—strange joy.
Lo! heights of night ringing with unseen larks.
Music showering our upturned list'ning faces.

Death could drop from the dark
As easily as song—
But song only dropped,
Like a blind man's dreams on the sand

203

By dangerous tides,
Like a girl's dark hair for she dreams no ruin lies there,
Or her kisses where a serpent hides.

1917

WILFRED OWEN
1893–1918

♪ 147   *Anthem for Doomed Youth*

What passing-bells for these who die as cattle?
  —Only the monstrous anger of the guns.
  Only the stuttering rifles' rapid rattle
Can patter out their hasty orisons.
No mockeries now for them; no prayers nor bells;
  Nor any voice of mourning save the choirs,—
The shrill, demented choirs of wailing shells;
  And bugles calling for them from sad shires.

What candles may be held to speed them all?
  Not in the hands of boys but in their eyes
Shall shine the holy glimmers of goodbyes.
  The pallor of girls' brows shall be their pall;
Their flowers the tenderness of patient minds,
And each slow dusk a drawing-down of blinds.

Craiglockhart, 1917

♪ 148   *Dulce Et Decorum Est*

Bent double, like old beggars under sacks,
Knock-kneed, coughing like hags, we cursed through sludge,
Till on the haunting flares we turned our backs
And towards our distant rest began to trudge.
Men marched asleep. Many had lost their boots
But limped on, blood-shod. All went lame; all blind;

Drunk with fatigue; deaf even to the hoots
Of tired, outstripped Five-Nines that dropped behind.

Gas! GAS! Quick, boys!—An ecstasy of fumbling,
Fitting the clumsy helmets just in time;
But someone still was yelling out and stumbling,
And flound'ring like a man in fire or lime...
Dim, through the misty panes and thick green light,
As under a green sea, I saw him drowning.
In all my dreams, before my helpless sight,
He plunges at me, guttering, choking, drowning.

If in some smothering dreams you too could pace
Behind the wagon that we flung him in,
And watch the white eyes writhing in his face,
His hanging face, like a devil's sick of sin;
If you could hear, at every jolt, the blood
Come gargling from the froth-corrupted lungs,
Obscene as cancer, bitter as the cud
Of vile, incurable sores on innocent tongues,—
My friend, you would not tell with such high zest
To children ardent for some desperate glory,
The old Lie: Dulce et decorum est
Pro patria mori.

1917–18

149   *Exposure*

Our brains ache, in the merciless iced east winds that knive us...
Wearied we keep awake because the night is silent...
Low, drooping flares confuse our memory of the salient...
Worried by silence, sentries whisper, curious, nervous,
        But nothing happens.

Watching, we hear the mad gusts tugging on the wire,
Like twitching agonies of men among its brambles.
Northward, incessantly, the flickering gunnery rumbles,
Far off, like a dull rumour of some other war.
        What are we doing here?

The poignant misery of dawn begins to grow ...
We only know war lasts, rain soaks, and clouds sag stormy.
Dawn massing in the east her melancholy army
Attacks once more in ranks on shivering ranks of grey,
      But nothing happens.

Sudden successive flights of bullets streak the silence.
Less deathly than the air that shudders black with snow,
With sidelong flowing flakes that flock, pause, and renew;
We watch them wandering up and down the wind's nonchalance,
      But nothing happens.

Pale flakes with fingering stealth come feeling for our faces—
We cringe in holes, back on forgotten dreams, and stare, snow-dazed,
Deep into grassier ditches. So we drowse, sun-dozed,
Littered with blossoms trickling where the blackbird fusses,
      —Is it that we are dying?

Slowly our ghosts drag home: glimpsing the sunk fires, glozed
With crusted dark-red jewels; crickets jingle there;
For hours the innocent mice rejoice: the house is theirs;
Shutters and doors, all closed: on us the doors are closed,—
      We turn back to our dying.

Since we believe not otherwise can kind fires burn;
Nor ever suns smile true on child, or field, or fruit.
For God's invincible spring our love is made afraid;
Therefore, not loath, we lie out here; therefore were born,
      For love of God seems dying.

Tonight, this frost will fasten on this mud and us,
Shrivelling many hands, puckering foreheads crisp.
The burying-party, picks and shovels in shaking grasp,
Pause over half-known faces. All their eyes are ice,
      But nothing happens.

1917–18

Insensibility

I

Happy are men who yet before they are killed
Can let their veins run cold.
Whom no compassion fleers
Or makes their feet
Sore on the alleys cobbled with their brothers.
The front line withers.
But they are troops who fade, not flowers,
For poets' tearful fooling:
Men, gaps for filling:
Losses, who might have fought
Longer; but no one bothers.

II

And some cease feeling
Even themselves or for themselves.
Dullness best solves
The tease and doubt of shelling,
And Chance's strange arithmetic
Comes simpler than the reckoning of their shilling.
They keep no check on armies' decimation.

III

Happy are these who lose imagination:
They have enough to carry with ammunition.
Their spirit drags no pack.
Their old wounds, save with cold, can not more ache.
Having seen all things red,
Their eyes are rid
Of the hurt of the colour of blood for ever.
And terror's first constriction over,
Their hearts remain small-drawn.
Their senses in some scorching cautery of battle
Now long since ironed,
Can laugh among the dying, unconcerned.

IV

Happy the soldier home, with not a notion
How somewhere, every dawn, some men attack,

And many sighs are drained.
Happy the lad whose mind was never trained:
His days are worth forgetting more than not.
He sings along the march
Which we march taciturn, because of dusk,
The long, forlorn, relentless trend
From larger day to huger night.

V

We wise, who with a thought besmirch
Blood over all our soul,
How should we see our task
But through his blunt and lashless eyes?
Alive, he is not vital overmuch;
Dying, not mortal overmuch;
Nor sad, nor proud,
Nor curious at all.
He cannot tell
Old men's placidity from his.

VI

But cursed are dullards whom no cannon stuns,
That they should be as stones.
Wretched are they, and mean
With paucity that never was simplicity.
By choice they made themselves immune
To pity and whatever moans in man
Before the last sea and the hapless stars;
Whatever mourns when many leave these shores;
Whatever shares
The eternal reciprocity of tears.

1917–18

151 *The Send-Off*

Down the close darkening lanes they sang their way
To the siding-shed,
And lined the train with faces grimly gay.

Their breasts were stuck all white with wreath and spray
As men's are, dead.

Dull porters watched them, and a casual tramp
Stood staring hard,
Sorry to miss them from the upland camp.

Then, unmoved, signals nodded, and a lamp
Winked to the guard.

So secretly, like wrongs hushed-up, they went.
They were not ours:
We never heard to which front these were sent;

Nor there if they yet mock what women meant
Who gave them flowers.

Shall they return to beating of great bells
In wild train-loads?
A few, a few, too few for drums and yells,

May creep back, silent, to village wells,
Up half-known roads.

1918

152   *Futility*

Move him into the sun—
Gently its touch awoke him once,
At home, whispering of fields half-sown.
Always it woke him, even in France,
Until this morning and this snow.
If anything might rouse him now
The kind old sun will know.

Think how it wakes the seeds—
Woke once the clays of a cold star.
Are limbs, so dear achieved, are sides
Full-nerved, still warm, too hard to stir?

Was it for this the clay grew tall?
—O what made fatuous sunbeams toil
To break earth's sleep at all?

May 1918

153   *Strange Meeting*

It seemed that out of battle I escaped
Down some profound dull tunnel, long since scooped
Through granites which titanic wars had groined.

Yet also there encumbered sleepers groaned,
Too fast in thought or death to be bestirred.
Then, as I probed them, one sprang up, and stared
With piteous recognition in fixed eyes,
Lifting distressful hands, as if to bless.
And by his smile, I knew that sullen hall,—
By his dead smile I knew we stood in Hell.
With a thousand pains that vision's face was grained;
Yet no blood reached there from the upper ground,
And no guns thumped, or down the flues made moan.
'Strange friend,' I said, 'here is no cause to mourn.'
'None,' said that other, 'save the undone years,
The hopelessness. Whatever hope is yours,
Was my life also; I went hunting wild
After the wildest beauty in the world,
Which lies not calm in eyes, or braided hair,
But mocks the steady running of the hour,
And if it grieves, grieves richlier than here.
For by my glee might many men have laughed,
And of my weeping something had been left,
Which must die now. I mean the truth untold,
The pity of war, the pity war distilled.
Now men will go content with what we spoiled,
Or, discontent, boil bloody, and be spilled.
They will be swift with swiftness of the tigress.
None will break ranks, though nations trek from progress.
Courage was mine, and I had mystery,
Wisdom was mine, and I had mastery:

To miss the march of this retreating world
Into vain citadels that are not walled.
Then, when much blood had clogged their chariot-wheels,
I would go up and wash them from sweet wells,
Even with truths that lie too deep for taint.
I would have poured my spirit without stint
But not through wounds; not on the cess of war.
Foreheads of men have bled where no wounds were.

'I am the enemy you killed, my friend.
I knew you in this dark: for so you frowned
Yesterday through me as you jabbed and killed.
I parried; but my hands were loath and cold.
Let us sleep now....'

1918

154   *The Sentry*

We'd found an old Boche dug-out, and he knew,
And gave us hell; for shell on frantic shell
Lit full on top, but never quite burst through.
Rain, guttering down in waterfalls of slime,
Kept slush waist-high and rising hour by hour,
And choked the steps too thick with clay to climb.
What murk of air remained stank old, and sour
With fumes from whizz-bangs, and the smell of men
Who'd lived there years, and left their curse in the den,
If not their corpses . . .
                   There we herded from the blast
Of whizz-bangs; but one found our door at last,—
Buffeting eyes and breath, snuffing the candles,
And thud! flump! thud! down the steep steps came thumping
And sploshing in the flood, deluging muck,
The sentry's body; then his rifle, handles
Of old Boche bombs, and mud in ruck on ruck.
We dredged it up, for dead, until he whined,
'O sir—my eyes,—I'm blind,—I'm blind,—I'm blind.'
Coaxing, I held a flame against his lids

And said if he could see the least blurred light
He was not blind; in time they'd get all right.
'I can't,' he sobbed. Eyeballs, huge-bulged like squids',
Watch my dreams still,—yet I forgot him there
In posting Next for duty, and sending a scout
To beg a stretcher somewhere, and flound'ring about
To other posts under the shrieking air.

Those other wretches, how they bled and spewed,
And one who would have drowned himself for good,—
I try not to remember these things now.
Let Dread hark back for one word only: how,
Half-listening to that sentry's moans and jumps,
And the wild chattering of his shivered teeth,
Renewed most horribly whenever crumps
Pummelled the roof and slogged the air beneath,—
Through the dense din, I say, we heard him shout
'I see your lights!'—But ours had long gone out.

1917–18

155   *Spring Offensive*

Halted against the shade of a last hill
They fed, and eased of pack-loads, were at ease;
And leaning on the nearest chest or knees
Carelessly slept.
                        But many there stood still
To face the stark blank sky beyond the ridge,
Knowing their feet had come to the end of the world.
Marvelling they stood, and watched the long grass swirled
By the May breeze, murmurous with wasp and midge;
And though the summer oozed into their veins
Like an injected drug for their bodies' pains,
Sharp on their souls hung the imminent ridge of grass,
Fearfully flashed the sky's mysterious glass.

Hour after hour they ponder the warm field
And the far valley behind, where buttercups
Had blessed with gold their slow boots coming up;
When even the little brambles would not yield
But clutched and clung to them like sorrowing arms.
They breathe like trees unstirred.

212

Till like a cold gust thrills the little word
At which each body and its soul begird
And tighten them for battle. No alarms
Of bugles, no high flags, no clamorous haste,—
Only a lift and flare of eyes that faced
The sun, like a friend with whom their love is done.
O larger shone that smile against the sun,—
Mightier than his whose bounty these have spurned.

So, soon they topped the hill, and raced together
Over an open stretch of herb and heather
Exposed. And instantly the whole sky burned
With fury against them; earth set sudden cups
In thousands for their blood; and the green slope
Chasmed and deepened sheer to infinite space.

Of them who running on that last high place
Breasted the surf of bullets, or went up
On the hot blast and fury of hell's upsurge,
Or plunged and fell away past this world's verge,
Some say God caught them even before they fell.

But what say such as from existence' brink
Ventured but drave too swift to sink,
The few who rushed in the body to enter hell,
And there out-fiending all its fiends and flames
With superhuman inhumanities,
Long-famous glories, immemorial shames—
And crawling slowly back, have by degrees
Regained cool peaceful air in wonder—
Why speak not they of comrades that went under?

July–September 1918

ROBERT GRAVES
1895–1985

156   *The Dead Fox Hunter*
*(In memory of Captain A. L. Samson, 2nd Battalion Royal Welch
Fusiliers, killed near Cuinchy, Sept. 25th, 1915)*

We found the little captain at the head;
   His men lay well aligned.
We touched his hand—stone cold—and he was dead,
   And they, all dead behind,
Had never reached their goal, but they died well;
They charged in line, and in the same line fell.

The well-known rosy colours of his face
   Were almost lost in grey.
We saw that, dying and in hopeless case,
   For others' sake that day
He'd smothered all rebellious groans: in death
His fingers were tight clenched between his teeth.

For those who live uprightly and die true
   Heaven has no bars or locks,
And serves all taste . . . or what's for him to do
   Up there, but hunt the fox?
Angelic choirs? No, Justice must provide
For one who rode straight and in hunting died.

So if Heaven had no Hunt before he came,
   Why, it must find one now:
If any shirk and doubt they know the game,
   There's one to teach them how;
And the whole host of Seraphim complete
Must jog in scarlet to his opening Meet.

1915

157   *Sergeant–Major Money*

It wasn't our battalion, but we lay alongside it,
   So the story is as true as the telling is frank.
They hadn't one Line-officer left, after Arras,
   Except a batty major and the Colonel, who drank.

'B' Company Commander was fresh from the Depot,
   An expert on gas drill, otherwise a dud;
So Sergeant-Major Money carried on, as instructed,
   And that's where the swaddies began to sweat blood.

His Old Army humour was so well-spiced and hearty
    That one poor sod shot himself, and one lost his wits;
But discipline's maintained, and back in rest-billets
    The Colonel congratulates 'B' company on their kits.

The subalterns went easy, as was only natural
    With a terror like Money driving the machine,
Till finally two Welshmen, butties from the Rhondda,
    Bayoneted their bugbear in a field-canteen.

Well, we couldn't blame the officers, they relied on Money;
    We couldn't blame the pitboys, their courage was grand;
Or, least of all, blame Money, an old stiff surviving
    In a New (bloody) Army he couldn't understand.

1917

158   *The Legion*

'Is that the Three-and-Twentieth, Strabo mine,
Marching below, and we still gulping wine?'
From the sad magic of his fragrant cup
The red-faced old centurion started up,
Cursed, battered on the table. 'No,' he said,
'Not that! The Three-and-Twentieth Legion's dead,
Dead in the first year of this damned campaign—
The Legion's dead, dead, and won't rise again.
Pity? Rome pities her brave lads that die,
But we need pity also, you and I,
Whom Gallic spear and Belgian arrow miss,
Who live to see the Legion come to this:
Unsoldierlike, slovenly, bent on loot,
Grumblers, diseased, unskilled to thrust or shoot.
O brown cheek, muscled shoulder, sturdy thigh!
Where are they now? God! watch it straggle by,
The sullen pack of ragged, ugly swine!
Is that the Legion, Gracchus? Quick, the wine!'
'Strabo,' said Gracchus, 'you are strange to-night.
The Legion is the Legion, it's all right.
If these new men are slovenly, in your thinking,
Hell take it! you'll not better them by drinking.

They all try, Strabo; trust their hearts and hands.
The Legion is the Legion while Rome stands,
And these same men before the autumn's fall
Shall bang old Vercingetorix out of Gaul.'

1916

159 *Recalling War*

Entrance and exit wounds are silvered clean,
The track aches only when the rain reminds.
The one-legged man forgets his leg of wood,
The one-armed man his jointed wooden arm.
The blinded man sees with his ears and hands
As much or more than once with both his eyes.
Their war was fought these twenty years ago
And now assumes the nature-look of time,
As when the morning traveller turns and views
His wild night-stumbling carved into a hill.

What, then, was war? No mere discord of flags
But an infection of the common sky
That sagged ominously upon the earth
Even when the season was the airiest May.
Down pressed the sky, and we, oppressed, thrust out
Boastful tongue, clenched fist and valiant yard.
Natural infirmities were out of mode,
For Death was young again: patron alone
Of healthy dying, premature fate-spasm.

Fear made fine bed-fellows. Sick with delight
At life's discovered transitoriness,
Our youth became all-flesh and waived the mind.
Never was such antiqueness of romance,
Such tasty honey oozing from the heart.
And old importances came swimming back—
Wine, meat, log-fires, a roof over the head,
A weapon at the thigh, surgeons at call.
Even there was a use again for God—
A word of rage in lack of meat, wine, fire,
In ache of wounds beyond all surgeoning.

War was return of earth to ugly earth,
War was foundering of sublimities,
Extinction of each happy art and faith
By which the world had still kept head in air.
Protesting logic or protesting love,
Until the unendurable moment struck—
The inward scream, the duty to run mad.

And we recall the merry ways of guns—
Nibbling the walls of factory and church
Like a child, piecrust; felling groves of trees
Like a child, dandelions with a switch!
Machine-guns rattle toy-like from a hill,
Down in a row the brave tin-soldiers fall:
A sight to be recalled in elder days
When learnedly the future we devote
To yet more boastful visions of despair.

1938

160   *The Persian Version*

Truth-loving Persians do not dwell upon
The trivial skirmish fought near Marathon.
As for the Greek theatrical tradition
Which represents that summer's expedition
Not as a mere reconnaissance in force
By three brigades of foot and one of horse
(Their left flank covered by some obsolete
Light craft detached from the main Persian fleet)
But as a grandiose, ill-starred attempt
To conquer Greece—they treat it with contempt;
And only incidentally refute
Major Greek claims, by stressing what repute
The Persian monarch and the Persian nation
Won by this salutary demonstration:
Despite a strong defence and adverse weather
All arms combined magnificently together.

1945

EDMUND BLUNDEN
1896–1974

161   *Two Voices*

'There's something in the air,' he said
    In the large parlour cool and bare;
The plain words in his hearers bred
    A tumult, yet in silence there
All waited; wryly gay, he left the phrase,
Ordered the march and bade us go our ways.

'We're going South, man'; as he spoke
    The howitzer with huge ping-bang
Racked the light hut; as thus he broke
    The death-news, bright the skylarks sang;
He took his riding-crop and humming went
Among the apple-trees all bloom and scent.

Now far withdraws the roaring night
    Which wrecked our flower after the first
Of those two voices; misty light
    Shrouds Thiepval Wood and all its worst:
But still 'There's something in the air' I hear,
And still 'We're going South, man,' deadly near.

                                                1916

162   *The Zonnebeke Road*

Morning, if this late withered light can claim
Some kindred with that merry flame
Which the young day was wont to fling through space!
Agony stares from each gray face.
And yet the day is come; stand down! stand down!
Your hands unclasp from rifles while you can;
The frost has pierced them to the bended bone?
Why, see old Stevens there, that iron man,
Melting the ice to shave his grotesque chin:
Go ask him, shall we win?

I never liked this bay, some foolish fear
Caught me the first time that I came in here;
That dugout fallen in awakes, perhaps,
Some formless haunting of some corpse's chaps.
True, and wherever we have held the line,
There were such corners, seeming-saturnine
For no good cause.
                Now where Haymarket starts,
That is no place for soldiers with weak hearts;
The minenwerfers have it to the inch.
Look, how the snow-dust whisks along the road,
Piteous and silly; the stones themselves must flinch
In this east wind; the low sky like a load
Hangs over—a dead-weight. But what a pain
Must gnaw where its clay cheek
Crushes the shell-chopped trees that fang the plain—
The ice-bound throat gulps out a gargoyle shriek.
The wretched wire before the village line
Rattles like rusty brambles or dead bine,
And then the daylight oozes into dun;
Black pillars, those are trees where roadways run.
Even Ypres now would warm our souls; fond fool,
Our tour's but one night old, seven more to cool!
O screaming dumbness, O dull clashing death,
Shreds of dead grass and willows, homes and men,
Watch as you will, men clench their chattering teeth
And freeze you back with that one hope, disdain.

1928

163   *Vlamertinghe: Passing the Château,*
July 1917

'And all her silken flanks with garlands drest'—
But we are coming to the sacrifice.
Must those have flowers who are not yet gone West?
May those have flowers who live with death and lice?
This must be the floweriest place
That earth allows; the queenly face
Of the proud mansion borrows grace for grace
Spite of those brute guns lowing at the skies.

Bold great daisies, golden lights,
Bubbling roses' pinks and whites—
Such a gay carpet! poppies by the million;
Such damask! such vermilion!
But if you ask me, mate, the choice of colour
Is scarcely right; this red should have been much duller.

1928

164   *Report on Experience*

I have been young, and now am not too old;
And I have seen the righteous forsaken,
His health, his honour and his quality taken.
   This is not what we were formerly told.

I have seen a green country, useful to the race,
Knocked silly with guns and mines, its villages vanished,
Even the last rat and last kestrel banished—
   God bless us all, this was peculiar grace.

I knew Seraphina; Nature gave her hue,
Glance, sympathy, note, like one from Eden.
I saw her smile warp, heard her lyric deaden;
   She turned to harlotry;—this I took to be new.

Say what you will, our God sees how they run.
These disillusions are His curious proving
That He loves humanity and will go on loving;
   Over these are faith, life, virtue in the sun.

1928

165   *1916 seen from 1921*

Tired with dull grief, grown old before my day,
I sit in solitude and only hear
Long silent laughters, murmurings of dismay,
The lost intensities of hope and fear;
In those old marshes yet the rifles lie,

On the thin breastwork flutter the grey rags,
The very books I read are there—and I
Dead as the men I loved, wait while life drags

Its wounded length from those sad streets of war
Into green places here, that were my own;
But now what once was mine is mine no more,
I seek such neighbours here and I find none.
With such strong gentleness and tireless will
Those ruined houses seared themselves in me,
Passionate I look for their dumb story still,
And the charred stub outspeaks the living tree.

I rise up at the singing of a bird
And scarcely knowing slink along the lane,
I dare not give a soul a look or word
Where all have homes and none's at home in vain:
Deep red the rose burned in the grim redoubt,
The self-sown wheat around was like a flood,
In the hot path the lizard lolled time out,
The saints in broken shrines were bright as blood.

Sweet Mary's shrine between the sycamores!
There we would go, my friend of friends and I,
And snatch long moments from the grudging wars,
Whose dark made light intense to see them by.
Shrewd bit the morning fog, the whining shots
Spun from the wrangling wire; then in warm swoon
The sun hushed all but the cool orchard plots,
We crept in the tall grass and slept till noon.

1921

RICHARD ALDINGTON
1892–1962

166   *Battlefield*

The wind is piercing chill
And blows fine grains of snow

Over this shell-rent ground;
Every house in sight
Is smashed and desolate.

But in this fruitless land,
Thorny with wire
And foul with rotting clothes and sacks,
The crosses flourish—
Ci-gît, ci-gît, ci-gît . . .
'Ci-gît 1 soldat Allemand,
Priez pour lui.'

1919

EDGELL RICKWORD
1898–1982

167   *Winter Warfare*

Colonel Cold strode up the Line
   (tabs of rime and spurs of ice);
stiffened all that met his glare:
   horses, men, and lice.

Visited a forward post,
   left them burning, ear to foot;
fingers stuck to biting steel,
   toes to frozen boot.

Stalked on into No Man's Land,
   turned the wire to fleecy wool,
iron stakes to sugar sticks
   snapping at a pull.

Those who watched with hoary eyes
   saw two figures gleaming there;
Hauptmann Kälte, Colonel Cold,
   gaunt in the grey air.

EDGELL RICKWORD

Stiffly, tinkling spurs they moved,
  glassy-eyed, with glinting heel
stabbing those who lingered there
  torn by screaming steel.

1921

168   *Trench Poets*

I knew a man, he was my chum,
but he grew blacker every day,
and would not brush the flies away,
nor blanch however fierce the hum
of passing shells; I used to read,
to rouse him, random things from Donne—
like 'Get with child a mandrake-root.'
But you can tell he was far gone,
for he lay gaping, mackerel-eyed,
and stiff and senseless as a post
even when that old poet cried
'I long to talk with some old lover's ghost.'

I tried the Elegies one day,
but he, because he heard me say:
'What needst thou have more covering than a man?'
grinned nastily, and so I knew
the worms had got his brains at last.
There was one thing that I might do
to starve the worms; I racked my head
for healthy things and quoted '*Maud.*'
His grin got worse and I could see
he sneered at passion's purity.
He stank so badly, though we were great chums
I had to leave him; then rats ate his thumbs.

1921

E. E. CUMMINGS
1894–1962

169

my sweet old etcetera
aunt lucy during the recent

war could and what
is more did tell you just
what everybody was fighting

for,
my sister

isabel created hundreds
(and
hundreds)of socks not to
mention shirts fleaproof earwarmers

etcetera wristers etcetera, my
mother hoped that

i would die etcetera
bravely of course my father used
to become hoarse talking about how it was
a privilege and if only he
could meanwhile my

self etcetera lay quietly
in the deep mud et

cetera
(dreaming,
et
    cetera, of
Your smile
eyes knees and of your Etcetera)

1926

170 'next to of course god america i
love you land of the pilgrims' and so forth oh
say can you see by the dawn's early my
country 'tis of centuries come and go
and are no more what of it we should worry
in every language even deafanddumb
thy sons acclaim your glorious name by gorry
by jingo by gee by gosh by gum
why talk of beauty what could be more beaut-
iful than these heroic happy dead
who rushed like lions to the roaring slaughter
they did not stop to think they died instead
then shall the voice of liberty be mute?'

He spoke.   And drank rapidly a glass of water

1926

171 i sing of Olaf glad and big
whose warmest heart recoiled at war:
a conscientious object-or

his wellbelovéd colonel(trig
westpointer most succinctly bred)
took erring Olaf soon in hand;
but—though an host of overjoyed
noncoms(first knocking on the head
him) do through icy waters roll
that helplessness which others stroke
with brushes recently employed
anent this muddy toiletbowl,
while kindred intellects evoke
allegiance per blunt instruments—
Olaf(being to all intents
a corpse and wanting any rag
upon what God unto him gave)
responds, without getting annoyed
'I will not kiss your f.ing flag'

straightway the silver bird looked grave
(departing hurriedly to shave)

225

but—though all kinds of officers
(a yearning nation's blueeyed pride)
their passive prey did kick and curse
until for wear their clarion
voices and boots were much the worse,
and egged the firstclassprivates on
his rectum wickedly to tease
by means of skilfully applied
bayonets roasted hot with heat—
Olaf(upon what were once knees)
does almost ceaselessly repeat
'there is some s. I will not eat'

our president, being of which
assertions duly notified
threw the yellowsonofabitch
into a dungeon, where he died

Christ(of His mercy infinite)
i pray to see; and Olaf, too

preponderatingly because
unless statistics lie he was
more brave than me:more blond than you.

1931

JOHN PEALE BISHOP
1892–1944

172   *In the Dordogne*

We stood up before day
And shaved by metal mirrors
In the faint flame of a faulty candle.
And we hurried down the wide stone stairs
With a clirr of spur chains
On stone. And we thought

When the cocks crew
That the ghosts of a dead dawn
Would rise and be off. But they stayed
Under the window, crouched on the staircase,
The windows now the color of morning.

The colonel slept in the bed of Sully
Slept on: but we descended
And saw in a niche in the white wall
A Virgin and Child, serene
Who were stone: we saw sycamores:
Three aged mages
Scattering gifts of gold.
But when the wind blew, there were autumn odors
And the shadowed trees
Had the dapplings of young fawns.

And each day one died or another
Died: each week we sent out thousands
That returned by hundreds
Wounded or gassed. And those that died
We buried close to the old wall
Within a stone's throw of Périgord
Under the tower of the troubadours.

And because we had courage;
Because there was courage and youth
Ready to be wasted; because we endured
And were prepared for all endurance;
We thought something must come of it:
That the Virgin would raise her Child and smile;
The trees gather up their gold and go;
That courage would avail something
And something we had never lost
Be regained through wastage, by dying,
By burying the others under the English tower.

The colonel slept on in the bed of Sully
Under the ravelling curtains; the leaves fell
And were blown away; the young men rotted
Under the shadow of the tower
In a land of small clear silent streams
Where the coming on of evening is

227

The letting down of blue and azure veils
Over the clear and silent streams
Delicately bordered by poplars.

1933

DAVID JONES
1895–1974

173   from *In Parenthesis*, part 7

But sweet sister death has gone debauched today and stalks
on this high ground with strumpet confidence, makes no coy
veiling of her appetite but leers from you to me with all her
parts discovered.

   By one and one the line gaps, where her fancy will—how-
soever they may howl for their virginity
she holds them—who impinge less on space
sink limply to a heap
nourish a lesser category of being
like those other who fructify the land
like Tristram
Lamorak de Galis
Alisand le Orphelin
Beaumains who was youngest
or all of them in shaft-shade
at strait Thermopylae
or the sweet brothers Balin and Balan
embraced beneath their single monument.
   Jonathan my lovely one
on Gelboe mountain
and the young man Absalom.
White Hart transfixed in his dark lodge.
Peredur of steel arms
and he who with intention took grass of that field to be for
him the Species of Bread.
   Taillefer the maker,
and on the same day,

228

thirty thousand other ranks.
And in the country of Béarn—Oliver
and all the rest—so many without memento
beneath the tumuli on the high hills
and under the harvest places.[1]

But how intolerably bright the morning is where we who are
alive and remain, walk lifted up, carried forward by an effect-
ive word.

But red horses now—blare every trump without economy,
burn boat and sever every tie every held thing goes west and
tethering snapt, bolts unshot and brass doors flung wide and
you go forward, foot goes another step further.

The immediate foreground sheers up, tilts toward,
like an high wall falling.
There she breaches black perpendiculars
where the counter-barrage warms to the seventh power where
the Three Children walk under the fair morning
and the Twin Brother[2]
and the high grass soddens through your puttees
and dew asperges the freshly dead.

There doesn't seem a soul about yet surely we walk already
near his preserves; there goes old Dawes as large as life and
there is Lazarus Cohen like on field-days, he always would
have his entrenching-tool-blade-carrier hung low, jogging
on his fat arse.
    They pass a quite ordinary message about keeping aligned
with No. 8.

You drop apprehensively—the sun gone out,
strange airs smite your body
and muck rains straight from heaven
and everlasting doors lift up for '02 Weavel.
    You cant see anything but sheen on drifting particles and
you move forward in your private bright cloud like
one assumed
who is borne up by an exterior volition.

You stumble on a bunch of six with Sergeant Quilter getting
them out again to the proper interval, and when the chemical
thick air dispels you see briefly and with great clearness what
kind of a show this is.

The gentle slopes are green to remind you
of South English places, only far wider and flatter spread and
grooved and harrowed criss-cross whitely and the disturbed
subsoil heaped up albescent.

Across upon this undulated board of verdure chequered bright
when you look to left and right
small, drab, bundled pawns severally make effort
moved in tenuous line
and if you looked behind—the next wave came slowly, as suc-
cessive surfs creep in to dissipate on flat shore;
and to your front, stretched long laterally,
and receded deeply,
the dark wood.

And now the gradient runs more flatly toward the separate
scared saplings, where they make fringe for the interior thicket
and you take notice.
    There between the thinning uprights
at the margin
straggle tangled oak and flayed sheeny beech-bole, and fragile
birch whose silver queenery is draggled and ungraced
and June shoots lopt
and fresh stalks bled
                runs the Jerry trench.
And cork-screw stapled trip-wire
to snare among the briars
and iron warp with bramble weft
with meadow-sweet and lady-smock
for a fair camouflage.

Mr Jenkins half inclined his head to them—he walked just
barely in advance of his platoon and immediately to the left of
Private Ball.

    He makes the conventional sign
and there is the deeply inward effort of spent men who would
make response for him,

and take it at the double.
He sinks on one knee
and now on the other,
his upper body tilts in rigid inclination
this way and back;
weighted lanyard runs to full tether,
    swings like a pendulum
    and the clock run down.
Lurched over, jerked iron saucer over tilted brow,
clampt unkindly over lip and chin
nor no ventaille to this darkening
    and masked face lifts to grope the air
and so disconsolate;
enfccbled fingering at a paltry strap—
buckle holds,
holds him blind against the morning.
 Then stretch still where weeds pattern the chalk predella
—where it rises to his wire[3]—and Sergeant T. Quilter takes
over.

1937

---

[1] *shaft-shade*. Cf. Herodotus, book vii, *Polymnia*, Dieneces' speech.
sweet brothers . . . monument. Cf. Malory, book ii, ch. 19.
White Hart transfixed. Cf. *Richard II*, Act v, Sc. vi.
Peredur of steel arms. Peredur. The *Percivale* of the romances called 'of steel arms' in the Triads, and by the Gododdin poet: 'Peredur with arms of steel . . . ' (he commemorates other warriors, and proceeds)' . . . though men might have slain them, they too were slayers, none returned to their homes.'
with intention . . . Species of Bread. In some battle of the Welsh, all reference to which escapes me, a whole army ate grass in token of the Body of the Lord. Also somewhere in the Malory, a single knight feeling himself at the point of death makes this same act.
Taillefer . . . other ranks. Cf. Wace, *Roman de Rou*: 'Then Taillefer, who sang right well, rode before the duke singing of Carlemaine and of Rollant, of Oliver and the vassals who died at Renchevals.'
country of Béarn . . . harvest places. Not that Roncesvalles is in the Béarn country, but I associate it with Béarn because, once, looking from a window in Salies-de-Béarn I could see a gap in the hills, which my hostess told me was indeed the pass where Roland fell. [DJ]
[2] *seventh power . . . Three Children . . . Twin Brother*. Cf. Book of Daniel, ch. iii. Here I identify 'The Great Twin Brethren' at the battle of Lake Regillus with the Second Person of the Blessed Trinity—who walked with the Three Children in the fiery furnace. [DJ]
[3] *chalk predella . . . his wire*. The approach to the German trenches here rose slightly, in low chalk ridges. [DJ]

LAURENCE BINYON
1869–1943

174   *For the Fallen*

With proud thanksgiving, a mother for her children,
England mourns for her dead across the sea.
Flesh of her flesh they were, spirit of her spirit,
Fallen in the cause of the free.

Solemn the drums thrill: Death august and royal
Sings sorrow up into immortal spheres.
There is music in the midst of desolation
And a glory that shines upon our tears.

They went with songs to the battle, they were young,
Straight of limb, true of eye, steady and aglow.
They were staunch to the end against odds uncounted,
They fell with their faces to the foe.

They shall grow not old, as we that are left grow old:
Age shall not weary them, nor the years condemn.
At the going down of the sun and in the morning
We will remember them.

They mingle not with their laughing comrades again;
They sit no more at familiar tables of home;
They have no lot in our labour of the day-time;
They sleep beyond England's foam.

But where our desires are and our hopes profound,
Felt as a well-spring that is hidden from sight,
To the innermost heart of their own land they are known
As the stars are known to the Night;

As the stars that shall be bright when we are dust,
Moving in marches upon the heavenly plain,
As the stars that are starry in the time of our darkness,
To the end, to the end, they remain.

1914

EZRA POUND
1885–1972

from *Hugh Selwyn Mauberley*
(Life and contacts)

These fought in any case,
and some believing,
            pro domo, in any case...

Some quick to arm,
some for adventure,
some from fear of weakness,
some from fear of censure,
some for love of slaughter, in imagination,
learning later...
some in fear, learning love of slaughter;
Died some, pro patria,
            non 'dulce' non 'et decor'...
walked eye-deep in hell
believing in old men's lies, then unbelieving
came home, home to a lie,
home to many deceits,
home to old lies and new infamy;
usury age-old and age-thick
and liars in public places.

Daring as never before, wastage as never before.
Young blood and high blood,
fair cheeks, and fine bodies;

fortitude as never before

frankness as never before,
disillusions as never told in the old days,
hysterias, trench confessions,
laughter out of dead bellies.

           *

There died a myriad,
And of the best, among them,

233

For an old bitch gone in the teeth,
For a botched civilization,

Charm, smiling at the good mouth,
Quick eyes gone under earth's lid,

For two gross of broken statues,
For a few thousand battered books.

1920

T. S. ELIOT
1888–1965

176   *Triumphal March*

Stone, bronze, stone, steel, stone, oakleaves, horses' heels
Over the paving.
And the flags. And the trumpets. And so many eagles.
How many? Count them. And such a press of people.
We hardly knew ourselves that day, or knew the City.
This is the way to the temple, and we so many crowding the way.
So many waiting, how many waiting? what did it matter, on such a day?
Are they coming? No, not yet. You can see some eagles.
    And hear the trumpets.
Here they come. Is he coming?
The natural wakeful life of our Ego is a perceiving.
We can wait with our stools and our sausages.
What comes first? Can you see? Tell us. It is
    5,800,000 rifles and carbines,
      102,000 machine guns,
       28,000 trench mortars,
       53,000 field and heavy guns,
I cannot tell how many projectiles, mines and fuses,
       13,000 aeroplanes,
       24,000 aeroplane engines,
       50,000 ammunition waggons,

now 55,000 army waggons,
  11,000 field kitchens,
   1,150 field bakeries.

What a time that took. Will it be he now? No,
Those are the golf club Captains, these the Scouts,
And now the *société gymnastique de Poissy*
And now come the Mayor and the Liverymen. Look
There he is now, look:
There is no interrogation in his eyes
Or in the hands, quiet over the horse's neck,
And the eyes watchful, waiting, perceiving, indifferent.
O hidden under the dove's wing, hidden in the turtle's breast,
Under the palmtree at noon, under the running water
At the still point of the turning world. O hidden.

Now they go up to the temple. Then the sacrifice.
Now come the virgins bearing urns, urns containing
Dust
Dust
Dust of dust, and now
Stone, bronze, stone, steel, stone, oakleaves, horses' heels
Over the paving.

That is all we could see. But how many eagles! and how many trumpets!
(And Easter Day, we didn't get to the country,
So we took young Cyril to church. And they rang a bell
And he said right out loud, *crumpets*.)
                         Don't throw away that sausage,
It'll come in handy. He's artful. Please, will you
Give us a light?
Light
Light
Et les soldats faisaient la haie? ILS LA FAISAIENT.

1931

G. K. CHESTERTON
1874–1936

177   *Elegy in a Country Churchyard*

The men that worked for England
They have their graves at home:
And bees and birds of England
About the cross can roam.

But they that fought for England,
Following a falling star,
Alas, alas for England
They have their graves afar.

And they that rule in England,
In stately conclave met,
Alas, alas for England
They have no graves as yet.

1922

RUDYARD KIPLING
1865–1936

178   *Mesopotamia 1917*

They shall not return to us, the resolute, the young,
    The eager and whole-hearted whom we gave:
But the men who left them thriftily to die in their own dung,
    Shall they come with years and honour to the grave?

They shall not return to us, the strong men coldly slain
    In sight of help denied from day to day:
But the men who edged their agonies and chid them in their pain,
    Are they too strong and wise to put away?

Our dead shall not return to us while Day and Night divide—
    Never while the bars of sunset hold.
But the idle-minded overlings who quibbled while they died,
    Shall they thrust for high employments as of old?

Shall we only threaten and be angry for an hour?
    When the storm is ended shall we find
How softly but how swiftly they have sidled back to power
    By the favour and contrivance of their kind?

Even while they soothe us, while they promise large amends,
    Even while they make a show of fear,
Do they call upon their debtors, and take counsel with their friends,
    To confirm and re-establish each career?

Their lives cannot repay us—their death could not undo—
    The shame that they have laid upon our race.
But the slothfulness that wasted and the arrogance that slew,
    Shall we leave it unabated in its place?

1917

179   from *Epitaphs of the War 1914–18*

A SERVANT

We were together since the War began.
He was my servant—and the better man.

A SON

My son was killed while laughing at some jest. I would I knew
What it was, and it might serve me in a time when jests are few.

AN ONLY SON

I have slain none except my Mother. She
(Blessing her slayer) died of grief for me.

HINDU SEPOY IN FRANCE

This man in his own country prayed we know not to what Powers.
We pray Them to reward him for his bravery in ours.

RUDYARD KIPLING

THE COWARD

I could not look on Death, which being known,
Men led me to him, blindfold and alone.

PELICANS IN THE WILDERNESS

A Grave near Halfa

The blown sand heaps on me, that none may learn
  Where I am laid for whom my children grieve....
O wings that beat at dawning, ye return
  Out of the desert to your young at eve!

TWO CANADIAN MEMORIALS

I

We giving all gained all.
  Neither lament us nor praise.
Only in all things recall,
  It is Fear, not Death that slays.

II

From little towns in a far land we came,
  To save our honour and a world aflame.
By little towns in a far land we sleep;
  And trust that world we won for you to keep!

THE BEGINNER

On the first hour of my first day
  In the front trench I fell.
(Children in boxes at a play
  Stand up to watch it well.)

NATIVE WATER-CARRIERS (M.E.F.)

Prometheus brought down fire to men.
  This brought up water.
The Gods are jealous—now, as then,
  Giving no quarter.

BOMBED IN LONDON

On land and sea I strove with anxious care
To escape conscription. It was in the air!

RUDYARD KIPLING

THE SLEEPY SENTINEL

Faithless the watch that I kept: now I have none to keep.
I was slain because I slept: now I am slain I sleep.
Let no man reproach me again, whatever watch is unkept—
I sleep because I am slain. They slew me because I slept.

BATTERIES OUT OF AMMUNITION

If any mourn us in the workshop, say
We died because the shift kept holiday.

COMMON FORM

If any question why we died,
Tell them, because our fathers lied.

A DEAD STATESMAN

I could not dig: I dared not rob:
Therefore I lied to please the mob.
Now all my lies are proved untrue
And I must face the men I slew.
What tale shall serve me here among
Mine angry and defrauded young?

A DRIFTER OFF TARENTUM

He from the wind-bitten North with ship and companions descended,
    Searching for eggs of death spawned by invisible hulls.
Many he found and drew forth. Of a sudden the fishery ended
    In flame and a clamorous breath known to the eye-pecking gulls.

DESTROYERS IN COLLISION

For Fog and Fate no charm is found
    To lighten or amend.
I, hurrying to my bride, was drowned—
    Cut down by my best friend.

CONVOY ESCORT

I was a shepherd to fools
    Causelessly bold or afraid.
They would not abide by my rules.
    Yet they escaped. For I stayed.

RUDYARD KIPLING

Headless, lacking foot and hand,
Horrible I come to land.
I beseech all women's sons
Know I was a mother once.

RAPED AND REVENGED

One used and butchered me: another spied
Me broken—for which thing an hundred died.
So it was learned among the heathen hosts
How much a freeborn woman's favour costs.

JOURNALISTS

On a Panel in the Hall of the Institute of Journalists

We have served our day.

1919

ELIZABETH DARYUSH

1887–1977

180   *Subalterns*

She said to one: 'How glows
My heart at the hot thought
Of battle's glorious throes!'
He said: 'For us who fought
Are icy memories
That must for ever freeze
The sunny hours they bought.'

She said to one: 'How light
Must be your freed heart now,
After the heavy fight!'
He said: 'Well, I don't know . . .
The war gave one a shake,
Somehow, knocked one awake . . .
Now, life's so deadly slow.'

1934

MAY WEDDERBURN CANNAN
1893–1973

August 1914

The sun rose over the sweep of the hill
  All bare for the gathered hay,
And a blackbird sang by the window-sill,
   And a girl knelt down to pray:
    'Whom Thou hast kept through the night, O Lord,
    Keep Thou safe through the day.'

The sun rose over the shell-swept height,
  The guns are over the way,
And a soldier turned from the toil of the night
  To the toil of another day,
    And a bullet sang by the parapet
    To drive in the new-turned clay.

The sun sank slow by the sweep of the hill,
  They had carried all the hay,
And a blackbird sang by the window-sill,
   And a girl knelt down to pray:
    'Keep Thou safe through the night, O Lord,
    Whom Thou hast kept through the day.'

The sun sank slow by the shell-swept height,
  The guns had prepared a way,
And a soldier turned to sleep that night
  Who would not wake for the day,
    And a blackbird flew from the window-sill,
    When a girl knelt down to pray.

March 1915

Rouen
26 April–25 May 1915

Early morning over Rouen, hopeful, high, courageous morning,
And the laughter of adventure and the steepness of the stair,
And the dawn across the river, and the wind across the bridges,
And the empty littered station and the tired people there.

Can you recall those mornings and the hurry of awakening,
And the long-forgotten wonder if we should miss the way,
And the unfamiliar faces, and the coming of provisions,
And the freshness and the glory of the labour of the day?

Hot noontide over Rouen, and the sun upon the city,
Sun and dust unceasing, and the glare of cloudless skies,
And the voices of the Indians and the endless stream of soldiers,
And the clicking of the tatties, and the buzzing of the flies.

Can you recall those noontides and the reek of steam and coffee,
Heavy-laden noontides with the evening's peace to win,
And the little piles of Woodbines, and the sticky soda bottles,
And the crushes in the 'Parlour', and the letters coming in?

Quiet night-time over Rouen, and the station full of soldiers,
All the youth and pride of England from the ends of all the earth;
And the rifles piled together, and the creaking of the sword-belts,
And the faces bent above them, and the gay, heart-breaking mirth.

Can I forget the passage from the cool white-bedded Aid Post
Past the long sun-blistered coaches of the khaki Red Cross train
To the truck train full of wounded, and the weariness and laughter,
And 'Good-bye, and thank you, Sister', and the empty yards again?

Can you recall the parcels that we made them for the railroad,
Crammed and bulging parcels held together by their string,
And the voices of the sergeants who called the Drafts together,
And the agony and splendour when they stood to save the King?

Can you forget their passing, the cheering and the waving,
The little group of people at the doorway of the shed,
The sudden awful silence when the last train swung to darkness,
And the lonely desolation, and the mocking stars o'erhead?

Can you recall the midnights, and the footsteps of night watchers,
Men who came from darkness and went back to dark again,
And the shadows on the rail–lines and the all-inglorious labour,
And the promise of the daylight firing blue the window-pane?

Can you recall the passing through the kitchen door to morning,
Morning very still and solemn breaking slowly on the town,
And the early coastways engines that had met the ships at daybreak,
And the Drafts just out from England, and the day shift coming down?

Can you forget returning slowly, stumbling on the cobbles,
And the white-decked Red Cross barges dropping seawards for the
    tide,
And the search for English papers, and the blessed cool of water,
And the peace of half-closed shutters that shut out the world outside?

Can I forget the evenings and the sunsets on the island,
And the tall black ships at anchor far below our balcony,
And the distant call of bugles, and the white wine in the glasses,
And the long line of the street lamps, stretching Eastwards to the sea?

... When the world slips slow to darkness, when the office fire burns
    lower,
My heart goes out to Rouen, Rouen all the world away;
When other men remember I remember our Adventure
And the trains that go from Rouen at the ending of the day.

1917

183   *'After the War'*

        After the War perhaps I'll sit again
        Out on the terrace where I sat with you,
        And see the changeless sky and hills beat blue
        And live an afternoon of summer through.

        I shall remember then, and sad at heart
        For the lost day of happiness we knew,
        Wish only that some other man were you
        And spoke my name as once you used to do.

February 1917

PHILIP LARKIN
1922–1985

MCMXIV

Those long uneven lines
Standing as patiently
As if they were stretched outside
The Oval or Villa Park,
The crowns of hats, the sun
On moustached archaic faces
Grinning as if it were all
An August Bank Holiday lark;

And the shut shops, the bleached
Established names on the sunblinds,
The farthings and sovereigns,
And dark-clothed children at play
Called after kings and queens,
The tin advertisements
For cocoa and twist, and the pubs
Wide open all day;

And the countryside not caring:
The place-names all hazed over
With flowering grasses, and fields
Shadowing Domesday lines
Under wheat's restless silence;
The differently-dressed servants
With tiny rooms in huge houses,
The dust behind limousines;

Never such innocence,
Never before or since,
As changed itself to past
Without a word—the men
Leaving the gardens tidy,
The thousands of marriages
Lasting a little while longer:
Never such innocence again.

1964

VERNON SCANNELL

1922–2007

185   *The Great War*

Whenever war is spoken of
I find
The war that was called Great invades the mind:
The grey militia marches over land
A darker mood of grey
Where fractured tree-trunks stand
And shells, exploding, open sudden fans
Of smoke and earth.
Blind murders scythe
The deathscape where the iron brambles writhe;
The sky at night
Is honoured with rosettes of fire,
Flares that define the corpses on the wire
As terror ticks on wrists at zero hour.
These things I see,
But they are only part
Of what it is that slyly probes the heart:
Less vivid images and words excite
The sensuous memory
And, even as I write,
Fear and a kind of love collaborate
To call each simple conscript up
For quick inspection:
Trenches' parapets
Paunchy with sandbags; bandoliers, tin-hats,
Candles in dug-outs,
Duckboards, mud and rats.
Then, like patrols, tunes creep into the mind:
A long, long, trail, The Rose of No Man's Land,
Home Fires and *Tipperary*;
And through the misty keening of a band
Of Scottish pipes the proper names are heard
Like fateful commentary of distant guns:
Passchendaele, Bapaume, and Loos, and Mons.
And now,
Whenever the November sky

VERNON SCANNELL

Quivers with a bugle's hoarse, sweet cry,
The reason darkens; in its evening gleam
Crosses and flares, tormented wire, grey earth
Splattered with crimson flowers,
And I remember,
Not the war I fought in
But the one called Great
Which ended in a sepia November
Four years before my birth.

1962

TED HUGHES

1930–1998

186 *Six Young Men*

The celluloid of a photograph holds them well,—
Six young men, familiar to their friends.
Four decades that have faded and ochre-tinged
This photograph have not wrinkled the faces or the hands.
Though their cocked hats are not now fashionable,
Their shoes shine. One imparts an intimate smile,
One chews a grass, one lowers his eyes, bashful,
One is ridiculous with cocky pride—
Six months after this picture they were all dead.

All are trimmed for a Sunday jaunt. I know
That bilberried bank, that thick tree, that black wall,
Which are there yet and not changed. From where these sit
You hear the water of seven streams fall
To the roarer in the bottom, and through all
The leafy valley a rumouring of air go.
Pictured here, their expressions listen yet,
And still that valley has not changed its sound
Though their faces are four decades under the ground.

This one was shot in an attack and lay
Calling in the wire, then this one, his best friend,

246

Went out to bring him in and was shot too;
And this one, the very moment he was warned
From potting at tin-cans in no-man's-land,
Fell back dead with his rifle-sights shot away.
The rest, nobody knows what they came to,
But come to the worst they must have done, and held it
Closer than their hope; all were killed.

Here see a man's photograph,
The locket of a smile, turned overnight
Into the hospital of his mangled last
Agony and hours; see bundled in it
His mightier-than-a-man dead bulk and weight:
And on this one place which keeps him alive
(In his Sunday best) see fall war's worst
Thinkable flash and rending, onto his smile
Forty years rotting into soil.

That man's not more alive whom you confront
And shake by the hand, see hale, hear speak loud,
Than any of these six celluloid smiles are,
Nor prehistoric or fabulous beast more dead;
No thought so vivid as their smoking blood:
To regard this photograph might well dement,
Such contradictory permanent horrors here
Smile from the single exposure and shoulder out
One's own body from its instant and heat.

1957

187   *Platform One**

Holiday squeals, as if all were scrambling for their lives,
Panting aboard the "Cornish Riviera".
Then overflow of relief and luggage and children,
Then ducking to smile out as the station moves.

* On platform number one of London's Paddington Station, Charles Sargeant
Jagger's larger-than-life-size bronze statue of the soldier described in this poem stands
as a memorial to the "Men and Women of the Great Western Railway who gave their
Lives for King and Country" in the World Wars of 1914–18 and 1939–45.

Out there on the platform, under the rain,
Under his rain-cape, helmet and full pack,
Somebody, head bowed reading something,
Doesn't know he's missing his train.

He's completely buried in that book.
He's forgotten utterly where he is.
He's forgotten Paddington, forgotten
Timetables, forgotten the long, rocking

Cradle of a journey into the golden West,
The coach's soft wingbeat—as light
And straight as a dove's flight.
Like a graveyard statue sentry cast

In blackened old bronze. Is he reading poems?
A letter? The burial service? The raindrops
Beaded along his helmet rim are bronze.
The words on his page are bronze. Their meanings bronze.

Sunk in his bronze world he stands, enchanted.
His bronze mind is deep among the dead.
Sunk so deep among the dead that, much
As he would like to remember us all, he cannot.

1995

DOUGLAS DUNN

1942–

188   *War Blinded*

For more than sixty years he has been blind
Behind that wall, these trees, with terrible
Longevity wheeled in the sun and wind
On pathways of the soldiers' hospital.

For half that time his story's troubled me—
That showroom by the ferry, where I saw

His basketwork, a touch-turned filigree
His fingers coaxed from charitable straw;

Or how he felt when young, enlisting at
Recruiting tables on the football pitch,
To end up slumped across a parapet,
His eye-blood running in a molten ditch;

Or how the light looked when I saw two men,
One blind, one in a wheelchair, in that park,
Their dignity, which I have not forgotten,
Which helps me struggle with this lesser dark.

That war's too old for me to understand
How he might think, nursed now in wards of want,
Remembering that day when his right hand
Gripped on the shoulder of the man in front.

1981

MICHAEL LONGLEY

1939–

189   *Wounds*

Here are two pictures from my father's head –
I have kept them like secrets until now:
First, the Ulster Division at the Somme
Going over the top with 'Fuck the Pope!'
'No Surrender!': a boy about to die,
Screaming 'Give 'em one for the Shankill!'
'Wilder than Gurkhas' were my father's words
Of admiration and bewilderment.
Next comes the London-Scottish padre
Resettling kilts with his swagger-stick,
With a stylish backhand and a prayer.
Over a landscape of dead buttocks
My father followed him for fifty years.

At last, a belated casualty,
He said—lead traces flaring till they hurt—
'I am dying for King and Country, slowly.'
I touched his hand, his thin head I touched.

Now, with military honours of a kind,
With his badges, his medals like rainbows,
His spinning compass, I bury beside him
Three teenage soldiers, bellies full of
Bullets and Irish beer, their flies undone.
A packet of Woodbines I throw in,
A lucifer, the Sacred Heart of Jesus
Paralysed as heavy guns put out
The night-light in a nursery for ever;
Also a bus-conductor's uniform—
He collapsed beside his carpet-slippers
Without a murmur, shot through the head
By a shivering boy who wandered in
Before they could turn the television down
Or tidy away the supper dishes.
To the children, to a bewildered wife,
I think 'Sorry Missus' was what he said.

1973

LOUIS MacNEICE

1907–1963

190   from *Autumn Journal*

And I remember Spain
    At Easter ripe as an egg for revolt and ruin
Though for a tripper the rain
    Was worse than the surly or the worried or the haunted faces
With writings on the walls—
    Hammer and sickle, Boicot, Viva, Muerra;
With café-au-lait brimming the waterfalls,
    With sherry, shellfish, omelettes.
With fretted stone the Moor

    Had chiselled for effects of sun and shadow;
With shadows of the poor,
    The begging cripples and the children begging.
The churches full of saints
    Tortured on racks of marble—
The old complaints
    Covered with gilt and dimly lit with candles.
With powerful or banal
    Monuments of riches or repression
And the Escorial
    Cold for ever within like the heart of Philip.
With ranks of dominoes
    Deployed on café tables the whole of Sunday;
With cabarets that call the tourist, shows
    Of thighs and eyes and nipples.
With slovenly soldiers, nuns,
    And peeling posters from the last elections
Promising bread or guns
    Or an amnesty or another
Order or else the old
    Glory veneered and varnished
As if veneer could hold
    The rotten guts and crumbled bones together.
And a vulture hung in air
    Below the cliffs of Ronda and below him
His hook-winged shadow wavered like despair
    Across the chequered vineyards.
And the boot-blacks in Madrid
    Kept us half an hour with polish and pincers
And all we did
    In that city was drink and think and loiter.
And in the Prado half-
    wit princes looked from the canvas they had paid for
(Goya had the laugh—
    But can what is corrupt be cured by laughter?)
And the day at Aranjuez
    When the sun came out for once on the yellow river
With Valdepeñas burdening the breath
    We slept a royal sleep in the royal gardens;
And at Toledo walked
    Around the ramparts where they throw the garbage
And glibly talked
    Of how the Spaniards lack all sense of business.

And Avila was cold
   And Segovia was picturesque and smelly
And a goat on the road seemed old
   As the rocks or the Roman arches.
And Easter was wet and full
   In Seville and in the ring on Easter Sunday
A clumsy bull and then a clumsy bull
   Nodding his banderillas died of boredom.
And the standard of living was low
   But that, we thought to ourselves, was not our business;
All that the tripper wants is the *status quo*
   Cut and dried for trippers.
And we thought the papers a lark
   With their party politics and blank invective;
And we thought the dark
   Women who dyed their hair should have it dyed more often.
And we sat in trains all night
   With the windows shut among civil guards and peasants
And tried to play piquet by a tiny light
   And tried to sleep bolt upright;
And cursed the Spanish rain
   And cursed their cigarettes which came to pieces
And caught heavy colds in Cordova and in vain
   Waited for the right light for taking photos.
And we met a Cambridge don who said with an air
   'There's going to be trouble shortly in this country,'
And ordered anis, pudgy and debonair,
   Glad to show off his mastery of the language.
But only an inch behind
   This map of olive and ilex, this painted hoarding,
Careless of visitors the people's mind
   Was tunnelling like a mole to day and danger.
And the day before we left
   We saw the mob in flower at Algeciras
Outside a toothless door, a church bereft
   Of its images and its aura.
And at La Linea while
   The night put miles between us and Gibraltar
We heard the blood-lust of a drunkard pile
   His heaven high with curses;
And next day took the boat
   For home, forgetting Spain, not realising
That Spain would soon denote

Our grief, our aspirations;
Not knowing that our blunt
    Ideals would find their whetstone, that our spirit
Would find its frontier on the Spanish front,
    Its body in a rag-tag army.

1939

JOHN CORNFORD
1915–1936

191   *A Letter from Aragon*

This is a quiet sector of a quiet front.

We buried Ruiz in a new pine coffin,
But the shroud was too small and his washed feet stuck out.
The stink of his corpse came through the clean pine boards
And some of the bearers wrapped handkerchiefs round their faces.
Death was not dignified.
We hacked a ragged grave in the unfriendly earth
And fired a ragged volley over the grave.

You could tell from our listlessness, no one much missed him.

This is a quiet sector of a quiet front.
There is no poison gas and no H. E.

But when they shelled the other end of the village
And the streets were choked with dust
Women came screaming out of the crumbling houses,
Clutched under one arm the naked rump of an infant.
I thought: how ugly fear is.

This is a quiet sector of a quiet front.
Our nerves are steady; we all sleep soundly.

In the clean hospital bed, my eyes were so heavy
Sleep easily blotted out one ugly picture,
A wounded militiaman moaning on a stretcher,

253

Now out of danger, but still crying for water,
Strong against death, but unprepared for such pain.

This on a quiet front.

But when I shook hands to leave, an Anarchist worker
Said: 'Tell the workers of England
This was a war not of our own making
We did not seek it.
But if ever the Fascists again rule Barcelona
It will be as a heap of ruins with us workers beneath it.'

1936

192   *Full Moon at Tierz:*
Before the Storming of Huesca

I

The past, a glacier, gripped the mountain wall,
And time was inches, dark was all.
But here it scales the end of the range,
The dialectic's point of change,
Crashes in light and minutes to its fall.

Time present is a cataract whose force
Breaks down the banks even at its source
And history forming in our hand's
Not plasticine but roaring sands,
Yet we must swing it to its final course.

The intersecting lines that cross both ways,
Time future, has no image in space,
Crooked as the road that we must tread,
Straight as our bullets fly ahead.
We are the future. The last fight let us face.

II

Where, in the fields by Huesca, the full moon
Throws shadows clear as daylight's, soon
The innocence of this quiet plain
Will fade in sweat and blood, in pain,
As our decisive hold is lost or won.

All round the barren hills of Aragon
Announce our testing has begun.
Here what the Seventh Congress said,
If true, if false, is live or dead,
Speaks in the Oviedo mausers tone.

Three years ago Dimitrov fought alone
And we stood taller when he won.
But now the Leipzig dragon's teeth
Sprout strong and handsome against death
And here an army fights where there was one.

We studied well how to begin this fight,
Our Maurice Thorez held the light.
But now by Monte Aragon
We plunge into the dark alone,
Earth's newest planet wheeling through the night.

III

Though Communism was my waking time,
Always before the lights of home
Shone clear and steady and full in view—
Here, if you fall, there's help for you—
Now, with my Party, I stand quite alone.

Then let my private battle with my nerves,
The fear of pain whose pain survives,
The love that tears me by the roots,
The loneliness that claws my guts,
Fuse in the welded front our fight preserves.

O be invincible as the strong sun,
Hard as the metal of my gun,
O let the mounting tempo of the train
Sweep where my footsteps slipped in vain,
October in the rhythm of its run.

IV

Now the same night falls over Germany
And the impartial beauty of the stars
Lights from the unfeeling sky
Oranienburg and freedom's crooked scars.

We can do nothing to ease that pain
But prove the agony was not in vain.

England is silent under the same moon,
From Clydeside to the gutted pits of Wales.
The innocent mask conceals that soon
Here, too, our freedom's swaying in the scales.
O understand before too late
Freedom was never held without a fight.

Freedom is an easily spoken word
But facts are stubborn things. Here, too, in Spain
Our fight's not won till the workers of all the world
Stand by our guard on Huesca's plain
Swear that our dead fought not in vain,
Raise the red flag triumphantly
For Communism and for liberty.

1936

193   *To Margot Heinemann*

Heart of the heartless world,
Dear heart, the thought of you
Is the pain at my side,
The shadow that chills my view.

The wind rises in the evening,
Reminds that autumn's near.
I am afraid to lose you,
I am afraid of my fear.

On the last mile to Huesca,
The last fence for our pride,
Think so kindly, dear, that I
Sense you at my side.

And if bad luck should lay my strength
Into the shallow grave,
Remember all the good you can;
Don't forget my love.

1936

GEORGE ORWELL

1903–1950

194   The Italian soldier shook my hand
Beside the guard-room table;
The strong hand and the subtle hand
Whose palms are only able

To meet within the sound of guns,
But oh! what peace I knew then
In gazing on his battered face
Purer than any woman's!

For the fly-blown words that make me spew
Still in his ears were holy,
And he was born knowing what I had learned
Out of books and slowly.

The treacherous guns had told their tale
And we both had bought it,
But my gold brick was made of gold—
Oh! who ever would have thought it?

Good luck go with you, Italian soldier!
But luck is not for the brave;
What would the world give back to you?
Always less than you gave.

Between the shadow and the ghost,
Between the white and the red,
Between the bullet and the lie,
Where would you hide your head?

For where is Manuel Gonzalez,
And where is Pedro Aguilar,
And where is Ramon Fenellosa?
The earthworms know where they are.

Your name and your deeds were forgotten
Before your bones were dry,

And the lie that slew you is buried
Under a deeper lie;

But the thing that I saw in your face
No power can disinherit:
No bomb that ever burst
Shatters the crystal spirit.

1939

ANONYMOUS

195 *[Stanzas found on a leaf of an International
Brigader's notebook]*

Eyes of men running, falling, screaming
Eyes of men shouting, sweating, bleeding
The eyes of the fearful, those of the sad
The eyes of exhaustion, and those of the mad.

Eyes of men thinking, hoping, waiting
Eyes of men loving, cursing, hating
The eyes of the wounded sodden in red
The eyes of the dying and those of the dead.

mid-1930s

LAURIE LEE

1914–1997

196 *A Moment of War*

It is night like a red rag
drawn across the eyes

the flesh is bitterly pinned
to desperate vigilance

the blood is stuttering with fear

O praise the security of worms
in cool crumbs of soil,
flatter the hidden sap
and the lost unfertilized spawn of fish!

The hands melt with weakness
into the gun's hot iron

the body melts with pity,

the face is braced for wounds
the odour and the kiss of final pain.

O envy the peace of women
giving birth and love like toys
into the hands of men!

The mouth chatters with pale curses

the bowels struggle like a nest of rats

the feet wish they were grass
spaced quietly.

O Christ and Mother!

But darkness opens like a knife for you
and you are marked down by your pulsing brain

and isolated

and your breathing,

your breathing is the blast, the bullet,
and the final sky.

Spanish Frontier, 1937

SYLVIA TOWNSEND WARNER
1893–1978

*Benicasim**

Here for a little we pause.
The air is heavy with sun and salt and colour.
On palm and lemon-tree, on cactus and oleander
a dust of dust and salt and pollen lies.
And the bright villas
sit in a row like perched macaws,
and rigid and immediate yonder
the mountains rise.

And it seems to me we have come
into a bright-painted landscape of Acheron.
For along the strand
in bleached cotton pyjamas, on rope-soled tread,
wander the risen-from-the-dead,
the wounded, the maimed, the halt.
Or they lay bare their hazarded flesh to the salt
air, the recaptured sun,
or bathe in the tideless sea, or sit fingering the sand.

But narrow is this place, narrow is this space
of garlanded sun and leisure and colour, of return
to life and release from living. Turn
(Turn not!) sight inland:
there, rigid as death and unforgiving, stand
the mountains—and close at hand.

1938

---

* At Benicasim on the east coast of Spain is the Rest Home for the convalescent
wounded of the Spanish People's Army, and the Villa dedicated to Ralph Fox,
supported by the Spanish Medical Aid. [STW]

W. H. AUDEN
1907–1973

Spain 1937

Yesterday all the past. The language of size
Spreading to China along the trade-routes; the diffusion
       Of the counting-frame and the cromlech;
Yesterday the shadow-reckoning in the sunny climates.

Yesterday the assessment of insurance by cards,
The divination of water; yesterday the invention
       Of cart-wheels and clocks, the taming of
Horses; yesterday the bustling world of the navigators.

Yesterday the abolition of fairies and giants;
The fortress like a motionless eagle eyeing the valley,
       The chapel built in the forest;
Yesterday the carving of angels and of frightening gargoyles;

The trial of heretics among the columns of stone;
Yesterday the theological feuds in the taverns
       And the miraculous cure at the fountain;
Yesterday the Sabbath of Witches. But today the struggle.

Yesterday the installation of dynamos and turbines;
The construction of railways in the colonial desert;
       Yesterday the classic lecture
On the origin of Mankind. But today the struggle.

Yesterday the belief in the absolute value of Greek;
The fall of the curtain upon the death of a hero;
       Yesterday the prayer to the sunset,
And the adoration of madmen. But today the struggle.

As the poet whispers, startled among the pines
Or, where the loose waterfall sings, compact, or upright
       On the crag by the leaning tower:
'O my vision. O send me the luck of the sailor.'

And the investigator peers through his instruments
At the inhuman provinces, the virile bacillus
      Or enormous Jupiter finished:
'But the lives of my friends. I inquire, I inquire.'

And the poor in their fireless lodgings dropping the sheets
Of the evening paper: 'Our day is our loss. O show us
      History the operator, the
Organiser, Time the refreshing river.'

And the nations combine each cry, invoking the life
That shapes the individual belly and orders
      The private nocturnal terror:
'Did you not found once the city state of the sponge,

'Raise the vast military empires of the shark
And the tiger, establish the robin's plucky canton?
      Intervene. O descend as a dove or
A furious papa or a mild engineer: but descend.'

And the life, if it answers at all, replies from the heart
And the eyes and the lungs, from the shops and squares of the city:
      'O no, I am not the Mover,
Not today, not to you. To you I'm the

'Yes-man, the bar-companion, the easily-duped:
I am whatever you do; I am your vow to be
      Good, your humorous story;
I am your business voice; I am your marriage.

'What's your proposal? To build the Just City? I will.
I agree. Or is it the suicide pact, the romantic
      Death? Very well, I accept, for
I am your choice, your decision: yes, I am Spain.'

Many have heard it on remote peninsulas,
On sleepy plains, in the aberrant fishermen's islands,
      In the corrupt heart of the city;
Have heard and migrated like gulls or the seeds of a flower.

They clung like burrs to the long expresses that lurch
Through the unjust lands, through the night, through the alpine
   tunnel;

They floated over the oceans;
They walked the passes: they came to present their lives.

On that arid square, that fragment nipped off from hot
Africa, soldered so crudely to inventive Europe,
        On that tableland scored by rivers,
Our fever's menacing shapes are precise and alive.

Tomorrow, perhaps, the future: the research on fatigue
And the movements of packers; the gradual exploring of all the
        Octaves of radiation;
Tomorrow the enlarging of consciousness by diet and breathing.

Tomorrow the rediscovery of romantic love;
The photographing of ravens; all the fun under
        Liberty's masterful shadow;
Tomorrow the hour of the pageant-master and the musician.

Tomorrow, for the young, the poets exploding like bombs,
The walks by the lake, the winter of perfect communion;
        Tomorrow the bicycle races
Through the suburbs on summer evenings: but today the struggle.

Today the inevitable increase in the chances of death;
The conscious acceptance of guilt in the fact of murder;
        Today the expending of powers
On the flat ephemeral pamphlet and the boring meeting.

Today the makeshift consolations; the shared cigarette;
The cards in the candle-lit barn and the scraping concert,
        The masculine jokes; today the
Fumbled and unsatisfactory embrace before hurting.

The stars are dead; the animals will not look:
We are left alone with our day, and the time is short and
        History to the defeated
May say Alas but cannot help or pardon.

1937; rev. 1940

STEPHEN SPENDER

1909–1995

199   *Two Armies*

Deep in the winter plain, two armies
Dig their machinery, to destroy each other.
Men freeze and hunger. No one is given leave
On either side, except the dead and wounded.
These have their leave; while new battalions wait
On time at last to bring them violent peace.

All have become so nervous and so cold
That each man hates the cause and distant words
That brought him here, more terribly than bullets.
Once a boy hummed a popular marching song,
Once a novice hand flapped their salute;
The voice was choked, the lifted hand fell,
Shot through the wrist by those of his own side.

From their numb harvest, all would flee, except
For discipline drilled once in an iron school
Which holds them at the point of the revolver.
Yet when they sleep, the images of home
Ride wishing horses of escape
Which herd the plain in a mass unspoken poem.

Finally, they cease to hate: for although hate
Bursts from the air and whips the earth with hail
Or shoots it up in fountains to marvel at,
And although hundreds fall, who can connect
The inexhaustible anger of the guns
With the dumb patience of those tormented animals?

Clean silence drops at night, when a little walk
Divides the sleeping armies, each
Huddled in linen woven by remote hands.
When the machines are stilled, a common suffering
Whitens the air with breath and makes both one
As though these enemies slept in each other's arms.

Only the lucid friend to aerial raiders
The brilliant pilot moon, stares down
Upon this plain she makes a shining bone
Cut by the shadows of many thousand bones.
Where amber clouds scatter on No Man's Land
She regards death and time throw up
The furious words and minerals which destroy.

1939

200   *Ultima Ratio Regum*

The guns spell money's ultimate reason
In letters of lead on the Spring hillside.
But the boy lying dead under the olive trees
Was too young and too silly
To have been notable to their important eye.
He was a better target for a kiss.

When he lived, tall factory hooters never summoned him
Nor did restaurant plate-glass doors revolve to wave him in.
His name never appeared in the papers.
The world maintained its traditional wall
Round the dead with their gold sunk deep as a well,
Whilst his life, intangible as a Stock Exchange rumour, drifted
    outside.

O too lightly he threw down his cap
One day when the breeze threw petals from the trees.
The unflowering wall sprouted with guns,
Machine-gun anger quickly scythed the grasses;
Flags and leaves fell from hands and branches;
The tweed cap rotted in the nettles.

Consider his life which was valueless
In terms of employment, hotel ledgers, news files.
Consider. One bullet in ten thousand kills a man.
Ask. Was so much expenditure justified
On the death of one so young, and so silly
Lying under the olive trees, O world, O death?

1939

BERNARD SPENCER
1909–1963

201   *A Thousand Killed*

I read of a thousand killed.
And am glad because the scrounging imperial paw
Was there so bitten:
As a man at elections is thrilled
When the results pour in, and the North goes with him
And the West breaks in the thaw.

(That fighting was a long way off.)

Forgetting therefore an election
Being fought with votes and lies and catch-cries
And orator's frowns and flowers and posters' noise,
Is paid for with cheques and toys:
Wars the most glorious
Victory-winged and steeple-uproarious
... With the lives, burned-off,
Of young men and boys.

                                                    1936

HERBERT READ
1893–1968

202   *To a Conscript of 1940*

Qui n'a pas une fois désespéré de l'honneur, ne sera
jamais un héros.

                                        Georges Bernanos

A soldier passed me in the freshly fallen snow
His footsteps muffled, his face unearthly grey;

And my heart gave a sudden leap
As I gazed on a ghost of five-and-twenty years ago.

I shouted Halt! and my voice had the old accustomed ring
And he obeyed it as it was obeyed
In the shrouded days when I too was one
Of an army of young men marching

Into the unknown. He turned towards me and I said:
'I am one of those who went before you
Five-and-twenty years ago: one of the many who never returned,
Of the many who returned and yet were dead.

'We went where you are going, into the rain and the mud;
We fought as you will fight
With death and darkness and despair;
We gave what you will give—our brains and our blood.

'We think we gave in vain. The world was not renewed.
There was hope in the homestead and anger in the streets
But the old world was restored and we returned
To the dreary field and workshop, and the immemorial feud

'Of rich and poor. Our victory was our defeat.
Power was retained where power had been misused
And youth was left to sweep away
The ashes that the fires had strewn beneath our feet.

'But one thing we learned: there is no glory in the deed
Until the soldier wears a badge of tarnished braid;
There are heroes who have heard the rally and have seen
The glitter of a garland round their head.

'Theirs is the hollow victory. They are deceived.
But you, my brother and my ghost, if you can go
Knowing that there is no reward, no certain use
In all your sacrifice, then honour is reprieved.

'To fight without hope is to fight with grace,
The self reconstructed, the false heart repaired.'
Then I turned with a smile, and he answered my salute
As he stood against the fretted hedge, which was like white lace.

1944

LOUIS ARAGON
1897–1983

The Lilacs and the Roses

O months of blossoming, months of transfigurations,
May without a cloud and June stabbed to the heart,
I shall not ever forget the lilacs or the roses
Nor those the Spring has kept folded away apart.

I shall not ever forget the tragic sleight-of-hand,
The cavalcade, the cries, the crowd, the sun,
The lorries loaded with love, the Belgian gifts,
The road humming with bees, the atmosphere that spun,
The feckless triumphing before the battle,
The scarlet blood the scarlet kiss bespoke
And those about to die bolt upright in the turrets
Smothered in lilac by a drunken folk.

I shall not ever forget the flower-gardens of France—
Illuminated scrolls from eras more than spent—
Nor forget the trouble of dusk, the sphinx-like silence,
The roses all along the way we went;
Flowers that gave the lie to the soldiers passing
On wings of fear, a fear importunate as a breeze,
And gave the lie to the lunatic push-bikes and the ironic
Guns and the sorry rig of the refugees.

But what I do not know is why this whirl
Of memories always comes to the same point and drops
At Sainte-Marthe . . . a general . . . a black pattern . . .
A Norman villa where the forest stops;
All is quiet here, the enemy rests in the night
And Paris has surrendered, so we have just heard—
I shall never forget the lilacs nor the roses
Nor those two loves whose loss we have incurred:

Bouquets of the first day, lilacs, Flanders lilacs,
Soft cheeks of shadow rouged by death—and you,
Bouquets of the Retreat, delicate roses, tinted
Like far-off conflagrations: roses of Anjou.

1939-40

Translated from the French by Louis MacNeice

C. DAY LEWIS
1904–1972

204   *The Stand-To*

Autumn met me today as I walked over Castle Hill.
The wind that had set our corn by the ears was blowing still:
Autumn, who takes the leaves and the long days, crisped the air
With a tang of action, a taste of death; and the wind blew fair

From the east for men and barges massed on the other side—
Men maddened by numbers or stolid by nature, they have their pride
As we in work and children, but now a contracting will
Crumples their meek petitions and holds them poised to kill.

Last night a Stand-To was ordered. Thirty men of us here
Came out to guard the star-lit village—my men who wear
Unwitting the season's beauty, the received truth of the spade—
Roadmen, farm labourers, masons, turned to another trade.

A dog barked over the fields, the candle stars put a sheen
On the rifles ready, the sandbags fronded with evergreen:
The dawn wind blew, the stars winked out on the posts where we lay,
The order came, Stand Down, and thirty went away.

Since a cold wind from Europe blows back the words in my teeth,
Since autumn shortens the days and the odds against our death,
And the harvest moon is waxing and high tides threaten harm,
Since last night may be the last night all thirty men go home,

I write this verse to record the men who have watched with me—
Spot who is good at darts, Squibby at repartee,
Mark and Cyril, the dead shots, Ralph with a ploughman's gait,
Gibson, Harris and Long, old hands for the barricade,

Whiller the lorry-driver, Francis and Rattlesnake,
Fred and Charl and Stan—these nights I have lain awake
And thought of my thirty men and the autumn wind that blows
The apples down too early and shatters the autumn rose.

Destiny, History, Duty, Fortitude, Honour—all
The words of the politicians seem too big or too small
For the ragtag fighters of lane and shadow, the love that has grown
Familiar as working-clothes, faithful as bone to bone.

Blow, autumn wind, upon orchard and rose! Blow leaves along
Our lanes, but sing through me for the lives that are worth a song!
Narrowing days have darkened the vistas that hurt my eyes,
But pinned to the heart of darkness a tattered fire-flag flies.

September 1940

205   *Where are the War Poets?*

They who in folly or mere greed
Enslaved religion, markets, laws,
Borrow our language now and bid
Us to speak up in freedom's cause.

It is the logic of our times,
No subject for immortal verse—
That we who lived by honest dreams
Defend the bad against the worse.

1943

DAVID GASCOYNE
1916–2001

206   *Ecce Homo*

Whose is this horrifying face,
This putrid flesh, discoloured, flayed,
Fed on by flies, scorched by the sun?
Whose are these hollow red-filmed eyes
And thorn-spiked head and spear-stuck side?
Behold the Man: He is Man's Son.

Forget the legend, tear the decent veil
That cowardice or interest devised
To make their mortal enemy a friend,
To hide the bitter truth all His wounds tell,
Lest the great scandal be no more disguised:
He is in agony till the world's end,

And we must never sleep during that time!
He is suspended on the cross-tree now
And we are onlookers at the crime,
Callous contemporaries of the slow
Torture of God. Here is the hill
Made ghastly by His spattered blood

Whereon He hangs and suffers still:
See, the centurions wear riding-boots,
Black shirts and badges and peaked caps,
Greet one another with raised-arm salutes;
They have cold eyes, unsmiling lips;
Yet these His brothers know not what they do.

And on his either side hang dead
A labourer and a factory hand,
Or one is maybe a lynched Jew
And one a Negro or a Red,
Coolie or Ethiopian, Irishman,
Spaniard or German democrat.

Behind His lolling head the sky
Glares like a fiery cataract
Red with the murders of two thousand years
Committed in His name and by
Crusaders, Christian warriors
Defending faith and property.

Amid the plain beneath His transfixed hands,
Exuding darkness as indelible
As guilty stains, fanned by funereal
And lurid airs, besieged by drifting sands
And clefted landslides our about-to-be
Bombed and abandoned cities stand.

He who wept for Jerusalem
Now sees His prophecy extend
Across the greatest cities of the world
A guilty panic reason cannot stem
Rising to raze them all as He foretold;
And He must watch this drama to the end.

Though often named, He is unknown
To the dark kingdoms at His feet
Where everything disparages His words,
And each man bears the common guilt alone
And goes blindfolded to his fate,
And fear and greed are sovereign lords.

The turning point of history
Must come. Yet the complacent and the proud
And who exploit and kill, may be denied—
Christ of Revolution and of Poetry—
The resurrection and the life
Wrought by your spirit's blood.

Involved in their own sophistry
The black priest and the upright man
Faced by subversive truth shall be struck dumb,
Christ of Revolution and of Poetry,
While the rejected and condemned become
Agents of the divine.

Not from a monstrance silver-wrought
But from the tree of human pain
Redeem our sterile misery,
Christ of Revolution and of Poetry,
That man's long journey through the night
May not have been in vain.

1943

207   *Spring MCMXL*

London Bridge is falling down, Rome's burnt, and Babylon
The Great is now but dust; and still Spring must

Swing back through Time's continual arc to earth.
Though every land become as a black field
Dunged with the dead, drenched by the dying's blood,
Still must a punctual goddess waken and ascend
The rocky stairs, up into earth's chilled air,
And pass upon her mission through those carrion ranks,
Picking her way among a maze of broken brick
To quicken with her footsteps the short sooty grass between
While now once more their futile matchwood empires flare and blaze
And through the smoke men gaze with bloodshot eyes
At the translucent apparition, clad in trembling nascent green,
Of one they can still recognize, though scarcely understand.

1940

CZESLAW MILOSZ

1911–2004

208   *A Book in the Ruins*

A dark building. Crossed boards, nailed up, create
A barrier at the entrance, or a gate
When you go in. Here, in the gutted foyer,
The ivy snaking down the walls is wire
Dangling. And over there the twisted metal
Columns rising from the undergrowth of rubble
Are tattered tree trunks. This could be the brick
Of the library, you don't know yet, or the sick
Grove of dry white aspen where, stalking birds,
You met a Lithuanian dusk stirred
From its silence only by the wails of hawks.
Now walk carefully. You see whole blocks
Of ceiling caved in by a recent blast.
And above, through jagged tiers of plaster,
A patch of blue. Pages of books lying
Scattered at your feet are like fern-leaves hiding
A moldy skeleton, or else fossils
Whitened by the secrets of Jurassic shells.

A remnant life so ancient and unknown
Compels a scientist, tilting a stone
Into the light, to wonder. He can't know
Whether it is some dead epoch's shadow
Or a living form. He looks again
At chalk spirals eroded by the rain,
The rust of tears. Thus, in a book picked up
From the ruins, you see a world erupt
And glitter with its distant sleepy past,
Green times of creatures tumbled to the vast
Abyss and backward: the brows of women,
An earring fixed with trembling hand, pearl button
On a glove, candelabra in the mirror.
The lanterns have been lit. A first shiver
Passes over the instruments. The quadrille
Begins to curl, subdued by the rustle
Of big trees swaying in the formal park.
She slips outside, her shawl floating in the dark,
And meets him in a bower overgrown
With vines. They sit close on a bench of stone
And watch the lanterns glowing in the jasmine.
Or here, this stanza: you hear a goose pen
Creak, the butterfly of an oil lamp
Flutters slowly over scrolls and parchment,
A crucifix, bronze busts. The lines complain,
In plangent rhythms, that desire is vain.
Here a city rises. In the market square
Signboards clang, a stagecoach rumbles in to scare
A flock of pigeons up. Under the town clock,
In the tavern, a hand pauses in the stock
Gesture of arrest—meanwhile workers walk
Home from the textile mill, townsfolk talk
On the steps—and the hand moves now to evoke
The fire of justice, a world gone up in smoke,
The voice quavering with the revenge of ages.
So the world seems to drift from these pages
Like the mist clearing on a field at dawn.
Only when two times, two forms are drawn
Together and their legibility
Disturbed, do you see that immortality
Is not very different from the present
And is for its sake. You pick a fragment
Of grenade which pierced the body of a song

On Daphnis and Chloe. And you long,
Ruefully, to have a talk with her,
As if it were what life prepared you for.
—How is it, Chloe, that your pretty skirt
Is torn so badly by the winds that hurt
Real people, you who, in eternity, sing
The hours, sun in your hair appearing
And disappearing? How is it that your breasts
Are pierced by shrapnel, and the oak groves burn,
While you, charmed, not caring at all, turn
To run through forests of machinery and concrete
And haunt us with the echoes of your feet?
If there is such an eternity, lush
Though short-lived, that's enough. But how . . . hush!
We were predestined to live when the scene
Grows dim and the outline of a Greek ruin
Blackens the sky. It is noon, and wandering
Through a dark building, you see workers sitting
Down to a fire a narrow ray of sunlight
Kindles on the floor. They have dragged out
Heavy books and made a table of them
And begun to cut their bread. In good time
A tank will clatter past, a streetcar chime.

Warsaw 1941

EDITH SITWELL
1887–1964

209   *Still Falls the Rain*
(The raids, 1940. Night and dawn)

Still falls the Rain—
Dark as the world of man, black as our loss—
Blind as the nineteen hundred and forty nails
Upon the Cross.

Still falls the Rain
With a sound like the pulse of the heart that is changed
   to the hammer-beat
In the Potter's Field, and the sound of the impious feet

On the Tomb:
        Still falls the Rain
In the Field of Blood where the small hopes breed and
  the human brain
Nurtures its greed, that worm with the brow of Cain.

Still falls the Rain
At the feet of the Starved Man hung upon the Cross.
Christ that each day, each night, nails there,
                      have mercy on us—
On Dives and on Lazarus:
Under the Rain the sore and the gold are as one.

Still falls the Rain—
Still falls the Blood from the Starved Man's wounded Side:
He bears in His Heart all wounds,—those of the light that died,
The last faint spark
In the self-murdered heart, the wounds of the sad
  uncomprehending dark,

The wounds of the baited bear,—
The blind and weeping bear whom the keepers beat
On his helpless flesh . . . the tears of the hunted hare.

Still falls the Rain—
Then—O Ile leape up to my God: who pulles me doune—
See, see where Christ's blood streames in the firmament:
It flows from the Brow we nailed upon the tree
Deep to the dying, to the thirsting heart
That holds the fires of the world,—dark-smirched with pain
As Caesar's laurel crown.

Then sounds the voice of One who like the heart of man
Was once a child who among beasts has lain—
'Still do I love, still shed my innocent light, my Blood, for thee.'

1942

H. D. [HILDA DOOLITTLE]
1886–1961

from *The Walls Do Not Fall*

An incident here and there,
and rails gone (for guns)
from your (and my) old town square:

mist and mist-grey, no colour,
still the Luxor bee, chick and hare
pursue unalterable purpose

in green, rose-red, lapis;
they continue to prophesy
from the stone papyrus:

there, as here, ruin opens
the tomb, the temple; enter,
there as here, there are no doors:

the shrine lies open to the sky,
the rain falls, here, there
sand drifts; eternity endures:

ruin everywhere, yet as the fallen roof
leaves the sealed room
open to the air,

so, through our desolation,
thoughts stir, inspiration stalks us
through gloom:

unaware, Spirit announces the Presence;
shivering overtakes us,
as of old, Samuel:

trembling at a known street-corner,
we know not nor are known;
the Pythian pronounces—we pass on

to another cellar, to another sliced wall
where poor utensils show
like rare objects in a museum;

Pompeii has nothing to teach us,
we know crack of volcanic fissure,
slow flow of terrible lava,

pressure on heart, lungs, the brain
about to burst its brittle case
(what the skull can endure!):

over us, Apocryphal fire,
under us, the earth sway, dip of a floor,
slope of a pavement

where men roll, drunk
with a new bewilderment,
sorcery, bedevilment:

the bone-frame was made for
no such shock knit within terror,
yet the skeleton stood up to it:

the flesh? it was melted away,
the heart burnt out, dead ember,
tendons, muscles shattered, outer husk dismembered,

yet the frame held:
we passed the flame: we wonder
what saved us? what for?

1944

LOUIS MacNEICE

1907–1963

211   *The Streets of Laredo*

O early one morning I walked out like Agag,
Early one morning to walk through the fire

278

Dodging the pythons that leaked on the pavements
With tinkle of glasses and tangle of wire;

When grimed to the eyebrows I met an old fireman
Who looked at me wryly and thus did he say:
'The streets of Laredo are closed to all traffic,
We won't never master this joker today.

'O hold the branch tightly and wield the axe brightly,
The bank is in powder, the banker's in hell,
But loot is still free on the streets of Laredo
And when we drive home we drive home on the bell.'

Then out from a doorway there sidled a cockney,
A rocking-chair rocking on top of his head:
'O fifty-five years I been feathering my love-nest
And look at it now—why, you'd sooner be dead.'

At which there arose from a wound in the asphalt,
His big wig a-smouldcr, Sir Christopher Wren
Saying: 'Let them make hay of the streets of Laredo;
When your ground-rents expire I will build them again.'

Then twangling their bibles with wrath in their nostrils
From Bonehill Fields came Bunyan and Blake:
'Laredo the golden is fallen, is fallen;
Your flame shall not quench nor your thirst shall not
    slake.'

'I come to Laredo to find me asylum',
Says Tom Dick and Harry the Wandering Jew;
'They tell me report at the first police station
But the station is pancaked—so what can I do?'

Thus eavesdropping sadly I strolled through Laredo
Perplexed by the dicta misfortunes inspire
Till one low last whisper inveigled my earhole—
The voice of the Angel, the voice of the fire:

O late, very late, have I come to Laredo
A whimsical bride in my new scarlet dress
But at last I took pity on those who were waiting
To see my regalia and feel my caress.

Now ring the bells gaily and play the hose daily,
Put splints on your legs, put a gag on your breath;
O you streets of Laredo, you streets of Laredo,
Lay down the red carpet—My dowry is death.

1948

R. N. CURREY

1907–2001

212   *Unseen Fire*

This is a damned inhuman sort of war.
I have been fighting in a dressing-gown
Most of the night; I cannot see the guns,
The sweating gun-detachments or the planes;

I sweat down here before a symbol thrown
Upon a screen, sift facts, initiate
Swift calculations and swift orders; wait
For the precise split-second to order fire.

We chant our ritual words; beyond the phones
A ghost repeats the orders to the guns:
One Fire . . . Two Fire . . . ghosts answer: the guns roar
Abruptly; and an aircraft waging war
Inhumanly from nearly five miles height
Meets our bouquet of death—and turns sharp right.

1945

KENNETH ALLOTT

1912–1973

213   *Prize for Good Conduct*

The worn-out voice of the clock breaks on the hour:
The State requires
          My wedding ring and my apostle spoons,
          My sons.

280

There will be a special service in the cathedral
After which the clergy will be disbanded
And the fane profaned and put to immediate service
To manufacture wooden legs for heroes
With a useful sideline in glass-eyes
And employment found for over two hundred widows.

The feverish wounded in the base hospital,
The nurse's coif becomes a phallic symbol,
He hears the red coal drop, and the cistern filling;
And the stripped dead buried in ungainly postures
Their lucky charms sent back with kindly letters,
The invalids sent home with eyesight failing
To sit on a waiting-list for operations
And never to be put off iron rations;
And the nervous shipwrecked bodies in lovely grounds
Set aside by old ladies with unearned incomes;
The cows are eating the shadows off the field,
The wasps buzz angrily in the stoppered bottle,
The devil comes daintily over the stepping-stones
As they sit in the sunshine, crying no rest for the wicked.

1938

HENRY REED

1914–1986

214   *Lessons of the War*
To Alan Michell

Vixi duellis nuper idoneus
Et militavi non sine gloria

I. NAMING OF PARTS

Today we have naming of parts. Yesterday,
We had daily cleaning. And tomorrow morning,
We shall have what to do after firing. But today,

Today we have naming of parts. Japonica
Glistens like coral in all of the neighbouring gardens,
    And today we have naming of parts.

This is the lower sling swivel. And this
Is the upper sling swivel, whose use you will see,
When you are given your slings. And this is the piling swivel,
Which in your case you have not got. The branches
Hold in the gardens their silent, eloquent gestures,
    Which in our case we have not got.

This is the safety-catch, which is always released
With an easy flick of the thumb. And please do not let me
See anyone using his finger. You can do it quite easy
If you have any strength in your thumb. The blossoms
Are fragile and motionless, never letting anyone see
    Any of them using their finger.

And this you can see is the bolt. The purpose of this
Is to open the breech, as you see. We can slide it
Rapidly backwards and forwards: we call this
Easing the spring. And rapidly backwards and forwards
The early bees are assaulting and fumbling the flowers:
    They call it easing the Spring.

They call it easing the Spring: it is perfectly easy
If you have any strength in your thumb: like the bolt,
And the breech, and the cocking-piece, and the point of balance,
Which in our case we have not got; and the almond-blossom
Silent in all of the gardens and the bees going backwards and forwards,
    For today we have naming of parts.

II. JUDGING DISTANCES

Not only how far away, but the way that you say it
Is very important. Perhaps you may never get
The knack of judging a distance, but at least you know
How to report on a landscape: the central sector,
The right of arc and that, which we had last Tuesday,
    And at least you know

That maps are of time, not place, so far as the army
Happens to be concerned—the reason being,

HENRY REED

Is one which need not delay us. Again, you know
There are three kinds of tree, three only, the fir and the poplar,
And those which have bushy tops to; and lastly
    That things only seem to be things.

A barn is not called a barn, to put it more plainly,
Or a field in the distance, where sheep may be safely grazing.
You must never be over-sure. You must say, when reporting:
At five o'clock in the central sector is a dozen
Of what appear to be animals; whatever you do,
    Don't call the bleeders *sheep*.

I am sure that's quite clear; and suppose, for the sake of example,
The one at the end, asleep, endeavours to tell us
What he sees over there to the west, and how far away,
After first having come to attention. There to the west,
On the fields of summer the sun and the shadows bestow
    Vestments of purple and gold.

The still white dwellings are like a mirage in the heat,
And under the swaying elms a man and a woman
Lie gently together. Which is, perhaps, only to say
That there is a row of houses to the left of arc,
And that under some poplars a pair of what appear to be humans
    Appear to be loving.

Well that, for an answer, is what we might rightly call
Moderately satisfactory only, the reason being,
Is that two things have been omitted, and those are important.
The human beings, now: in what direction are they,
And how far away, would you say? And do not forget
    There may be dead ground in between.

There may be dead ground in between; and I may not have got
The knack of judging a distance; I will only venture
A guess that perhaps between me and the apparent lovers,
(Who, incidentally, appear by now to have finished,)
At seven o'clock from the houses, is roughly a distance
    Of about one year and a half.

III. UNARMED COMBAT

In due course of course you will all be issued with
Your proper issue; but until tomorrow,
You can hardly be said to need it; and until that time,
We shall have unarmed combat. I shall teach you.
The various holds and rolls and throws and breakfalls
     Which you may sometimes meet.

And the various holds and rolls and throws and breakfalls
Do not depend on any sort of weapon,
But only on what I might coin a phrase and call
The ever-important question of human balance,
And the ever-important need to be in a strong
     Position at the start.

There are many kinds of weakness about the body,
Where you would least expect, like the ball of the foot.
But the various holds and rolls and throws and breakfalls
Will always come in useful. And never be frightened
To tackle from behind: it may not be clean to do so,
     But this is global war.

So give them all you have, and always give them
As good as you get; it will always get you somewhere.
(You may not know it, but you can tie a Jerry
Up without rope; it is one of the things I shall teach you.)
Nothing will matter if only you are ready for him.
     The readiness is all.

The readiness is all. How can I help but feel
I have been here before? But somehow then,
I was the tied-up one. How to get out
Was always then my problem. And even if I had
A piece of rope I was always the sort of person
     Who threw the rope aside.

And in my time I have given them all I had,
Which was never as good as I got, and it got me nowhere.
And the various holds and rolls and throws and breakfalls
Somehow or other I always seemed to put
In the wrong place. And as for war, my wars
     Were global from the start.

Perhaps I was never in a strong position,
Or the ball of my foot got hurt, or I had some weakness
Where I had least expected. But I think I see your point.
While awaiting a proper issue, we must learn the lesson
Of the ever-important question of human balance.
        It is courage that counts.

Things may be the same again; and we must fight
Not in the hope of winning but rather of keeping
Something alive: so that when we meet our end,
It may be said that we tackled wherever we could,
That battle-fit we lived, and though defeated,
        Not without glory fought.

1945

ALUN LEWIS

1915–1944

215   *All day it has rained ...*

All day it has rained, and we on the edge of the moors
Have sprawled in our bell-tents, moody and dull as boors,
Groundsheets and blankets spread on the muddy ground
And from the first grey wakening we have found
No refuge from the skirmishing fine rain
And the wind that made the canvas heave and flap
And the taut wet guy-ropes ravel out and snap.
All day the rain has glided, wave and mist and dream,
Drenching the gorse and heather, a gossamer stream
Too light to stir the acorns that suddenly
Snatched from their cups by the wild south-westerly
Pattered against the tent and our upturned dreaming faces.
And we stretched out, unbuttoning our braces,
Smoking a Woodbine, darning dirty socks,
Reading the Sunday papers—I saw a fox
And mentioned it in the note I scribbled home;—
And we talked of girls, and dropping bombs on Rome,

And thought of the quiet dead and the loud celebrities
Exhorting us to slaughter, and the herded refugees;
—Yet thought softly, morosely of them, and as indifferently
As of ourselves or those whom we
For years have loved, and will again
Tomorrow maybe love; but now it is the rain
Possesses us entirely, the twilight and the rain.

And I can remember nothing dearer or more to my heart
Than the children I watched in the woods on Saturday
Shaking down burning chestnuts for the schoolyard's merry
    play,
Or the shaggy patient dog who followed me
By Sheet and Steep and up the wooded scree
To the Shoulder o' Mutton where Edward Thomas brooded
    long
On death and beauty—till a bullet stopped his song.

1942

216   *Dawn on the East Coast*

From Orford Ness to Shingle Street
The grey disturbance spreads
Washing the icy seas on Deben Head.

Cock pheasants scratch the frozen fields,
Gulls lift thin horny legs and step
Fastidiously among the rusted mines.

The soldier leaning on the sandbagged wall
Hears in the combers' curling rush and crash
His single self-centred monotonous wish;

And time is a froth of such transparency
His drowning eyes see what they wish to see;
A girl laying his table with a white cloth.

.   .   .

The light assails him from a flank,
Two carbons touching in his brain
Crumple the cellophane lanterns of his dream.

And then the day, grown feminine and kind,
Stoops with the gulfing motion of the tide
And pours his ashes in a tiny urn.

From Orford Ness to Shingle Street
The grey disturbance lifts its head
And one by one, reluctantly,
The living come back slowly from the dead.

1945

217   *Goodbye*

So we must say Goodbye, my darling,
And go, as lovers go, for ever;
Tonight remains, to pack and fix on labels
And make an end of lying down together.

I put a final shilling in the gas,
And watch you slip your dress below your knees
And lie so still I hear your rustling comb
Modulate the autumn in the trees.

And all the countless things I shall remember
Lay mummy-cloths of silence round my head;
I fill the carafe with a drink of water;
You say 'We paid a guinea for this bed,'

And then, 'We'll leave some gas, a little warmth
For the next resident, and these dry flowers,'
And turn your face away, afraid to speak
The big word, that Eternity is ours.

Your kisses close my eyes and yet you stare
As though God struck a child with nameless fears;
Perhaps the water glitters and discloses
Time's chalice and its limpid useless tears.

Everything we renounce except our selves;
Selfishness is the last of all to go;

Our sighs are exhalations of the earth,
Our footprints leave a track across the snow.

We made the universe to be our home,
Our nostrils took the wind to be our breath,
Our hearts are massive towers of delight,
We stride across the seven seas of death.

Yet when all's done you'll keep the emerald
I placed upon your finger in the street;
And I will keep the patches that you sewed
On my old battledress tonight, my sweet.

1945

218   *Song*
            (*On seeing dead bodies floating off the Cape*)

The first month of his absence
I was numb and sick
And where he'd left his promise
Life did not turn or kick.
The seed, the seed of love was sick.

The second month my eyes were sunk
In the darkness of despair,
And my bed was like a grave
And his ghost was lying there.
And my heart was sick with care.

The third month of his going
I thought I heard him say
'Our course deflected slightly
On the thirty-second day—'
The tempest blew his words away.

And he was lost among the waves,
His ship rolled helpless in the sea,
The fourth month of his voyage
He shouted grievously
'Beloved, do not think of me.'

ALUN LEWIS

The flying fish like kingfishers
Skim the sea's bewildered crests,
The whales blow steaming fountains,
The seagulls have no nests
Where my lover sways and rests.

We never thought to buy and sell
This life that blooms or withers in the leaf,
And I'll not stir, so he sleeps well,
Though cell by cell the coral reef
Builds an eternity of grief.

But oh! the drag and dullness of my Self;
The turning seasons wither in my head;
All this slowness, all this hardness,
The nearness that is waiting in my bed,
The gradual self-effacement of the dead.

1945

SIDNEY KEYES

1922–1943

219   from *The Foreign Gate*

The moon is a poor woman.
The moon returns to weep with us. The crosses
Burn raw and white upon the night's stiff banners.
The wooden crosses and the marble trees
Shrink from the foreign moon.
The iron gate glitters. Here the soldiers lie.
Fold up the flags, muffle the soldier's drum;
Silence the calling fife. O drape
The soldier's drum with heavy crêpe;
With mourning weeds muffle the soldier's girl.
It's a long way and a long march

To the returning moon and to the soil
No time at all.
                    O call
The soldier's glory by another name:
Shroud up the soldier's common shame
And drape the soldier's drum, but spare
The steel-caged brain, the feet that walk to war.

Once striding under a horsehair plume
Once beating the taut drums for war
The sunlight rang from brass and iron;
History was an angry play—
The boy grew tall and rode away;
The door hung slack; the pale girl wept
And cursed the company he kept.
And dumb men spoke
Through the glib mouths of smoke;
The servile learned to strike
The proud to shriek;
And strangled in their lovers' lips
The young fell short of glory in the sand
Raking for graves among the scattered sand;
The tattered flags strained at the wind
Scaring the thrifty kite, mocking the dead.
But muffle the soldier's drum, hide his pale head,
His face a spider's web of blood. O fold
The hands that grip a splintered gun.
                    The glittering gate
Baffles him still, his starvecrow soul. O drape
The soldier's drum and cry, who never dare
Defy the ironbound brain, the feet that walk to war.

The cold hand clenches. The stupid mouth
Writhes like a ripple. Now the field is full
Of noises and dead voices . . .
                              'My rags flap
Though the great flags are trampled . . .'
                              'My mouth speaks
Terror and truth, instead of hard command.'
'Remember the torn lace, the fine coats slashed
With steel instead of velvet. Künersdorf
Fought in the shallow sand was my relief.'
'I rode to Naseby' . . . 'And the barren land

Of Tannenberg drank me. Remember now
The grey and jointed corpses in the snow,
The struggle in the drift, the numb hands freezing
Into the bitter iron . . . '
                              'At Dunkirk I
Rolled in the shallows, and the living trod
Across me for a bridge . . . '
                              'Let me speak out
Against this sham of policy, for pain
Alone is true. I was a general
Who fought the cunning Africans, returned
Crowned with harsh laurel, frantically cheered
Through Roman streets. I spoke of fame and glory.
Women grabbed at my robe. Great poets praised me.
I died of cancer, screaming, in a year.'
'I fell on a black Spanish hillside
Under the thorn-hedge, fighting for a dream
That troubled me in Paris; vomited
My faith and courage out among the stones . . . '
'I was a barb of light, a burning cross
Of wood and canvas, falling through the night.'
'I was shot down at morning, in a yard.'

The moon regards them without shame. The wind
Rises and twitters through the wreck of bone . . .
                              'It is so hard to be alone
Continually, watching the great stars march
Their circular unending route; sharp sand
Straying about the eyes, blinding the quick-eyed spirit.'
A soldier's death is hard;
There's no prescribed or easy word
For dissolution in the Army books.
The uniform of pain with pain put on is straiter
Than any lover's garment; yet the death
Of these is different, and their glory greater.
Once men, then moving figures on a map,
Patiently giving time and strength and vision
Even identity
Into the future's keeping;
Nourished on wounds and weeping
Faces and laughing flags and pointed laurels,
Their pain cries down the noise of poetry.

So muffle the soldier's drum, forget the battles;
Remember only fame's a way of living:
The writing may be greater than the speaking
And every death for something different
From time's compulsion, is a written word.
Whatever gift, it is the giving
Remains significant: whatever death
It is the dying matters.
                    Emblematic
Bronze eagle or bright banner or carved name
Of fighting ancestor; these never pardon
The pain and sorrow. It is the dying pardons,
For something different from man or emblem.
Then drape the soldier's drum
And carry him down
Beyond the moon's inspection, and the noise
Of bands and banners and the striking sun.
Scatter the soldier's emblems and his fame:
Shroud up the shattered face, the empty name;
Speak out the word and drape the drum and spare
The captive brain, the feet that walk to war
The ironbound brain, the hand unskilled in war
The shrinking brain, sick of an inner war.

February–March 1942

220   *Timoshenko**

Hour ten he rose, ten-sworded, every finger
A weighted blade, and strapping round his loins
The courage of attack, he threw the window
Open to look on his appointed night.

Where lay, beneath the winds and creaking flares
Tangled like lovers or alone assuming
The wanton postures of the drunk with sleep,

---

* In June 1940, the Russian Marshal Semyon Konstantinovich Timoshenko was appointed commissar for defence. He achieved renown in the Second World War for recapturing Rostov from the Germans (November 1941), and for his command on the north-west front (1942), in the Caucasus (1942), and in Bessarabia (1944).

An army of twisted limbs and hollow faces
Thrown to and fro between the winds and shadows.
O hear the wind, the wind that shakes the dawn.
And there before the night, he was aware
Of the flayed fields of home, and black with ruin
The helpful earth under the tracks of tanks.
His bladed hand, in pity falling, mimicked
The crumpled hand lamenting the broken plow;
And the oracular metal lips in anger
Squared to the shape of the raped girl's yelling mouth.
He heard the wind explaining nature's sorrow
And humming in the wire hair of the dead.

He turned, and his great shadow on the wall
Swayed like a tree. His eyes grew cold as lead.
Then, in a rage of love and grief and pity,
He made the pencilled map alive with war.

September 1942

221   from *The Wilderness*

The red rock wilderness
Shall be my dwelling-place.

Where the wind saws at the bluffs
And the pebble falls like thunder
I shall watch the clawed sun
Tear the rocks asunder.

The seven-branched cactus
Will never sweat wine:
My own bleeding feet
Shall furnish the sign.

The rock says 'Endure.'
The wind says 'Pursue.'
The sun says 'I will suck your bones
And afterwards bury you.'

Here where the horned skulls mark the limit
Of instinct and intransigent desire
I beat against the rough-tongued wind
Towards the heart of fire.

So knowing my youth, which was yesterday,
And my pride which shall be gone tomorrow,
I turn my face to the sun, remembering gardens
Planted by others—Longinus, Guillaume de Lorris
And all love's gardeners, in an early May.
O sing, small ancient bird, for I am going
Into the sun's garden, the red rock desert
I have dreamt of and desired more than the lilac's promise.
The flowers of the rock shall never fall.

O speak no more of love and death
And speak no word of sorrow:
My anger's eaten up my pride
And both shall die tomorrow.

Knowing I am no lover, but destroyer,
I am content to face the destroying sun.
There shall be no more journeys, nor the anguish
Of meeting and parting, after the last great parting
From the images of dancing and the gardens
Where the brown bird chokes in its song:
Until that last great meeting among mountains
Where the metal bird sings madly from the fire.

O speak no more of ceremony,
Speak no more of fame:
My heart must seek a burning land
To bury its foolish pain.

By the dry river at the desert edge
I regret the speaking rivers I have known;
The sunlight shattered under the dark bridge
And many tongues of rivers in the past.
Rivers and gardens, singing under the willows,
The glowing moon. . . .
                    And all the poets of summer
Must lament another spirit's passing over.

O never weep for me, my love,
Or seek me in this land:
But light a candle for my luck
And bear it in your hand.

1942-43

JOHN MANIFOLD

1915–1985

222   *The Tomb of Lt John Learmonth, AIF*

'*At the end on Crete he took to the hills, and said he'd fight it out with
only a revolver. He was a great soldier...*'

One of his men in a letter

This is not sorrow, this is work: I build
A cairn of words over a silent man,
My friend John Learmonth whom the Germans killed.

There was no word of hero in his plan;
Verse should have been his love and peace his trade,
But history turned him to a partisan.

Far from the battle as his bones are laid
Crete will remember him. Remember well,
Mountains of Crete, the Second Field Brigade!

Say Crete, and there is little more to tell
Of muddle tall as treachery, despair
And black defeat resounding like a bell;

But bring the magnifying focus near
And in contempt of muddle and defeat
The old heroic virtues still appear.

Australian blood where hot and icy meet
(James Hogg and Lermontov were of his kin)
Lie still and fertilise the fields of Crete.

*

Schoolboy, I watched his ballading begin:
Billy and bullocky and billabong,
Our properties of childhood, all were in.

I heard the air though not the undersong,
the fierceness and resolve; but all the same
They're the tradition, and tradition's strong.

Swagman and bushranger die hard, die game,
Die fighting, like that wild colonial boy—
Jack Dowling, says the ballad, was his name.

He also spun his pistol like a toy,
Turned to the hills like wolf or kangaroo,
And faced destruction with a bitter joy.

His freedom gave him nothing else to do
But set his back against his family tree
And fight the better for the fact he knew

He was as good as dead. Because the sea
Was closed and the air dark and the land lost,
'They'll never capture me alive,' said he.

*

That's courage chemically pure, uncrossed
With sacrifice or duty or career,
Which counts and pays in ready coin the cost

Of holding course. Armies are not its sphere
Where all's contrived to achieve its counterfeit;
It swears with discipline, it's volunteer.

I could as hardly make a moral fit
Around it as around a lighting flash.
There is no moral, that's the point of it,

No moral. But I'm glad of this panache
That sparkles, as from flint, from us and steel,
True to no crown nor presidential sash

Nor flag nor fame. Let others mourn and feel
He died for nothing: nothings have their place.
While thus the kind and civilised conceal

This spring of unsuspected inward grace
And look on death as equals, I am filled
With queer affection for the human race.

1946

KEITH DOUGLAS

1920–1944

223   *John Anderson**

John Anderson, a scholarly gentleman
advancing with his company in the attack,
received some bullets through him as he ran.

So his creative brain whirled, and he fell back
in the bloody dust—it was a fine day there
and warm. Blood turned his tunic black

while past his desperate final stare
the other simple soldiers run
and leave the hero unaware.

Apt epitaph or pun
he could not hit upon, to grace
a scholar's death; he only eyed the sun.

But I think, the last moment of his gaze
beheld the Father of Gods and Men,
Zeus, leaning from heaven as he dies.

* See p. 3 below.

Whom in his swoon he hears again
summon Apollo in the Homeric tongue:
Descend Phoebus and cleanse the stain

of dark blood from the body of John Anderson.
Give him to Death and Sleep,
who'll bear him as they can

out of the range of darts, to the broad vale
of Lycia; there lay him in a deep
solemn content on some bright dale.

And the brothers, Sleep and Death
lift up John Anderson at his last breath.

1940

224   *Gallantry*

The Colonel in a casual voice
spoke into the microphone a joke
which through a hundred earphones broke
into the ears of a doomed race.

Into the ears of the doomed boy, the fool
whose perfectly mannered flesh fell
in opening the door for a shell
as he had learnt to do at school.

Conrad luckily survived the winter:
he wrote a letter to welcome
the auspicious spring: only his silken
intentions severed with a single splinter.

Was George fond of little boys?
We always suspected it,
but who will say: since George was hit
we never mention our surmise.

It was a brave thing the Colonel said,
but the whole sky turned too hot

and the three heroes never heard what
it was, gone deaf with steel and lead.

But the bullets cried with laughter,
the shells were overcome with mirth,
plunging their heads in steel and earth—
(the air commented in a whisper).

1943

225   *Vergissmeinnicht*

Three weeks gone and the combatants gone
returning over the nightmare ground
we found the place again, and found
the soldier sprawling in the sun.

The frowning barrel of his gun
overshadowing. As we came on
that day, he hit my tank with one
like the entry of a demon.

Look. Here in the gunpit spoil
the dishonoured picture of his girl
who has put: *Steffi. Vergissmeinnicht*
in a copybook gothic script.

We see him almost with content,
abased, and seeming to have paid
and mocked at by his own equipment
that's hard and good when he's decayed.

But she would weep to see today
how on his skin the swart flies move;
the dust upon the paper eye
and the burst stomach like a cave.

For here the lover and killer are mingled
who had one body and one heart.
And death who had the soldier singled
has done the lover mortal hurt.

1943

226 *Aristocrats*
'I think I am becoming a God'

The noble horse with courage in his eye
clean in the bone, looks up at a shellburst:
away fly the images of the shires
but he puts the pipe back in his mouth.

Peter was unfortunately killed by an 88:
it took his leg away, he died in the ambulance.
I saw him crawling on the sand, he said
It's most unfair, they've shot my foot off.

How can I live among this gentle
obsolescent breed of heroes, and not weep?
Unicorns, almost,
for they are fading into two legends
in which their stupidity and chivalry
are celebrated. Each, fool and hero, will be an immortal.

These plains were their cricket pitch
and in the mountains the tremendous drop fences
brought down some of the runners. Here then
under the stones and earth they dispose themselves,
I think with their famous unconcern.
It is not gunfire I hear, but a hunting horn.

1943

JOHN JARMAIN
1911–1944

227 *El Alamein*

There are flowers now, they say, at Alamein;
Yes, flowers in the minefields now.
So those that come to view that vacant scene,
Where death remains and agony has been
Will find the lilies grow—
Flowers, and nothing that we know.

So they rang the bells for us and Alamein,
Bells which we could not hear:
And to those that heard the bells what could it mean,
That name of loss and pride, El Alamein?
—Not the murk and harm of war,
But their hope, their own warm prayer.

It will become a staid historic name,
That crazy sea of sand!
Like Troy or Agincourt its single fame
Will be the garland for our brow, our claim,
On us a fleck of glory to the end:
And there our dead will keep their holy ground.

But this is not the place that we recall,
The crowded desert crossed with foaming tracks,
The one blotched building, lacking half a wall,
The grey-faced men, sand powdered over all;
The tanks, the guns, the trucks,
The black, dark-smoking wrecks.

So be it: none but us has known that land:
El Alamein will still be only ours
And those ten days of chaos in the sand.
Others will come who cannot understand,
Will halt beside the rusty minefield wires
And find there—flowers.

Mareth, Tunisia, March 1943

NORMAN CAMERON

1905–1953

228   *Green, Green is El Aghir*

Sprawled on the crates and sacks in the rear of the truck,
I was gummy-mouthed from the sun and the dust of the track,

And the two Arab soldiers I'd taken on as hitch-hikers
At a torrid petrol-dump, had been there on their hunkers
Since early morning. I said, in a kind of French
'On m'a dit, qu'il y a une belle source d'eau fraîche,
Plus loin, à El Aghir'...

               It was eighty more kilometres
Until round a corner we heard a splashing of waters,
And there, in a green, dark street, was a fountain with two faces
Discharging both ways, from full-throated faucets
Into basins, thence into troughs and thence into brooks.
Our negro corporal driver slammed his brakes,
And we yelped and leapt from the truck and went at the double
To fill our bidons and bottles and drink and dabble.
Then, swollen with water, we went to an inn for wine.
The Arabs came, too, though their faith might have stood between.
'After all,' they said, 'it's a boisson,' without contrition.

Green, green is El Aghir. It has a railway-station,
And the wealth of its soil has borne many another fruit,
A mairie, a school and an elegant Salle de Fêtes.
Such blessings, as I remarked, in effect, to the waiter,
Are added unto them that have plenty of water.

1950

F. T. PRINCE

1912–2003

229   *Soldiers Bathing*

The sea at evening moves across the sand.
Under a reddening sky I watch the freedom of a band
Of soldiers who belong to me. Stripped bare
For bathing in the sea, they shout and run in the warm air;
Their flesh worn by the trade of war, revives
And my mind towards the meaning of it strives.

All's pathos now. The body that was gross,
Rank, ravenous, disgusting in the act or in repose,

All fever, filth and sweat, its bestial strength
And bestial decay, by pain and labour grows at length
Fragile and luminous. 'Poor bare forked animal,'
Conscious of his desires and needs and flesh that rise and fall,
Stands in the soft air, tasting after toil
The sweetness of his nakedness: letting the sea-waves coil
Their frothy tongues about his feet, forgets
His hatred of the war, its terrible pressure that begets
A machinery of death and slavery,
Each being a slave and making slaves of others: finds that he
Remembers his old freedom in a game
Mocking himself, and comically mimics fear and shame.

He plays with death and animality;
And reading in the shadows of his pallid flesh, I see
The idea of Michelangelo's cartoon
Of soldiers bathing, breaking off before they were half done
At some sortie of the enemy, an episode
Of the Pisan wars with Florence. I remember how he showed
Their muscular limbs that clamber from the water,
And heads that turn across the shoulder, eager for the slaughter,
Forgetful of their bodies that are bare,
And hot to buckle on and use the weapons lying there.
—And I think too of the theme another found
When, shadowing men's bodies on a sinister red ground,
Another Florentine, Pollaiuolo,
Painted a naked battle: warriors, straddled, hacked the foe,
Dug their bare toes into the ground and slew
The brother-naked man who lay between their feet and drew
His lips back from his teeth in a grimace.

They were Italians who knew war's sorrow and disgrace
And showed the thing suspended, stripped: a theme
Born out of the experience of war's horrible extreme
Beneath a sky where even the air flows
With lacrimae Christi. For that rage, that bitterness, those blows,
That hatred of the slain, what could they be
But indirectly or directly a commentary
On the Crucifixion? And the picture burns
With indignation and pity and despair by turns,
Because it is the obverse of the scene
Where Christ hangs murdered, stripped, upon the Cross. I mean,
That is the explanation of its rage.

And we too have our bitterness and pity that engage
Blood, spirit, in this war. But night begins,
Night of the mind: who nowadays is conscious of our sins?
Though every human deed concerns our blood,
And even we must know, what nobody has understood,
That some great love is over all we do,
And that is what has driven us to this fury, for so few
Can suffer all the terror of that love:
The terror of that love has set us spinning in this groove
Greased with our blood.

            These dry themselves and dress,
Combing their hair, forget the fear and shame of nakedness.
Because to love is frightening we prefer
The freedom of our crimes. Yet, as I drink the dusky air,
I feel a strange delight that fills me full,
Strange gratitude, as if evil itself were beautiful,
And kiss the wound in thought, while in the west
I watch a streak of red that might have issued from Christ's breast.

1954

ROY FULLER

1912–1991

230   *The Middle of a War*

My photograph already looks historic.
The promising youthful face, the matelot's collar,
Say 'This one is remembered for a lyric.
His place and period—nothing could be duller.'

Its position is already indicated—
The son or brother in the album; pained
The expression and the garments dated,
His fate so obviously pre-ordained.

The original turns away; as horrible thoughts,
Loud fluttering aircraft slope above his head
At dusk. The ridiculous empires break like biscuits.

Ah, life has been abandoned by the boats—
Only the trodden island and the dead
Remain, and the once inestimable caskets.

1942

STANLEY KUNITZ

1905–2006

231 *Careless Love*

Who have been lonely once
Are comforted by their guns.
Affectionately they speak
To the dark beauty, whose cheek
Beside their own cheek glows.
They are calmed by such repose,
Such power held in hand;
Their young bones understand
The shudder in that frame.
Without nation, without name,
They give the load of love,
And it's returned, to prove
How much the husband heart
Can hold of it: for what
This nymphomaniac enjoys
Inexhaustibly is boys.

1944

In Distrust of Merits

Strengthened to live, strengthened to die for
   medals and positioned victories?
They're fighting, fighting, fighting the blind
   man who thinks he sees,—
who cannot see that the enslaver is
enslaved; the hater, harmed. O shining O
   firm star, O tumultuous
      ocean lashed till small things go
   as they will, the mountainous
      wave makes us who look, know

depth. Lost at sea before they fought! O
   star of David, star of Bethlehem,
O black imperial lion
   of the Lord—emblem
of a risen world—be joined at last, be
joined. There is hate's crown beneath which all is
   death; there's love's without which none
      is king; the blessed deeds bless
   the halo. As contagion
      of sickness makes sickness,

contagion of trust can make trust. They're
   fighting in deserts and caves, one by
one, in battalions and squadrons;
   they're fighting that I
may yet recover from the disease, My
Self; some have it lightly; some will die. 'Man
   wolf to man' and we devour
      ourselves. The enemy could not
   have made a greater breach in our
      defences. One pilot-

ing a blind man can escape him, but
   Job disheartened by false comfort knew

that nothing can be so defeating
    as a blind man who
can see. O alive who are dead, who are
proud not to see, O small dust of the earth
      that walks so arrogantly,
          trust begets power and faith is
      an affectionate thing. We
        vow, we make this promise

to the fighting—it's a promise—'We'll
    never hate black, white, red, yellow, Jew,
Gentile, Untouchable.' We are
    not competent to
make our vows. With set jaw they are fighting,
fighting, fighting,—some we love whom we know,
      some we love but know not—that
        hearts may feel and not be numb.
      It cures me; or am I what
        I can't believe in? Some

in snow, some on crags, some in quicksands,
    little by little, much by much, they
are fighting fighting fighting that where
    there was death there may
be life. 'When a man is prey to anger,
he is moved by outside things; when he holds
      his ground in patience patience
        patience, that is action or
      beauty', the soldier's defence
      and hardest armour for

the fight. The world's an orphans' home. Shall
    we never have peace without sorrow?
without pleas of the dying for
    help that won't come? O
quiet form upon the dust, I cannot
look and yet I must. If these great patient
      dyings—all these agonies
        and woundbearings and bloodshed—
      can teach us how to live, these
      dyings were not wasted.

Hate-hardened heart, O heart of iron,
    iron is iron till it is rust.
There never was a war that was
    not inward; I must
fight till I have conquered in myself what
causes war, but I would not believe it.
        I inwardly did nothing.
           O Iscariotlike crime!
      Beauty is everlasting
        and dust is for a time.

1944

RICHARD EBERHART

1904–2005

233   *The Fury of Aerial Bombardment*

You would think the fury of aerial bombardment
Would rouse God to relent; the infinite spaces
Are still silent. He looks on shock-pried faces.
History, even, does not know what is meant.

You would feel that after so many centuries
God would give man to repent; yet he can kill
As Cain could, but with multitudinous will,
No farther advanced than in his ancient furies.

Was man made stupid to see his own stupidity?
Is God by definition indifferent, beyond us all?
Is the eternal truth man's fighting soul
Wherein the Beast ravens in its own avidity?

Of Van Wettering I speak, and Averill,
Names on a list, whose faces I do not recall
But they are gone to early death, who late in school
Distinguished the belt feed lever from the belt holding pawl.

1944

RANDALL JARRELL
1914–1965

Eighth Air Force

If, in an odd angle of the hutment,
A puppy laps the water from a can
Of flowers, and the drunk sergeant shaving
Whistles O *Paradiso!*—shall I say that man
Is not as men have said: a wolf to man?

The other murderers troop in yawning;
Three of them play Pitch, one sleeps, and one
Lies counting missions, lies there sweating
Till even his heart beats: One; One; One.
O murderers! ... Still, this is how it's done:

This is a war.... But since these play, before they die,
Like puppies with their puppy; since, a man,
I did as these have done, but did not die—
I will content the people as I can
And give up these to them: Behold the man!

I have suffered, in a dream, because of him,
Many things; for this last saviour, man,
I have lied as I lie now. But what is lying?
Men wash their hands, in blood, as best they can:
I find no fault in this just man.

1948

The Death of the Ball Turret Gunner

From my mother's sleep I fell into the State,
And I hunched in its belly till my wet fur froze.
Six miles from earth, loosed from its dream of life,
I woke to black flak and the nightmare fighters.
When I died they washed me out of the turret with a hose.

1945

I walk beside the prisoners to the road.
Load on puffed load,
Their corpses, stacked like sodden wood,
Lie barred or galled with blood

By the charred warehouse. No one comes today
In the old way
To knock the fillings from their teeth;
The dark, coned, common wreath

Is plaited for their grave—a kind of grief.
The living leaf
Clings to the planted profitable
Pine if it is able;

The boughs sigh, mile on green, calm, breathing mile,
From this dead file
The planners ruled for them. . . . One year
They sent a million here:

Here men were drunk like water, burnt like wood.
The fat of good
And evil, the breast's star of hope
Were rendered into soap.

I paint the star I sawed from yellow pine—
And plant the sign
In soil that does not yet refuse
Its usual Jews

Their first asylum. But the white, dwarfed star—
This dead white star—
Hides nothing, pays for nothing; smoke
Fouls it, a yellow joke,

The needles of the wreath are chalked with ash,
A filmy trash
Litters the black woods with the death
Of men; and one last breath

Curls from the monstrous chimney.... I laugh aloud
Again and again;
The star laughs from its rotting shroud
Of flesh. O star of men!

1948

237   *A Front*

Fog over the base: the beams ranging
From the five towers pull home from the night
The crews cold in fur, the bombers banging
Like lost trucks down the levels of the ice.
A glow drifts in like mist (how many tons of it?),
Bounces to a roll, turns suddenly to steel
And tires and turrets, huge in the trembling light.
The next is high, and pulls up with a wail,
Comes round again—no use. And no use for the rest
In drifting circles out along the range;
Holding no longer, changed to a kinder course,
The flights drone southward through the steady rain.
The base is closed.... But one voice keeps on calling,
The lowering pattern of the engines grows;
The roar gropes downward in its shaky orbit
For the lives the season quenches. Here below
They beg, order, are not heard; and hear the darker
Voice rising: *Can't you hear me? Over. Over—*
All the air quivers, and the east sky glows.

1945

W. D. SNODGRASS

1926–2009

238   *'After Experience Taught Me ...'*

After experience taught me that all the ordinary
Surroundings of social life are futile and vain;

I'm going to show you something very
Ugly: someday, it might save your life.

Seeing that none of the things I feared contain
In themselves anything either good or bad

What if you get caught without a knife;
Nothing—even a loop of piano wire;

Excepting only in the effect they had
Upon my mind, I resolved to inquire

Take the first two fingers of this hand;
Fork them out—kind of a 'V for Victory'—

Whether there might be something whose discovery
Would grant me supreme, unending happiness.

And jam them into the eyes of your enemy.
You have to do this hard. Very hard. Then press

No virtue can be thought to have priority
Over this endeavor to preserve one's being.

Both fingers down around the cheekbone
And setting your foot high into the chest

No man can desire to act rightly, to be blessed,
To live rightly, without simultaneously

You must call up every strength you own
And you can rip off the whole facial mask.

Wishing to be, to act, to live. He must ask
First, in other words, to actually exist.

And you, whiner, who wastes your time
Dawdling over the remorseless earth,
What evil, what unspeakable crime
Have you made your life worth?

1968

239 *Returned to Frisco, 1946*

We shouldered like pigs along the rail to try
And catch that first gray outline of the shore
Of our first life. A plane hung in the sky
From which a girl's voice sang: '... you're home once more.'

For that one moment, we were dulled and shaken
By fear. What could still catch us by surprise?
We had known all along we would be taken
By hawkers, known what authoritative lies

Would plan us as our old lives had been planned.
We had stood years and, then, scrambled like rabbits
Up hostile beaches; why should we fear this land
Intent on luxuries and its old habits?

A seagull shrieked for garbage. The Bay Bridge,
Busy with noontime traffic, rose ahead.
We would have liberty, the privilege
Of lingering over steak and white, soft bread

Served by women, free to get drunk or fight,
Free, if we chose, to blow in our back pay
On smart girls or trinkets, free to prowl all night
Down streets giddy with lights, to sleep all day,

Pay our own way and make our own selections;
Free to choose just what they meant we should;
To turn back finally to our old affections,
The ties that lasted and which must be good.

Off the port side, through haze, we could discern
Alcatraz, lavender with flowers. Barred,
The Golden Gate, fading away astern,
Stood like the closed gate of your own backyard.

1959

LOUIS SIMPSON
1923–2012

240

*Carentan O Carentan**

Trees in the old days used to stand
And shape a shady lane
Where lovers wandered hand in hand
Who came from Carentan.

This was the shining green canal
Where we came two by two
Walking at combat-interval.
Such trees we never knew.

The day was early June, the ground
Was soft and bright with dew.
Far away the guns did sound,
But here the sky was blue.

The sky was blue, but there a smoke
Hung still above the sea
Where the ships together spoke
To towns we could not see.

Could you have seen us through a glass
You would have said a walk
Of farmers out to turn the grass,
Each with his own hay-fork.

The watchers in their leopard suits
Waited till it was time,
And aimed between the belt and boot
And let the barrel climb.

I must lie down at once, there is
A hammer at my knee.
And call it death or cowardice,
Don't count again on me.

* Carentan was the site of a battle in the invasion of Normandy in June 1944.

314

Everything's all right, Mother,
Everyone gets the same
At one time or another.
It's all in the game.

I never strolled, nor ever shall,
Down such a leafy lane.
I never drank in a canal,
Nor ever shall again.

There is a whistling in the leaves
And it is not the wind,
The twigs are falling from the knives
That cut men to the ground.

Tell me, Master–Sergeant,
The way to turn and shoot.
But the Sergeant's silent
That taught me how to do it.

O Captain, show us quickly
Our place upon the map.
But the Captain's sickly
And taking a long nap.

Lieutenant, what's my duty,
My place in the platoon?
He too's a sleeping beauty,
Charmed by that strange tune.

Carentan O Carentan
Before we met with you
We never yet had lost a man
Or known what death could do.

1949

241   *Memories of a Lost War*

The guns know what is what, but underneath
In fearful file

315

We go around burst boots and packs and teeth
That seem to smile.

The scene jags like a strip of celluloid,
A mortar fires,
Cinzano falls, Michelin is destroyed,
The man of tires.

As darkness drifts like fog in from the sea
Somebody says
'We're digging in.' Look well, for this may be
The last of days.

Hot lightnings stitch the blind eye of the moon,
The thunder's blunt.
We sleep. Our dreams pass in a faint platoon
Toward the front.

Sleep well, for you are young. Each tree and bush
Drips with sweet dew,
And earlier than morning June's cool hush
Will waken you.

The riflemen will wake and hold their breath.
Though they may bleed
They will be proud a while of something death
Still seems to need.

1955

242   *The Battle*

Helmet and rifle, pack and overcoat
Marched through a forest. Somewhere up ahead
Guns thudded. Like the circle of a throat
The night on every side was turning red.

They halted and they dug. They sank like moles
Into the clammy earth between the trees.
And soon the sentries, standing in their holes,
Felt the first snow. Their feet began to freeze.

At dawn the first shell landed with a crack.
Then shells and bullets swept the icy woods.
This lasted many days. The snow was black.
The corpses stiffened in their scarlet hoods.

Most clearly of that battle I remember
The tiredness in eyes, how hands looked thin
Around a cigarette, and the bright ember
Would pulse with all the life there was within.

1955

243   *The Heroes*

I dreamed of war-heroes, of wounded war-heroes
With just enough of their charms shot away
To make them more handsome. The women moved nearer
To touch their brave wounds and their hair streaked with gray.

I saw them in long ranks ascending the gang-planks;
The girls with the doughnuts were cheerful and gay.
They minded their manners and muttered their thanks;
The Chaplain advised them to watch and to pray.

They shipped these rapscallions, these sea-sick battalions
To a patriotic and picturesque spot;
They gave them new bibles and marksmen's medallions,
Compasses, maps, and committed the lot.

A fine dust has settled on all that scrap metal.
The heroes were packaged and sent home in parts
To pluck at a poppy and sew on a petal
And count the long night by the stroke of their hearts.

1955

317

RICHARD WILBUR

1921–

First Snow in Alsace

The snow came down last night like moths
Burned on the moon; it fell till dawn,
Covered the town with simple cloths.

Absolute snow lies rumpled on
What shellbursts scattered and deranged,
Entangled railings, crevassed lawn.

As if it did not know they'd changed,
Snow smoothly clasps the roofs of homes
Fear-gutted, trustless and estranged.

The ration stacks are milky domes;
Across the ammunition pile
The snow has climbed in sparkling combs.

You think: beyond the town a mile
Or two, this snowfall fills the eyes
Of soldiers dead a little while.

Persons and persons in disguise,
Walking the new air white and fine,
Trade glances quick with shared surprise.

At children's windows, heaped, benign,
As always, winter shines the most,
And frost makes marvellous designs.

The night guard coming from his post,
Ten first-snows back in thought, walks slow
And warms him with a boyish boast:

He was the first to see the snow.

1947

245 *Terza Rima*

In this great form, as Dante proved in Hell,
There is no dreadful thing that can't be said
In passing. Here, for instance, one could tell

How our jeep skidded sideways toward the dead
Enemy soldier with the staring eyes,
Bumping a little as it struck his head,

And then flew on, as if toward Paradise.

2010

LINCOLN KIRSTEIN
1907–1996

246 *Rank*

Differences between rich and poor, king and queen,
Cat and dog, hot and cold, day and night, now and then,
Are less clearly distinct than all those between
Officers and us: enlisted men.

Not by brass may you guess nor their private latrine
Since distinctions obtain in any real well-run war;
It's when off duty, drunk, one acts nice or mean
In a sawdust-strewn bistro-type bar.

Ours was on a short street near the small market square;
Farmers dropped by for some beer or oftener to tease
The Gargantuan bartender Jean-Pierre
About his sweet wife, Marie-Louise.

GI's got the habit who liked French movies or books,
Tried to talk French or were happy to be left alone;
It was our kinda club; we played chess in nooks
With the farmers. We made it our own.

To this haven one night came an officer bold;
Crocked and ugly, he'd had it in five bars before.
A lurid luster glazed his eye which foretold
He'd better stay out of our shut door,

319

But did not. He barged in, slung his cap on the zinc:
'Dewbelle veesky,' knowing well there was little but beer.
Jean-Pierre showed the list of what one could drink:
'What sorta jerk joint you running here?'

Jean-Pierre had wine but no whisky to sell.
Wine loves the soul. Hard liquor hots up bloody fun,
And it's our rule noncommissioned personnel
Must keep by them their piece called a gun.

As well we are taught, enlisted soldiers may never
Ever surrender this piece—MI, carbine, or rifle—
With which no mere officer whomsoever
May freely or foolishly trifle.

A porcelain stove glowed in its niche, white and warm.
Jean-Pierre made jokes with us French-speaking boys.
Marie-Louise lay warm in bed far from harm;
Upstairs, snored through the ensuing noise.

This captain swilled beer with minimal grace. He began:
'Shit. What you-all are drinkin's not liquor. It's piss.'
Two privates (first class) now consider some plan
To avoid what may result from this.

Captain Stearnes is an Old Army joe. Eighteen years
In the ranks, man and boy; bad luck, small promotion;
Without brains or cash, not the cream of careers.
Frustration makes plenty emotion.

'Now, Mac,' Stearnes grins (Buster's name is not Mac; it is Jack),
'Toss me your gun an' I'll show you an old army trick;
At forty feet, with one hand, I'll crack that stove, smack.'
'Let's not,' drawls Jack back, scared of this prick.

'You young punk,' Stearnes now storms, growing moody but mean,
'Do you dream I daren't pull my superior rank?'
His hand snatches Jack's light clean bright carbine.
What riddles the roof is no blank.

The rifle is loaded as combat zones ever require.
His arm kicks back without hurt to a porcelain stove.

Steel drilling plaster and plank, thin paths of fire
Plug Marie-Louise sleeping above.

Formal enquiry subsequent to this shootin'
Had truth and justice separately demanded.
Was Stearnes found guilty? You are darned tootin':
Fined, demoted. More: reprimanded.

The charge was not murder, mayhem, mischief malicious,
Yet something worse, and this they brought out time and again:
Clearly criminal and caddishly vicious
Was his: Drinking With Enlisted Men.

I'm serious. It's what the Judge Advocate said:
Strict maintenance of rank or our system is sunk.
Stearnes saluted. Jean-Pierre wept his dead.
Jack and I got see-double drunk.

1964

VERNON SCANNELL

1922–2007

247   *Walking Wounded*

A mammoth morning moved grey flanks and groaned.
In the rusty hedges pale rags of mist hung;
The gruel of mud and leaves in the mauled lane
Smelled sweet, like blood. Birds had died or flown,
Their green and silent attics sprouting now
With branches of leafed steel, hiding round eyes
And ripe grenades ready to drop and burst.
In the ditch at the cross-roads the fallen rider lay
Hugging his dead machine and did not stir
At crunch of mortar, tantrum of a Bren
Answering a Spandau's manic jabber.
Then into sight the ambulances came,
Stumbling and churning past the broken farm,
The amputated sign-post and smashed trees,

Slow wagonloads of bandaged cries, square trucks
That rolled on ominous wheels, vehicles
Made mythopoeic by their mortal freight
And crimson crosses on the dirty white.
This grave procession passed, though, for a while,
The grinding of their engines could be heard,
A dark noise on the pallor of the morning,
Dark as dried blood; and then it faded, died.
The road was empty, but it seemed to wait—
Like a stage which knows the cast is in the wings—
Wait for a different traffic to appear.
The mist still hung in snags from dripping thorns;
Absent-minded guns still sighed and thumped.
And then they came, the walking wounded,
Straggling the road like convicts loosely chained,
Dragging at ankles exhaustion and despair.
Their heads were weighted down by last night's lead,
And eyes still drank the dark. They trailed the night
Along the morning road. Some limped on sticks;
Others wore rough dressings, splints and slings;
A few had turbanned heads, the dirty cloth
Brown-badged with blood. A humble brotherhood,
Not one was suffering from a lethal hurt,
They were not magnified by noble wounds,
There was no splendour in that company.
And yet, remembering after eighteen years,
In the heart's throat a sour sadness stirs;
Imagination pauses and returns
To see them walking still, but multiplied
In thousands now. And when heroic corpses
Turn slowly in their decorated sleep
And every ambulance has disappeared
The walking wounded still trudge down that lane,
And when recalled they must bear arms again.

1965

PAUL DEHN

1912–1976

248   *St Aubin D'Aubigné*

It was only a small place and they had cheered us too much,
A couple of allies, chance symbol of Freedom new-found.
They were eager to beckon, to back-slap, even to touch;
They put flowers in my helmet and corn-coloured wine in my hand.

The boy from Dakota and I, we had suffered too little
To deserve all the flowers, the kisses, the wine and the thanks.
We both felt ashamed; till the kettledrum clangour of metal
On cobble and kerbstone proclaimed the arrival of tanks.

Who saw them first, the exiles returning, the fighters,
The Croix de Lorraine and the Tricolour flown from the hull?
Who saw us moving more fitly to join the spectators,
The crazy, the crying, the silent whose hearts were full?

It was only a small place, but a bugle was blowing.
I remember the Mayor performing an intricate dance
And the boy from Dakota most gravely, most quietly, throwing
The flowers from his helmet toward the deserving of France.

1949

DYLAN THOMAS

1914–1953

249   *The hand that signed the paper*

The hand that signed the paper felled a city;
Five sovereign fingers taxed the breath,
Doubled the globe of dead and halved a country;
These five kings did a king to death.

The mighty hand leads to a sloping shoulder,
The finger joints are cramped with chalk;
A goose's quill has put an end to murder
That put an end to talk.

The hand that signed the treaty bred a fever,
And famine grew, and locusts came;
Great is the hand that holds dominion over
Man by a scribbled name.

The five kings count the dead but do not soften
The crusted wound nor stroke the brow;
A hand rules pity as a hand rules heaven;
Hands have no tears to flow.

1936

JAMES DICKEY
1923–1997

250   *The Firebombing*

> Denke daran, dass nach den grossen Zerstörungen
> Jedermann beweisen wird, dass er unschuldig war.
> *Günter Eich*
> Or hast thou an arm like God?
> *The Book of Job*

Homeowners unite.

All families lie together, though some are burned alive.
The others try to feel
For them. Some can, it is often said.

Starve and take off

Twenty years in the suburbs, and the palm trees willingly leap
Into the flashlights,
And there is beneath them also

A booted crackling of snailshells and coral sticks.
There are cowl flaps and the tilt cross of propellers,
The shovel-marked clouds' far sides against the moon,
The enemy filling up the hills
With ceremonial graves. At my somewhere among these,

Snap, a bulb is tricked on in the cockpit

And some technical-minded stranger with my hands
Is sitting in a glass treasure-hole of blue light,
Having potential fire under the undeodorized arms
Of his wings, on thin bomb-shackles,
The 'tear-drop-shaped' 300-gallon drop-tanks
Filled with napalm and gasoline.

Thinking forward ten minutes
From that, there is also the burst straight out
Of the overcast into the moon; there is now
The moon-metal-shine of propellers, the quarter-
moonstone, aimed at the waves,
Stopped on the cumulus.

There is then this re-entry
Into cloud, for the engines to ponder their sound.
In white dark the aircraft shrinks; Japan

Dilates around it like a thought.
Coming out, the one who is here is over
Land, passing over the all-night grainfields,
In dark paint over
The woods with one silver side,
Rice-water calm at all levels
Of the terraced hill.

               Enemy rivers and trees
Sliding off me like snakeskin,
Strips of vapor spooled from the wingtips
Going   invisible   passing   over   on
Over   bridges   roads for nightwalkers
Sunday night in the enemy's country   absolute
Calm   the moon's face   coming   slowly
About
         the inland sea

Slants   is woven with wire thread
Levels out   holds together like a quilt
Off the starboard wing   cloud flickers
At my glassed-off forehead   the moon's now and again
Uninterrupted face going forward
Over the waves in a glide-path
Lost into land.

Going:going with it

Combat booze by my side in a cratered canteen,
Bourbon frighteningly mixed
With GI pineapple juice,
Dogs trembling under me for hundreds of miles, on many
Islands, sleep-smelling that ungodly mixture
Of napalm and high-octane fuel,
Good bourbon and GI juice.

Rivers circling behind me around
Come to the fore, and bring
A town with everyone darkened.
Five thousand people are sleeping off
An all-day American drone.
Twenty years in the suburbs have not shown me
Which ones were hit and which not.

Haul on the wheel   racking slowly
The aircraft blackly around
In a dark dream   that   that is
That is like flying inside someone's head

Think of this   think of this

I did not think of my house
But think of my house now

Where the lawn mower rests on its laurels
Where the diet exists
For my own good   where I try to drop
Twenty years, eating figs in the pantry
Blinded by each and all
Of the eye-catching cans that gladly have caught my wife's eye
Until I cannot say
Where the screwdriver is   where the children

Get off the bus   where the new
Scoutmaster lives   where the fly
Hones his front legs   where the hammock folds
Its erotic daydreams   where the Sunday
School text for the day has been put   where the fire
Wood is   where the payments
For everything under the sun
Pile peacefully up,

But in this half-paid-for pantry
Among the red lids that screw off
With an easy half-twist to the left
And the long drawers crammed with dim spoons,
I still have charge—secret charge—
Of the fire developed to cling
To everything: to golf carts and fingernail
Scissors as yet unborn   tennis shoes
Grocery baskets   toy fire engines
New Buicks stalled by the half-moon
Shining at midnight on crossroads   green paint
Of jolly garden tools   red Christmas ribbons:

Not atoms, these, but glue inspired
By love of country to burn,
The apotheosis of gelatin.

Behind me having risen the Southern Cross
Set up by chaplains in the Ryukyus—
Orion, Scorpio, the immortal silver
Like the myths of king-
insects at swarming time—
One mosquito, dead drunk
On altitude, drones on, far under the engines,
And bites between
The oxygen mask and the eye.
The enemy-colored skin of families
Determines to hold its color
In sleep, as my hand turns whiter
Than ever, clutching the toggle—
The ship shakes   bucks
Fire hangs   not yet fire
In the air above Beppu
For I am fulfilling

327

An 'anti-morale' raid upon it.
All leashes of dogs
Break under the first bomb, around those
In bed, or late in the public baths: around those
Who inch forward on their hands
Into medicinal waters.
Their heads come up with a roar
Of Chicago fire:
Come up with the carp pond showing
The bathhouse upside down,
Standing stiller to show it more
As I sail artistically over
The resort town followed by farms,
Singing and twisting
All the handles in heaven   kicking
The small cattle off their feet
In a red costly blast
Flinging jelly over the walls
As in a chemical war-
fare field demonstration.
With fire of mine like a cat

Holding onto another man's walls,
My hat should crawl on my head
In streetcars, thinking of it,
The fat on my body should pale.

Gun down
The engines, the eight blades sighing
For the moment when the roofs will connect
Their flames, and make a town burning with all
American fire.
                              Reflections of houses catch;
Fire shuttles from pond to pond
In every direction, till hundreds flash with one death.
With this in the dark of the mind,
Death will not be what it should;
Will not, even now, even when
My exhaled face in the mirror
Of bars, dilates in a cloud like Japan.
The death of children is ponds
Shutter-flashing; responding mirrors; it climbs

The terraces of hills
Smaller and smaller, a mote of red dust
At a hundred feet; at a hundred and one it goes out.
That is what should have got in
To my eye
And shown the insides of houses, the low tables
Catch fire from the floor mats,
Blaze up in gas around their heads
Like a dream of suddenly growing
Too intense for war. Ah, under one's dark arms
Something strange-scented falls—when those on earth
Die, there is not even sound;
One is cool and enthralled in the cockpit,
Turned blue by the power of beauty,
In a pale treasure-hole of soft light
Deep in aesthetic contemplation,
Seeing the ponds catch fire
And cast it through ring after ring
Of land: O death in the middle
Of acres of inch-deep water!   Useless

Firing   small arms
Speckles   from the river
Bank   one ninety-millimeter
Misses   far down   wrong petals   gone

It is this detachment,
The honored aesthetic evil,
The greatest sense of power in one's life,
That must be shed in bars, or by whatever
Means, by starvation
Visions in well-stocked pantries:
The moment when the moon sails in between
The tail-booms   the rudders nod   I swing
Over   directly over the heart
The *heart* of the fire. A mosquito burns out on my cheek
With the cold of my face   there are the eyes
In blue light   bar light
All masked but them   the moon
Crossing from left to right   in the streams below
Oriental fish form quickly
In the chemical shine,

In their eyes one tiny seed
Of deranged, Old Testament light.

Letting go   letting go
The plane rises gently   dark forms
Glide off me   long water   pales
In safe zones   a new cry enters
The voice box of chained family dogs

We buck   leap over something
Not there   settle back
Leave it   leave it clinging and crying
It consumes them in a hot
Body-flash, old age or menopause
Of children, clings and burns
                              eating through
And when a reed mat catches fire
From me, it explodes through field after field
Bearing its sleeper   another

Bomb finds a home
And clings to it like a child. And so

Goodbye to the grassy mountains
To cloud streaming from the night engines
Flags   pennons   curved silks
Of air   myself streaming also
My body covered
With flags, the air of flags
Between the engines.
Forever I do sleep in that position,
Forever in a turn
For home that breaks out streaming banners
From my wingtips,
Wholly in position to admire.

O then I knock it off
And turn for home over the black complex thread worked through
The silver night-sea,
Following the huge, moon-washed steppingstones
Of the Ryukyus south,
The nightgrass of mountains billowing softly
In my rising heat.
                    Turn and tread down

The yellow stones of the islands
To where Okinawa burns,
Pure gold, on the radar screen,
Beholding, beneath, the actual island form
In the vast water-silver poured just above solid ground,
An inch of water extending for thousands of miles
Above flat ploughland. Say 'down,' and it is done.

All this, and I am still hungry,
Still twenty years overweight, still unable
To get down there or see
What really happened.
                                    But it may be that I could not,
If I tried, say to any
Who lived there, deep in my flames: say, in cold
Grinning sweat, as to another
Of these homeowners who are always curving
Near me down the different-grassed street: say
As though to the neighbor
I borrowed the hedge-clippers from
On the darker-grassed side of the two,
Come in, my house is yours, come in
If you can, if you
Can pass this unfired door. It is that I can imagine
At the threshold nothing
With its ears crackling off
Like powdery leaves,
Nothing with children of ashes, nothing not
Amiable, gentle, well-meaning,
A little nervous for no
Reason   a little worried   a little too loud
Or too easygoing   nothing I haven't lived with
For twenty years, still nothing not as
American as I am, and proud of it.

Absolution? Sentence? No matter;
The thing itself is in that.

1967

EPHIM FOGEL

1920–1992

251   *Shipment to Maidanek*

Arrived from scattered cities, several lands,
intact from sea land, mountain land, and plain.
Item: six surgeons, slightly mangled hands.
Item: three poets, hopelessly insane.

Item: a Russian mother and her child,
the former with five gold teeth and usable shoes,
the latter with seven dresses, peasant-styled.

Item: another hundred thousand Jews.

Item: a crippled Czech with a handmade crutch.
Item: a Spaniard with a subversive laugh;
seventeen dozen Danes, nine gross of Dutch.

Total: precisely a million and a half.

They are sorted and marked—the method is up to you.
The books must be balanced, the disposition stated.
Take care that all accounts are neat and true.

Make sure that they are thoroughly cremated.

1945

W. H. AUDEN

1907–1973

252   from *Sonnets from China*

Here war is harmless like a monument:
A telephone is talking to a man;

Flags on a map declare that troops were sent;
A boy brings milk in bowls. There is a plan

For living men in terror of their lives,
Who thirst at nine who were to thirst at noon,
Who can be lost and are, who miss their wives
And, unlike an idea, can die too soon.

Yet ideas can be true, although men die:
For we have seen a myriad faces
Ecstatic from one lie,

And maps can really point to places
Where life is evil now.
Nanking. Dachau.

1939

ANTHONY HECHT

1923–2004

253   *'More Light! More Light!'*
         for Heinrich Blücher and Hannah Arendt

Composed in the Tower before his execution
These moving verses, and being brought at that time
Painfully to the stake, submitted, declaring thus:
'I implore my God to witness that I have made no crime.'

Nor was he forsaken of courage, but the death was horrible,
The sack of gunpowder failing to ignite.
His legs were blistered sticks on which the black sap
Bubbled and burst as he howled for the Kindly Light.

And that was but one, and by no means one of the worst;
Permitted at least his pitiful dignity;
And such as were by made prayers in the name of Christ,
That shall judge all men, for his soul's tranquillity.

We move now to outside a German wood.
Three men are there commanded to dig a hole
In which the two Jews are ordered to lie down
And be buried alive by the third, who is a Pole.

Not light from the shrine at Weimar beyond the hill
Nor light from heaven appeared. But he did refuse.
A Lüger settled back deeply in its glove.
He was ordered to change places with the Jews.

Much casual death had drained away their souls.
The thick dirt mounted toward the quivering chin.
When only the head was exposed the order came
To dig him out again and to get back in.

No light, no light in the blue Polish eye.
When he finished a riding boot packed down the earth.
The Lüger hovered lightly in its glove.
He was shot in the belly and in three hours bled to death.

No prayers or incense rose up in those hours
Which grew to be years, and every day came mute
Ghosts from the ovens, sifting through crisp air,
And settled upon his eyes in a black soot.

1967

254   *The Book of Yolek*

   Wir haben ein Gesetz, und nach dem Gesetz soll er sterben.

The dowsed coals fume and hiss after your meal
Of grilled brook trout, and you saunter off for a walk
Down the fern trail, it doesn't matter where to,
Just so you're weeks and worlds away from home,
And among midsummer hills have set up camp
In the deep bronze glories of declining day.

You remember, peacefully, an earlier day
In childhood, remember a quite specific meal:

334

A corn roast and bonfire in summer camp.
That summer you got lost on a Nature Walk;
More than you dared admit, you thought of home;
No one else knows where the mind wanders to.

The fifth of August, 1942.
It was morning and very hot. It was the day
They came at dawn with rifles to The Home
For Jewish Children, cutting short the meal
Of bread and soup, lining them up to walk
In close formation off to a special camp.

How often you have thought about that camp,
As though in some strange way you were driven to,
And about the children, and how they were made to walk,
Yolek who had bad lungs, who wasn't a day
Over five years old, commanded to leave his meal
And shamble between armed guards to his long home.

We're approaching August again. It will drive home
The regulation torments of that camp
Yolek was sent to, his small, unfinished meal,
The electric fences, the numeral tattoo,
The quite extraordinary heat of the day
They all were forced to take that terrible walk.

Whether on a silent, solitary walk
Or among crowds, far off or safe at home,
You will remember, helplessly, that day,
And the smell of smoke, and the loudspeakers of the camp.
Wherever you are, Yolek will be there, too.
His unuttered name will interrupt your meal.

Prepare to receive him in your home some day.
Though they killed him in the camp they sent him to,
He will walk in as you're sitting down to a meal.

1990

THOM GUNN

1929–2004

Claus Von Stauffenberg
of the bomb-plot on Hitler, 1944

What made the place a landscape of despair,
History stunned beneath, the emblems cracked?
Smell of approaching snow hangs on the air;
The frost meanwhile can be the only fact.

They chose the unknown, and the bounded terror,
As a corrective, who corrected live
Surveying without choice the bounding error:
An unsanctioned present must be primitive.

A few still have the vigour to deny
Fear is a natural state; their motives neither
Of doctrinaire, of turncoat, nor of spy.
Lucidity of thought draws them together.

The maimed young Colonel who can calculate
On two remaining fingers and a will,
Takes lessons from the past, to detonate
A bomb that Brutus rendered possible.

Over the maps a moment, face to face:
Across from Hitler, whose grey eyes have filled
A nation with the illogic of their gaze,
The rational man is poised, to break, to build.

And though he fails, honour personified
In a cold time where honour cannot grow,
He stiffens, like a statue, in mid-stride
—Falling toward history, and under snow.

1961

CHARLES CAUSLEY

1917–2003

Armistice Day

I stood with three comrades in Parliament Square
November her freights of grey fire unloading,
No sound from the city upon the pale air
Above us the sea-bell eleven exploding.

Down by the bands and the burning memorial
Beats all the brass in a royal array,
But at our end we are not so sartorial:
Out of (as usual) the rig of the day.

Starry is wearing a split pusser's flannel
Rubbed, as he is, by the regular tide;
Oxo the ducks that he ditched in the Channel
In June, 1940 (when he was inside).

Kitty recalls his abandon-ship station,
Running below at the Old Man's salute
And (with a deck-watch) going down for duration
Wearing his oppoe's pneumonia-suit.

Comrades, for you the black captain of carracks
Writes in Whitehall his appalling decisions,
But as was often the case in the Barracks
Several ratings are not at Divisions.

Into my eyes the stiff sea-horses stare,
Over my head sweeps the sun like a swan.
As I stand alone in Parliament Square
A cold bugle calls, and the city moves on.

1957

257   *At the British War Cemetery, Bayeux*

I walked where in their talking graves
And shirts of earth five thousand lay,
When history with ten feasts of fire
Had eaten the red air away.

I am Christ's boy, I cried, I bear
In iron hands the bread, the fishes.
I hang with honey and with rose
This tidy wreck of all your wishes.

On your geometry of sleep
The chestnut and the fir-tree fly,
And lavender and marguerite
Forge with their flowers an English sky.

Turn now towards the belling town
Your jigsaws of impossible bone,
And rising read your rank of snow
Accurate as death upon the stone.

About your easy heads my prayers
I said with syllables of clay.
What gift, I asked, shall I bring now
Before I weep and walk away?

Take, they replied, the oak and laurel.
Take our fortune of tears and live
Like a spendthrift lover. All we ask
Is the one gift you cannot give.

1957

SIR JOHN BETJEMAN
1906–1984

In Memory of Basil, Marquess of
Dufferin and Ava

On such a morning as this
    with birds ricocheting their music
Out of the whelming elms
    to a copper beech's embrace
And a sifting sound of leaves
    from multitudinous branches
Running across the park
    to a chequer of light on the lake,
On such a morning as this
    with *The Times* for June the eleventh
Left with coffee and toast
    you opened the breakfast-room window
And, sprawled on the southward terrace,
    Said: 'That means war in September.'

Friend of my youth, you are dead!
    and the long peal pours from the steeple
Over this sunlit quad
    in our University city
And soaks in Headington stone.
    Motionless stand the pinnacles
Under a flying sky
    as though they too listened and waited
Like me for your dear return
    with a Bullingdon noise of an evening
In a Sports-Bugatti from Thame
    that belonged to a man in Magdalen.
Friend of my youth, you are dead!
    and the quads are empty without you.

Then there were people about.
    Each hour, like an Oxford archway,
Opened on long green lawns
    and distant unvisited buildings
And you my friend were explorer

SIR JOHN BETJEMAN

and so you remained to me always
Humorous, reckless, loyal—
   my kind, heavy-lidded companion.
Stop, oh many bells, stop
   pouring on roses and creeper
Your unremembering peal
   this hollow, unhallowed V.E. day,—
I am deaf to your notes and dead
   by a soldier's body in Burma.

1945

HOWARD NEMEROV

1920-1991

259   *The War in the Air*

For a saving grace, we didn't see our dead,
Who rarely bothered coming home to die
But simply stayed away out there
In the clean war, the war in the air.

Seldom the ghosts came back bearing their tales
Of hitting the earth, the incompressible sea,
But stayed up there in the relative wind,
Shades fading in the mind,

Who had no graves but only epitaphs
Where never so many spoke for never so few:
Per ardua, said the partisans of Mars,
Per aspera, to the stars.

That was the good war, the war we won
As if there were no death, for goodness' sake,
With the help of the losers we left out there
In the air, in the empty air.

1987

260 *Redeployment*

They say the war is over. But water still
Comes bloody from the taps, and my pet cat
In his disorder vomits worms which crawl
Swiftly away. Maybe they leave the house.
These worms are white, and flecked with the cat's blood.

The war may be over. I know a man
Who keeps a pleasant souvenir, he keeps
A soldier's dead blue eyeballs that he found
Somewhere—hard as chalk, and blue as slate.
He clicks them in his pocket while he talks.

And now there are cockroaches in the house,
They get slightly drunk on DDT,
Are fast, hard, shifty—can be drowned but not
Without you hold them under quite some time.
People say the Mexican kind can fly.

The end of the war. I took it quietly
Enough. I tried to wash the dirt out of
My hair and from under my fingernails,
I dressed in clean white clothes and went to bed.
I heard the dust falling between the walls.

1950

ARCHIBALD MacLEISH
1892–1982

261 *Memorial Rain*
for Kenneth MacLeish

Ambassador Puser the ambassador
Reminds himself in French, felicitous tongue
What these (young men no longer) lie here for
In rows that once, and somewhere else, were young...

ARCHIBALD MacLEISH

All night in Brussels the wind had tugged at my door:
I had heard the wind at my door and the trees strung
Taut, and to me who had never been before
In that country it was a strange wind, blowing
Steadily, stiffening the walls, the floor,
The roof of my room. I had not slept for knowing
He too, dead, was a stranger in that land
And felt beneath the earth in the wind's flowing
A tightening of roots and would not understand,
Remembering lake winds in Illinois,
That strange wind. I had felt his bones in the sand
Listening.

> ... *Reflects that these enjoy*
> *Their country's gratitude, that deep repose,*
> *That peace no pain can break, no hurt destroy,*
> *That rest, that sleep* ...

                          At Ghent the wind rose.
There was a smell of rain and a heavy drag
Of wind in the hedges but not as the wind blows
Over fresh water when the waves lag
Foaming and the willows huddle and it will rain:
I felt him waiting.

> ... *Indicates the flag*
> *Which (may he say) enisles in Flanders plain*
> *This little field these happy, happy dead*
> *Have made America* ...

                          In the ripe grain
The wind coiled glistening, darted, fled,
Dragging its heavy body: at Waereghem
The wind coiled in the grass above his head:
Waiting—listening ...

> ... *Dedicates to them*
> *This earth their bones have hallowed, this last gift*
> *A grateful country* ...

                          Under the dry grass stem
The words are blurred, are thickened, the words sift
Confused by the rasp of the wind, by the thin grating

342

Of ants under the grass, the minute shift
And tumble of dusty sand separating
From dusty sand. The roots of the grass strain,
Tighten, the earth is rigid, waits—he is waiting—

And suddenly, and all at once, the rain!

1926

JOHN PUDNEY
1909–1977

262 *For Johnny*

Do not despair
For Johnny-head-in-air;
He sleeps as sound
As Johnny underground.

Fetch out no shroud
For Johnny-in-the-cloud;
And keep your tears
For him in after years.

Better by far
For Johnny-the-bright-star,
To keep your head,
And see his children fed.

1941

JAMES TATE
1943–

263 *The Lost Pilot*
for my father, 1922–1944

Your face did not rot
like the others—the co-pilot,
for example, I saw him

yesterday. His face is corn-
mush: his wife and daughter,
the poor ignorant people, stare

as if he will compose soon.
He was more wronged than Job.
But your face did not rot

like the others—it grew dark,
and hard like ebony;
the features progressed in their

distinction. If I could cajole
you to come back for an evening,
down from your compulsive

orbiting, I would touch you,
read your face as Dallas,
your hoodlum gunner, now,

with the blistered eyes, reads
his braille editions. I would
touch your face as a disinterested

scholar touches an original page.
However frightening, I would
discover you, and I would not

turn you in; I would not make
you face your wife, or Dallas,
or the co-pilot, Jim. You

could return to your crazy
orbiting, and I would not try
to fully understand what

it means to you. All I know
is this: when I see you,
as I have seen you at least

once every year of my life,
spin across the wilds of the sky
like a tiny, African god,

I feel dead. I feel as if I were
the residue of a stranger's life,
that I should pursue you.

My head cocked toward the sky,
I cannot get off the ground,
and, you, passing over again,

fast, perfect, and unwilling
to tell me that you are doing
well, or that it was mistake

that placed you in that world,
and me in this; or that misfortune
placed these worlds in us.

1967

GEORGE MacBETH

1932–1992

264   *The Land-Mine*

It fell when I was sleeping. In my dream
    It brought the garden to the house
And let it in. I heard no parrot scream
    Or lion roar, but there were flowers
And water flowing where the cellared mouse
Was all before. And air moved as in bowers

Of cedar with a scented breath of smoke
    And fire. I rubbed scales from my eyes
And white with brushed stone in my hair half-woke
    In fear. I saw my father kneel
On glass that scarred the ground. And there were flies
Thick on that water, weeds around his heel

Where he was praying. And I knew that night
  Had cataracted through the wall
And loosed fine doors whose hinges had been tight
  And made each window weep glass tears
That clawed my hands. I climbed through holes. My hall
Where I had lain asleep with stoppered ears

Was all in ruins, planted thick with grime
  Of war. I walked as if in greaves
Through fire, lay down in gutters choked with lime
  And spoke for help. Alas, those birds
That dived in light above me in the leaves
Were birds of prey, and paid no heed to words.

Now I was walking, wearing on my brow
  What moved before through fireless coal
And held my father's head. I touch it now
  And feel my dream go. And no sound
That flying birds can make, or burrowing mole,
Will bring my garden back, or break new ground.

The war is over and the mine has gone
  That filled the air with whinnying fire
And no more nights will I lie waiting on
  Cold metal or cold stone to freeze
Before it comes again. That day of ire,
If it shall come, will find me on my knees.

1967

ALAN ROSS

1922–2001

265   *Off Brighton Pier*

I saw him a squat man with red hair,
Grown into sideburns, fishing off Brighton pier:
Suddenly he bent, and in a lumpy bag

Rummaged for bait, letting his line dangle,
And I noticed the stiffness of his leg
That thrust out, like a tripod, at an angle.
Then I remembered: the sideburns, that gloss
Of slicked-down ginger on a skin like candy floss.
He was there, not having moved, as last,
On a windless night, leaning against the mast,
I saw him, groping a bag for numbers.
And the date was the 17th of September,
15 years back, and we were playing Tombola
During the last Dog, someone beginning to holler
'Here you are' for a full card, and I remember
He'd just called 'Seven and six, she was worth it,'
When—without contacts or warning—we were hit.
Some got away with it, a few bought it.
And I recall now, when they carried him ashore,
Fishing gear lashed to his hammock, wishing
Him luck, and his faint smile, more
To himself than to me, when he saluted
From the stretcher, and, cadging a fag,
Cracked 'I'm quids in, it's only one leg,
They'll pension me off to go fishing.'

1958

ANDREW MOTION
1952–

266   *Now Then*

It was not my war, but all the same
my father handed over the harness
of his Sam Browne for me to polish,
and his enormous boots. There was
no way I could ever make the toes
brighter than they were already.

*

Years later I was riding a train south
from Gdansk to Warsaw at 4.00 am.
The pine forest swarmed beside me,
lit by the gentle glow of our carriages
and sometimes by devilish icy sparks
which flew from our wheels at points.

*

Tell him about the smell, my mother said,
working hard on his buttons with Brasso
at the window-end of the kitchen table.
She meant the smell of Belsen, the first
my father had known of any such place.
He slowly shook his head. *I don't think so.*

*

The forest lasted for miles. Miles and miles.
Then for a second I saw deep into the heart
of a clearing: there was this swine-herd
lolling against the wall of his pine cabin
wearing the helmet of a German soldier.
And pigs rootling in the husky moonlight.

*

Why not? my mother continued her polishing.
Surely the boy is old enough to know history?
My father sighed: *Now then, you know the reason.*
That ended it. I kept my eyes down and attention
fixed on the long face looming in his toe-caps,
convinced my efforts would never pass muster.

*

Eventually I slept, dreaming through what remained
of the great pine forest of Europe, while my father
pounded along in the dark outside my carriage.
At Warsaw he fell away from me, but not before
passing his boots through the window and asking
would I mind giving them a last quick once-over.

2010

348

GEOFFREY HILL

1932–

267   *September Song*
born 19.6.32–deported 24.9.42

Undesirable you may have been, untouchable
you were not. Not forgotten
or passed over at the proper time.

As estimated, you died. Things marched,
sufficient, to that end.
Just so much Zyklon and leather, patented
terror, so many routine cries.

(I have made
an elegy for myself it
is true)

September fattens on vines. Roses
flake from the wall. The smoke
of harmless fires drifts to my eyes.

This is plenty. This is more than enough.

1968

W. H. AUDEN

1907–1973

268   *The Shield of Achilles*

She looked over his shoulder
    For vines and olive trees,
Marble well-governed cities
    And ships upon untamed seas,
But there on the shining metal
    His hands had put instead

W. H. AUDEN

An artificial wilderness
And a sky like lead.

A plain without a feature, bare and brown,
   No blade of grass, no sign of neighborhood,
Nothing to eat and nowhere to sit down,
   Yet, congregated on its blankness, stood
   An unintelligible multitude,
A million eyes, a million boots in line,
Without expression, waiting for a sign.

Out of the air a voice without a face
   Proved by statistics that some cause was just
In tones as dry and level as the place:
   No one was cheered and nothing was discussed;
   Column by column in a cloud of dust
They marched away enduring a belief
Whose logic brought them, somewhere else, to grief.

         She looked over his shoulder
            For ritual pieties,
         White flower-garlanded heifers,
            Libation and sacrifice,
         But there on the shining metal
            Where the altar should have been,
         She saw by his flickering forge-light
            Quite another scene.

Barbed wire enclosed an arbitrary spot
   Where bored officials lounged (one cracked a joke)
And sentries sweated for the day was hot:
   A crowd of ordinary decent folk
   Watched from without and neither moved nor spoke
As three pale figures were led forth and bound
To three posts driven upright in the ground.

The mass and majesty of this world, all
   That carries weight and always weighs the same
Lay in the hands of others; they were small
   And could not hope for help and no help came:
   What their foes liked to do was done, their shame
Was all the worst could wish; they lost their pride
And died as men before their bodies died.

She looked over his shoulder
   For athletes at their games,
Men and women in a dance
   Moving their sweet limbs
Quick, quick, to music,
   But there on the shining shield
His hands had set no dancing-floor
   But a weed-choked field.

A ragged urchin, aimless and alone,
   Loitered about that vacancy; a bird
Flew up to safety from his well-aimed stone:
   That girls are raped, that two boys knife a third,
   Were axioms to him, who'd never heard
Of any world where promises were kept,
Or one could weep because another wept.

   The thin-lipped armorer,
      Hephaestos, hobbled away,
   Thetis of the shining breasts
      Cried out in dismay
   At what the god had wrought
      To please her son, the strong
   Iron-hearted man-slaying Achilles
      Who would not live long.

1955

ANDREI VOZNESENSKY

1933–2010

269   *I am Goya*

I am Goya
of the bare field, by the enemy's beak gouged
till the craters of my eyes gape
I am grief

I am the tongue
of war, the embers of cities
on the snows of the year 1941
I am hunger

I am the gullet
of a woman hanged whose body like a bell
tolled over a blank square
I am Goya

O grapes of wrath!
I have hurled westward
                      the ashes of the uninvited guest!
and hammered stars into the unforgetting sky—like nails
I am Goya

1960

Translated from the Russian by Stanley Kunitz

ROBERT LOWELL

1917–1977

270   *Fall 1961*

Back and forth, back and forth
goes the tock, tock, tock
of the orange, bland, ambassadorial
face of the moon
on the grandfather clock.

All autumn, the chafe and jar
of nuclear war;
we have talked our extinction to death.
I swim like a minnow
behind my studio window.

Our end drifts nearer,

the moon lifts,
radiant with terror.
The state
is a diver under a glass bell.

A father's no shield
for his child.
We are like a lot of wild
spiders crying together,
but without tears.

Nature holds up a mirror.
One swallow makes a summer.
It's easy to tick
off the minutes,
but the clockhands stick.

Back and forth!
Back and forth, back and forth—
my one point of rest
is the orange and black
oriole's swinging nest!

1965

271   *For the Union Dead*
          '*Relinquunt Omnia Servare Rem Publicam.*'

The old South Boston Aquarium stands
in a Sahara of snow now. Its broken windows are boarded.
The bronze weathervane cod has lost half its scales.
The airy tanks are dry.

Once my nose crawled like a snail on the glass;
my hand tingled
to burst the bubbles
drifting from the noses of the cowed, compliant fish.

My hand draws back. I often sigh still
for the dark downward and vegetating kingdom

of the fish and reptile. One morning last March,
I pressed against the new barbed and galvanized

fence on the Boston Common. Behind their cage,
yellow dinosaur steamshovels were grunting
as they cropped up tons of mush and grass
to gouge their underworld garage.

Parking spaces luxuriate like civic
sandpiles in the heart of Boston.
A girdle of orange, Puritan-pumpkin colored girders
braces the tingling Statehouse,

shaking over the excavations, as it faces Colonel Shaw
and his bell-cheeked Negro infantry
on St. Gaudens' shaking Civil War relief,
propped by a plank splint against the garage's earthquake.

Two months after marching through Boston,
half the regiment was dead;
at the dedication,
William James could almost hear the bronze Negroes breathe.

Their monument sticks like a fishbone
in the city's throat.
Its Colonel is as lean
as a compass-needle.

He has an angry wrenlike vigilance,
a greyhound's gentle tautness;
he seems to wince at pleasure,
and suffocate for privacy.

He is out of bounds now. He rejoices in man's lovely,
peculiar power to choose life and die—
when he leads his black soldiers to death,
he cannot bend his back.

On a thousand small town New England greens,
the old white churches hold their air
of sparse, sincere rebellion; frayed flags
quilt the graveyards of the Grand Army of the Republic.

The stone statues of the abstract Union Soldier
grow slimmer and younger each year—
wasp-waisted, they doze over muskets
and muse through their sideburns...

Shaw's father wanted no monument
except the ditch,
where his son's body was thrown
and lost with his 'niggers.'

The ditch is nearer.
There are no statues for the last war here;
on Boylston Street, a commercial photograph
shows Hiroshima boiling

over a Mosler Safe, the 'Rock of Ages'
that survived the blast. Space is nearer.
When I crouch to my television set,
the drained faces of Negro school-children rise like balloons.

Colonel Shaw
is riding on his bubble,
he waits
for the blessèd break.

The Aquarium is gone. Everywhere,
giant finned cars nose forward like fish;
a savage servility
slides by on grease.

1965

ALLEN GINSBERG

1926–1997

272   *A Vow*

I will haunt these States
with beard bald head

355

eyes staring out plane window,
hair hanging in Greyhound bus midnight

leaning over taxicab seat to admonish
    an angry cursing driver
      hand lifted to calm
        his outraged vehicle
that I pass with the Green Light of common law.

Common Sense, Common law, common tenderness
        & common tranquillity
our means in America to control the money munching
      war machine, bright lit industry
everywhere digesting forests & excreting soft pyramids
    of newsprint, Redwood and Ponderosa patriarchs
    silent in Meditation murdered & regurgitated as smoke,
      sawdust, screaming ceilings of Soap Opera,
      thick dead Lifes, slick Advertisements
        for Gubernatorial big guns
        burping Napalm on palm rice tropic greenery.

Dynamite in forests,
    boughs fly slow motion
      thunder down ravine,
      Helicopters roar over National Park, Mekong Swamp,
      Dynamite fire blasts thru Model Villages,
Violence screams at Police, Mayors get mad over radio,
    Drop the Bomb on Niggers!
        drop Fire on the gook China
        Frankenstein Dragon
    waving its tail over Bayonne's domed Aluminum
                oil reservoir!

I'll haunt these States all year
    gazing bleakly out train windows, blue airfield
      red TV network on evening plains,
      decoding radar Provincial editorial paper message,
      deciphering Iron Pipe laborers' curses as
      clanging hammers they raise steamshovel claws
over Puerto Rican agony lawyers' screams in slums.

11 October 1966

DENISE LEVERTOV

1923–1997

What Were They Like?

1) Did the people of Vietnam
   use lanterns of stone?
2) Did they hold ceremonies
   to reverence the opening of buds?
3) Were they inclined to quiet laughter?
4) Did they use bone and ivory,
   jade and silver, for ornament?
5) Had they an epic poem?
6) Did they distinguish between speech and singing?

1) Sir, their light hearts turned to stone.
   It is not remembered whether in gardens
   stone lanterns illumined pleasant ways.
2) Perhaps they gathered once to delight in blossom,
   but after the children were killed
   there were no more buds.
3) Sir, laughter is bitter to the burned mouth.
4) A dream ago, perhaps. Ornament is for joy.
   All the bones were charred.
5) It is not remembered. Remember,
   most were peasants; their life
   was in rice and bamboo.
   When peaceful clouds were reflected in the paddies
   and the water buffalo stepped surely along terraces,
   maybe fathers told their sons old tales.
   When bombs smashed those mirrors
   there was time only to scream.
6) There is an echo yet
   of their speech which was like a song.
   It was reported their singing resembled
   the flight of moths in moonlight.
   Who can say? It is silent now.

1967

ADRIAN MITCHELL

1932–2008

To Whom It May Concern

I was run over by the truth one day.
Ever since the accident I've walked this way
    So stick my legs in plaster
    Tell me lies about Vietnam.

Heard the alarm clock screaming with pain,
Couldn't find myself so I went back to sleep again
    So fill my ears with silver
    Stick my legs in plaster
    Tell me lies about Vietnam.

Every time I shut my eyes all I see is flames.
Made a marble phone book and I carved all the names
    So coat my eyes with butter
    Fill my ears with silver
    Stick my legs in plaster
    Tell me lies about Vietnam.

I smell something burning, hope it's just my brains.
They're only dropping peppermints and daisy-chains
    So stuff my nose with garlic
    Coat my eyes with butter
    Fill my ears with silver
    Stick my legs in plaster
    Tell me lies about Vietnam.

Where were you at the time of the crime?
Down by the Cenotaph drinking slime
    So chain my tongue with whisky
    Stuff my nose with garlic
    Coat my eyes with butter
    Fill my ears with silver
    Stick my legs in plaster
    Tell me lies about Vietnam.

ADRIAN MITCHELL

You put your bombers in, you put your conscience out,
You take the human being and you twist it all about
    So scrub my skin with women
    Chain my tongue with whisky
    Stuff my nose with garlic
    Coat my eyes with butter
    Fill my ears with silver
    Stick my legs in plaster
    Tell me lies about Vietnam.

1968

YUSEF KOMUNYAKAA

1947–

275   *Facing It*

My black face fades,
hiding inside the black granite.
I said I wouldn't
dammit: No tears.
I'm stone. I'm flesh.
My clouded reflection eyes me
like a bird of prey, the profile of night
slanted against morning. I turn
this way—the stone lets me go.
I turn that way—I'm inside
the Vietnam Veterans Memorial
again, depending on the light
to make a difference.
I go down the 58,022 names,
half-expecting to find
my own in letters like smoke.
I touch the name Andrew Johnson;
I see the booby trap's white flash.
Names shimmer on a woman's blouse
but when she walks away
the names stay on the wall.
Brushstrokes flash, a red bird's
wings cutting across my stare.

The sky. A plane in the sky.
A white vet's image floats
closer to me, then his pale eyes
look through mine. I'm a window.
He's lost his right arm
inside the stone. In the black mirror
a woman's trying to erase names:
No, she's brushing a boy's hair.

1988

276   *Starlight Scope Myopia*

Gray-blue shadows lift
shadows onto an oxcart.

Making night work for us,
the starlight scope brings
men into killing range.

The river under Vi Bridge
takes the heart away

like the Water God
riding his dragon.
Smoke-colored

Viet Cong
move under our eyelids,

lords over loneliness
winding like coral vine through
sandalwood & lotus,

inside our lowered heads
years after this scene

ends. The brain closes
down. What looks like
one step into the trees,

they're lifting crates of ammo
& sacks of rice, swaying

under their shared weight.
Caught in the infrared,
what are they saying?

Are they talking about women
or calling the Americans

beaucoup dien cai dau?
One of them is laughing.
You want to place a finger

to his lips & say "shhhh."
You try reading ghost talk

on their lips. They say
"up-up we go," lifting as one.
This one, old, bowlegged,

you feel you could reach out
& take him into your arms. You

peer down the sights of your M-16,
seeing the full moon
loaded on an oxcart.

1988

W. D. EHRHART
1948–

277   *Beautiful Wreckage*

What if I didn't shoot the old lady
running away from our patrol,
or the old man in the back of the head,
or the boy in the marketplace?

Or what if the boy—but he didn't
have a grenade, and the woman in Hue
didn't lie in the rain in a mortar pit
with seven Marines just for food,

Gaffney didn't get hit in the knee,
Ames didn't die in the river, Ski
didn't die in a medevac chopper
between Con Thien and Da Nang.

In Vietnamese, Con Thien means
place of angels. What if it really was
instead of the place of rotting sandbags,
incoming heavy artillery, rats and mud.

What if the angels were Ames and Ski,
or the lady, the man, and the boy,
and they lifted Gaffney out of the mud
and healed his shattered knee?

What if none of it happened the way I said?
Would it all be a lie?
Would the wreckage be suddenly beautiful?
Would the dead rise up and walk?

1999

BRUCE WEIGL

1949–

278
Song of Napalm
for my wife

After the storm, after the rain stopped pounding,
we stood in the doorway watching horses
walk off lazily across the pasture's hill.
We stared through the black screen,
our vision altered by the distance

so I thought I saw a mist
kicked up around their hooves when they faded
like cut-out horses
away from us.
The grass was never more blue in that light, more
scarlet; beyond the pasture
trees scraped their voices into the wind, branches
crisscrossed the sky like barbed wire
but you said they were only branches.

Okay. The storm stopped pounding.
I am trying to say this straight: for once
I was sane enough to pause and breathe
outside my wild plans and after the hard rain
I turned my back on the old curses. I believed
they swung finally away from me . . .

But still the branches are wire
and thunder is the pounding mortar,
still I close my eyes and see the girl
running from her village, napalm
stuck to her dress like jelly,
her hands reaching for the no one
who waits in waves of heat before her.

So I can keep on living,
so I can stay here beside you,
I try to imagine she runs down the road and wings
beat inside her until she rises
above the stinking jungle and her pain
eases, and your pain, and mine.

But the lie swings back again.
The lie works only as long as it takes to speak
and the girl runs only as far
as the napalm allows
until her burning tendons and crackling
muscles draw her up
into that final position
burning bodies so perfectly assume. Nothing
can change that, she is burned behind my eyes

and not your good love and not the rain-swept air
and not the jungle-green
pasture unfolding before us can deny it.

1985

JOHN BALABAN

1943–

279   *After Our War*

After our war, the dismembered bits
—all those pierced eyes, ear slivers, jaw splinters,
gouged lips, odd tibias, skin flaps, and toes—
came squinting, wobbling, jabbering back.
The genitals, of course, were the most bizarre,
inching along roads like glowworms and slugs.
The living wanted them back but good as new.
The dead, of course, had no use for them.
And the ghosts, the tens of thousands of abandoned souls
who had appeared like swamp fog in the city streets,
on the evening altars, and on doorsills of cratered homes,
also had no use for the scraps and bits
because, in their opinion, they looked good without them.
Since all things naturally return to their source,
these snags and tatters arrived, with immigrant uncertainty,
in the United States. It was almost home.
So, now, one can sometimes see a friend or a famous man talking
with an extra pair of lips glued and yammering on his cheek,
and this is why handshakes are often unpleasant,
why it is better, sometimes, not to look another in the eye,
why, at your daughter's breast thickens a hard keloidal scar.
After the war, with such Cheshire cats grinning in our trees,
will the ancient tales still tell us new truths?
Will the myriad world surrender new metaphor?
After our war, how will love speak?

1974

In Celebration of Spring

Our Asian war is over; others have begun.
Our elders, who tried to mortgage lies,
are disgraced, or dead, and already
the brokers are picking their pockets
for the keys and the credit cards.

In delta swamp in a united Vietnam,
a Marine with a bullfrog for a face,
rots in equatorial heat. An eel
slides through the cage of his bared ribs.
At night, on the old battlefield, ghosts,
like patches of fog, lurk into villages
to maunder on doorsills of cratered homes,
while all across the U.S.A.
the wounded walk about and wonder where to go.

And today, in the simmer of lyric sunlight,
the chrysalis pulses in its mushy cocoon,
under the bark on a gnarled root of an elm.
In the brilliant creek, a minnow flashes
delirious with gnats. The turtle's heart
quickens its raps in the warm bank sludge.
As she chases a frisbee spinning in sunlight,
a girl's breasts bounce full and strong;
a boy's stomach, as he turns, is flat and strong.

Swear by the locust, by dragonflies on ferns,
by the minnow's flash, the tremble of a breast,
by the new earth spongy under our feet;
that as we grow old, we will not grow evil,
that although our garden seeps with sewage,
and our elders think it's up for auction—swear
by this dazzle that does not wish to leave us—
that we will be keepers of a garden, nonetheless.

1997

NGO VINH LONG

1944–

281   *Untitled*

On this land
   Where each blade of grass is human hair
Each foot of soil is human flesh
   Where it rains blood
Hails bones
   Life must flower

1970

JAMES FENTON

1949–

282   *Dead Soldiers*

When His Excellency Prince Norodom Chantaraingsey
Invited me to lunch on the battlefield
I was glad of my white suit for the first time that day.
They lived well, the mad Norodoms, they had style.
The brandy and the soda arrived in crates.
Bricks of ice, tied around with raffia,
Dripped from the orderlies' handlebars.

And I remember the dazzling tablecloth
As the APCs fanned out along the road,
The dishes piled high with frogs' legs,
Pregnant turtles, their eggs boiled in the carapace,
Marsh irises in fish sauce
And inflorescence of a banana salad.

On every bottle, Napoleon Bonaparte
Pleaded for the authenticity of the spirit.
They called the empties Dead Soldiers
And rejoiced to see them pile up at our feet.

Each diner was attended by one of the other ranks
Whirling a table-napkin to keep off the flies.
It was like eating between rows of morris dancers—
Only they didn't kick.

On my left sat the prince;
On my right, his drunken aide.
The frogs' thighs leapt into the sad purple face
Like fish to the sound of a Chinese flute.
I wanted to talk to the prince. I wish now
I had collared his aide, who was Saloth Sar's brother.
We treated him as the club bore. He was always
Boasting of his connections, boasting with a head-shake
Or by pronouncing of some doubtful phrase.
And well might he boast. Saloth Sar, for instance,
Was Pol Pot's real name. The APCs
Fired into the sugar palms but met no resistance.

In a diary, I refer to Pol Pot's brother as the Jockey Cap.
A few weeks later, I find him 'in good form
And very skeptical about Chantaraingsey.'
'But one eats well there,' I remark.
'So one should,' says the Jockey Cap:
'The tiger always eats well,
It eats the raw flesh of the deer,
And Chantaraingsey was born in the year of the tiger.
So, did they show you the things they do
With the young refugee girls?'

And he tells me how he will one day give me the gen.
He will tell me how the prince financed the casino
And how the casino brought Lon Nol to power.
He will tell me this.
He will tell me all these things.
All I must do is drink and listen.

In those days, I thought that when the game was up
The prince would be far, far away—

In a limestone faubourg, on the promenade at Nice,
Reduced in circumstances but well enough provided for.
In Paris, he would hardly require his private army.
The Jockey Cap might suffice for café warfare,
And matchboxes for APCs.

But we were always wrong in these predictions.
It was a family war. Whatever happened,
The principals were obliged to attend its issue.
A few were cajoled into leaving, a few were expelled,
And there were villains enough, but none of them
Slipped away with the swag.

For the prince was fighting Sihanouk, his nephew,
And the Jockey Cap was ranged against his brother
Of whom I remember nothing more
Than an obscure reputation for virtue.
I have been told that the prince is still fighting
Somewhere in the Cardamoms or the Elephant Mountains.
But I doubt that the Jockey Cap would have survived his good
    connections.
I think the lunches would have done for him—
Either the lunches or the dead soldiers.

1982

SEAMUS HEANEY

1939–2013

283   *Requiem for the Croppies*

The pockets of our great coats full of barley—
No kitchens on the run, no striking camp—
We moved quick and sudden in our own country.
The priest lay behind ditches with the tramp.
A people, hardly marching—on the hike—
We found new tactics happening each day:
We'd cut through reins and rider with the pike

And stampede cattle into infantry,
Then retreat through hedges where cavalry must be thrown.
Until, on Vinegar Hill, the fatal conclave.
Terraced thousands died, shaking scythes at cannon.
The hillside blushed, soaked in our broken wave.
They buried us without shroud or coffin
And in August the barley grew up out of the grave.

1969

284   *Whatever You Say Say Nothing*

I

I'm writing just after an encounter
With an English journalist in search of 'views
On the Irish thing'. I'm back in winter
Quarters where bad news is no longer news,

Where media-men and stringers sniff and point,
Where zoom lenses, recorders and coiled leads
Litter the hotels. The times are out of joint
But I incline as much to rosary beads

As to the jottings and analyses
Of politicians and newspapermen
Who've scribbled down the long campaign from gas
And protest to gelignite and sten,

Who proved upon their pulses 'escalate',
'Backlash' and 'crack down', 'the provisional wing',
'Polarization' and 'long-standing hate'.
Yet I live here, I live here too, I sing,

Expertly civil tongued with civil neighbours
On the high wires of first wireless reports,
Sucking the fake taste, the stony flavours
Of those sanctioned, old, elaborate retorts:

'Oh, it's disgraceful, surely, I agree,'
'Where's it going to end?' 'It's getting worse.'

'They're murderers.' 'Internment, understandably . . . '
The 'voice of sanity' is getting hoarse.

II

Men die at hand. In blasted street and home
The gelignite's a common sound effect:
As the man said when Celtic won, 'The Pope of Rome
's a happy man this night.' His flock suspect

In their deepest heart of hearts the heretic
Has come at last to heel and to the stake.
We tremble near the flames but want no truck
With the actual firing. We're on the make

As ever. Long sucking the hind tit
Cold as a witch's and as hard to swallow
Still leaves us fork-tongued on the border bit:
The liberal papist note sounds hollow

When amplified and mixed in with the bangs
That shake all hearts and windows day and night.
(It's tempting here to rhyme on 'labour pangs'
And diagnose a rebirth in our plight

But that would be to ignore other symptoms.
Last night you didn't need a stethoscope
To hear the eructation of Orange drums
Allergic equally to Pearse and Pope.)

On all sides 'little platoons' are mustering—
The phrase is Cruise O'Brien's via that great
Backlash, Burke—while I sit here with a pestering
Drouth for words at once both gaff and bait

To lure the tribal shoals to epigram
And order. I believe any of us
Could draw the line through bigotry and sham
Given the right line, *aere perennius.*

III

'Religion's never mentioned here,' of course.
'You know them by their eyes,' and hold your tongue.
'One side's as bad as the other,' never worse.
Christ, it's near time that some small leak was sprung

In the great dykes the Dutchman made
To dam the dangerous tide that followed Seamus.
Yet for all this art and sedentary trade
I am incapable. The famous

Northern reticence, the tight gag of place
And times: yes, yes. Of the 'wee six' I sing
Where to be saved you only must save face
And whatever you say, you say nothing.

Smoke-signals are loud-mouthed compared with us:
Manoeuvrings to find out name and school,
Subtle discrimination by addresses
With hardly an exception to the rule

That Norman, Ken and Sidney signalled Prod
And Seamus (call me Sean) was sure-fire Pape.
O land of password, handgrip, wink and nod,
Of open minds as open as a trap,

Where tongues lie coiled, as under flames lie wicks,
Where half of us, as in a wooden horse
Were cabin'd and confined like wily Greeks,
Besieged within the siege, whispering morse.

IV

This morning from a dewy motorway
I saw the new camp for the internees:
A bomb had left a crater of fresh clay
In the roadside, and over in the trees

Machine-gun posts defined a real stockade.
There was that white mist you get on a low ground
And it was déjà-vu, some film made
Of Stalag 17, a bad dream with no sound.

Is there a life before death? That's chalked up
In Ballymurphy. Competence with pain,
Coherent miseries, a bit and sup,
We hug our little destiny again.

1975

285   *The Strand at Lough Beg*
         *In memory of Colum McCartney**

All round this little island, on the strand
Far down below there, where the breakers strive,
Grow the tall rushes from the oozy sand.
                    Dante, *Purgatorio*, i. 100–3

Leaving the white glow of filling stations
And a few lonely streetlamps among fields
You climbed the hills towards Newtownhamilton
Past the Fews Forest, out beneath the stars—
Along that road, a high, bare pilgrim's track
Where Sweeney fled before the bloodied heads,
Goat-beards and dogs' eyes in a demon pack
Blazing out of the ground, snapping and squealing.
What blazed ahead of you? A faked road block?
The red lamp swung, the sudden brakes and stalling
Engine, voices, heads hooded and the cold-nosed gun?
Or in your driving mirror, tailing headlights
That pulled out suddenly and flagged you down
Where you weren't known and far from what you knew:
The lowland clays and waters of Lough Beg,
Church Island's spire, its soft treeline of yew.

There you used hear guns fired behind the house
Long before rising time, when duck shooters
Haunted the marigolds and bulrushes,

* Colum McCartney, a relative of the author, was the victim of a random sectarian
killing in the late summer of 1975.
    Sweeney is the hero of a Middle Irish prose and poem sequence, one part of which
takes place in Fews in Co. Armagh. [SH]

But still were scared to find spent cartridges,
Acrid, brassy, genital, ejected,
On your way across the strand to fetch the cows.
For you and yours and yours and mine fought shy,
Spoke an old language of conspirators
And could not crack the whip or seize the day:
Big-voiced scullions, herders, feelers round
Haycocks and hindquarters, talkers in byres,
Slow arbitrators of the burial ground.
Across that strand of yours the cattle graze
Up to their bellies in an early mist
And now they turn their unbewildered gaze
To where we work our way through squeaking sedge
Drowning in dew. Like a dull blade with its edge
Honed bright, Lough Beg half shines under the haze.
I turn because the sweeping of your feet
Has stopped behind me, to find you on your knees
With blood and roadside muck in your hair and eyes,
Then kneel in front of you in brimming grass
And gather up cold handfuls of the dew
To wash you, cousin. I dab you clean with moss
Fine as the drizzle out of a low cloud.
I lift you under the arms and lay you flat.
With rushes that shoot green again, I plait
Green scapulars to wear over your shroud.

1979

CAROLYN FORCHÉ

1951–

286   *The Colonel*

What you have heard is true. I was in his house. His wife carried a tray
of coffee and sugar. His daughter filed her nails, his son went out for
the night. There were daily papers, pet dogs, a pistol on the cushion
beside him. The moon swung bare on its black cord over the house. On
the television was a cop show. It was in English. Broken bottles were

embedded in the walls around the house to scoop the kneecaps from a man's legs or cut his hands to lace. On the windows there were gratings like those in liquor stores. We had dinner, rack of lamb, good wine, a gold bell was on the table for calling the maid. The maid brought green mangoes, salt, a type of bread. I was asked how I enjoyed the country. There was a brief commercial in Spanish. His wife took everything away. There was some talk then of how difficult it had become to govern. The parrot said hello on the terrace. The colonel told it to shut up, and pushed himself from the table. My friend said to me with his eyes: say nothing. The colonel returned with a sack used to bring groceries home. He spilled many human ears on the table. They were like dried peach halves. There is no other way to say this. He took one of them in his hands, shook it in our faces, dropped it into a water glass. It came alive there. I am tired of fooling around he said. As for the rights of anyone, tell your people they can go fuck themselves. He swept the ears to the floor with his arm and held the last of his wine in the air. Something for your poetry, no? he said. Some of the ears on the floor caught this scrap of his voice. Some of the ears on the floor were pressed to the ground.

May 1978

DAVID HARSENT

1942–

287   *Snapshots (1)*

Troopers dead in a trench and a river of rats
Topers dead in a bar and a flood of reflections
Lovers dead in bed and a shift of maggots
Snipers dead in the trees and a cowl of crows
Travellers dead on the bridge and a gaggle of gawpers
Oldsters dead on a porch and a downpour of flies
Deserters dead in a ditch and a raft of chiggers
Foragers dead in a field and a jostle of foxes
Children dead at their desks and a month of Sundays

2005

288   *The Piss-pail*

We were dug in, just light of an apple orchard. You got
a faint scent from the whin until the dew burned off, and
     bird-
song out of the branches, or else a bullet.
One went up for a look-see, then another, then a third
as the trickster in the tree got off a shot
and clipped, as if he'd meant to, the piss-pail that stood
on the lip of the trench, which rose in the air and flipped
     like a lucky bet
once, then again, to come down flush over the third
     man's head
who buckled and blacked out, thinking he'd been hit.

We laid him under a flag. Kyrie eleison, we sang,
Christi eleison, until the earthworks rang,
and he opened his eyes to a world of light
such as he'd never seen, the cryptic white-on-white
of clouds and sky, white of gunsmoke, white of the
     trench walls,
whites of our eyes as we knelt and called to bring him
     back,
of his wife's shift, her steady smile, the slack
of her breasts as she stooped to gather windfalls.

2005

PETER WYTON

1944–

289   *Unmentioned in Dispatches*

Some of them never come home to fanfares,
they dump their kitbags down at the door,
kiss their wives and let their children
wrestle them down to the kitchen floor,
switch the telly on, pour out a whiskey,
search for the local football score.

Some of them skip the quayside welcome,
dodge the bunting and cannonade,
make their landfall in silent harbours,
nod to the coastguard, but evade
the searchlight of public scrutiny
like those engaged in the smuggling trade.

Some of them land at lonely airfields
far removed from the celebration,
hang their flying gear in a locker,
cadge a lift to the railway station,
make for home and take for granted
the short-lived thanks of a grateful nation.

Some of them miss the royal salute,
the victory parade along the Mall,
the fly-past, the ships in formation passing
the cheering crowds on the harbour wall.
Remembered only by friends and relatives,
some of them never come home at all.

Iraq, 1991

RICHARD WILBUR

1921–

290   *Advice to a Prophet*

When you come, as you soon must, to the streets of our city,
Mad-eyed from stating the obvious,
Not proclaiming our fall but begging us
In God's name to have self-pity,

Spare us all word of the weapons, their force and range,
The long numbers that rocket the mind;
Our slow, unreckoning hearts will be left behind,
Unable to fear what is too strange.

Nor shall you scare us with talk of the death of the race.
How should we dream of this place without us?—
The sun mere fire, the leaves untroubled about us,
A stone look on the stone's face?

Speak of the world's own change. Though we cannot conceive
Of an undreamt thing, we know to our cost
How the dreamt cloud crumbles, the vines are blackened by frost,
How the view alters. We could believe,

If you told us so, that the white-tailed deer will slip
Into perfect shade, grown perfectly shy,
The lark avoid the reaches of our eye,
The jack-pine lose its knuckled grip

On the cold ledge, and every torrent burn
As Xanthus once, its gliding trout
Stunned in a twinkling. What should we be without
The dolphin's arc, the dove's return,

These things in which we have seen ourselves and spoken?
Ask us, prophet, how we shall call
Our natures forth when that live tongue is all
Dispelled, that glass obscured or broken

In which we have said the rose of our love and the clean
Horse of our courage, in which beheld
The singing locust of the soul unshelled,
And all we mean or wish to mean.

Ask us, ask us whether with the worldless rose
Our hearts shall fail us; come demanding
Whether there shall be lofty or long standing
When the bronze annals of the oak-tree close.

1961

WILLIAM STAFFORD
1914–1993

291 *At the Bomb Testing Site*

At noon in the desert a panting lizard
waited for history, its elbows tense,
watching the curve of a particular road
as if something might happen.

It was looking at something farther off
than people could see, an important scene
acted in stone for little selves
at the flute end of consequences.

There was just a continent without much on it
under a sky that never cared less.
Ready for a change, the elbows waited.
The hands gripped hard on the desert.

1960

PETER PORTER
1929–2010

292 *Your Attention Please*

The Polar DEW has just warned that
A nuclear rocket strike of
At least one thousand megatons
Has been launched by the enemy
Directly at our major cities.
This announcement will take
Two and a quarter minutes to make,
You therefore have a further
Eight and a quarter minutes
To comply with the shelter

Requirements published in the Civil
Defence Code—section Atomic Attack.
A specially shortened Mass
Will be broadcast at the end
Of this announcement—
Protestant and Jewish services
Will begin simultaneously—
Select your wavelength immediately
According to instructions
In the Defence Code. Do not
Take well-loved pets (including birds)
Into your shelter—they will consume
Fresh air. Leave the old and bed-
ridden, you can do nothing for them.
Remember to press the sealing
Switch when everyone is in
The shelter. Set the radiation
Aerial, turn on the geiger barometer.
Turn off your Television now.
Turn off your radio immediately
The Services end. At the same time
Secure explosion plugs in the ears
Of each member of your family. Take
Down your plasma flasks. Give your children
The pills marked one and two
In the C.D. green container, then put
Them to bed. Do not break
The inside airlock seals until
The radiation All Clear shows
(Watch for the cuckoo in your
Perspex panel), or your District
Touring Doctor rings your bell.
If before this, your air becomes
Exhausted or if any of your family
Is critically injured, administer
The capsules marked 'Valley Forge'
(Red pocket in No. 1 Survival Kit)
For painless death. (Catholics
Will have been instructed by their priests
What to do in this eventuality.)
This announcement is ending. Our President
Has already given order for
Massive retaliation—it will be

Decisive. Some of us may die.
Remember, statistically
It is not likely to be you.
All flags are flying fully dressed
On Government buildings—the sun is shining.
Death is the least we have to fear.
We are all in the hands of God,
Whatever happens happens by His Will.
Now go quickly to your shelters.

1962

NOTES AND REFERENCES

TEXTS are based on the author's final version, with a few exceptions noted below. Spelling and punctuation have been modernized except for the extract from Spenser's *Astrophel*, whose spelling is part of its deliberate archaism.

The sources of passages excerpted from longer works are set out below. No references are given for poems by authors whose collected poems are easily available, since these can be found by consulting first-line indexes. The sources of poems in copyright may be found in the section of Acknowledgements (pp. 385–395).

1, 2. The Book of Exodus, 15: 1–18, and the Second Book of Samuel, 1: 19–27.

3. Homer. *The Iliad*, trans. Robert Fitzgerald (1974), xvi, ll. 666–83; xxii, ll. 309–515.

4. Simonides. 'Thermopylae', William Tirebuck, ed., *The Poetical Works of Bowles, Lamb and Hartley Coleridge* (1887).

5. Anonymous. 'Hymn to the Fallen', trans. Arthur Waley, *Chinese Poems* (1946, fifth impression 1976).

6. Virgil. *The Aeneid*, trans. Allen Mandelbaum (1971), xii, ll. 1178–1271.

7. Horace. *The Odes*, trans. James Michie (1963), ii. 7 and iii. 2.

8. Aneirin. 'The Gododdin', trans. Joseph P. Clancy, *Medieval Welsh Poems* (2003), stanzas vi–xi and xxi.

9. Rihaku. 'Lament of the Frontier Guard', trans. Ezra Pound, *Personae: Collected Poems* (1926, rev. 1949).

10, 12. Anonymous. 'The Finnesburh Fragment' and 'The Battle of Maldon', trans. Kevin Crossley-Holland and Bruce Mitchell, *The Battle of Maldon and other Old English Poems* (1965).

13. Anonymous. *The Song of Roland*, trans. Dorothy L. Sayers (1957), sections 161–3.

14. Anonymous. 'The Lament of Maev Leith-Dherg', Stopford A. Brook and T. W. Rolleston, eds., *A Treasury of Irish Poetry in the English Tongue* (1932).

16. Geoffrey Chaucer. 'The Knight's Tale', trans. John Dryden, *Fables, Ancient and Modern* (1700), ll. 1967–2038.

18. Edmund Spenser. *Astrophel, A Pastorall Elegie Upon the Death of the Most Noble and Valorous Knight, Sir Philip Sidney*, ll. 85–138.

19. Samuel Daniel. *The Civil Wars between the Two Houses of Lancaster and York*, bk. 8, stanzas 14–22.

21. George Gascoigne. 'The Fruits of War', stanzas 155–72.

22. George Peele. 'Farewell to Arms', *Polyhymnia* (1590).

28. John Milton. *Paradise Lost*, bk. 6, ll. 296–353.

29. Charles Sackville, Earl of Dorset. 'Song. Written at Sea in the First Dutch War (1665), the night before an Engagement', *Works* (1749).

30. John Dryden. 'Annus Mirabilis', stanzas 186–202.

31. Daniel Defoe. 'The Spanish Descent'. Text from Frank H. Ellis, ed., *Anthology of Poems on Affairs of State: Augustan Satirical Verse, 1660–1714*, vol. 6 (1970), ll. 269–344.

32. Joseph Addison. 'The Campaign: A Poem to His Grace the Duke of Marlborough', ll. 283–302.

34. James Thomson. 'Rule Brittania!' From the masque, *Alfred* (1740) by James Thomson and David Mallet. This song is probably, but not certainly, by Thomson.

35. Samuel Johnson. 'The Vanity of Human Wishes', ll. 191–222.

36. John Scott of Amwell. 'The Drum', *Poetical Works* (1782).

44. Percy Bysshe Shelley. *The Revolt of Islam*, canto 5, stanzas i–xiii.

45. Charles Wolfe. 'The Burial of Sir John Moore after Corunna'. Text from *Newry Telegraph*, 19 April 1817.

46. Joel Barlow. 'Advice to a Raven in Russia'. Text from Leon Howard, 'Joel Barlow and Napoleon', *The Huntington Library Quarterly*, vol. 2, no. 1, October 1938, pp. 37–51.

47. Adam Mickiewicz. 'The Year 1812', trans. Donald Davie, *The Forests of Lithuania* (1959).

48. Victor Hugo. 'Russia 1812', trans. Robert Lowell, *Imitations* (1961).

49. Fyodor Tyutchev. 'At Vshchizh', trans. Charles Tomlinson, *Selected Poems 1951–1974* (1978).

51. Thomas Hardy. *The Dynasts*, part 3, act VI, scene viii.

53, 54. Lord Byron. *Childe Harold's Pilgrimage*, canto 3, stanzas xxi–xxviii; and *Don Juan*, canto 7, stanzas xli and lxxix–lxxxvii.

56. Lord Macaulay. 'Horatius', stanzas xlii–lxiv.

57. William Edmonstoune Aytoun. 'Edinburgh after Flodden', sections x and xi.

58. Matthew Arnold. 'Sohrab and Rustum', ll. 495–539 and 827–92.

61. Alfred, Lord Tennyson. 'Maud', part III, vi.

62. William Makepeace Thackeray. 'The Due of the Dead'. Text from *Punch*, vol. xxvii (July–December 1854), p. 173.

77. James Russell Lowell. 'Ode Recited at the Harvard Commemoration', sections i and x–xi.

79. Rainer Maria Rilke. 'Last Evening', trans. J. B. Leishman: R. M. Rilke, *Selected Works*, vol. ii (1960).

80. Arthur Rimbaud. 'Eighteen-Seventy', trans. Robert Lowell, *Imitations* (1961), sections i–iii, vii–viii.

96. T. W. H. Crosland. 'Slain'. Text from M. van Wyk Smith, *Drummer Hodge. The Poetry of the Anglo-Boer War, 1899–1902* (1978), pp. 113–14.

97. Edgar Wallace. 'War', *Writ in Barracks* (1900).

100. Herbert Asquith. 'The Volunteer', *Poems 1912–33* (1933).

108. Julian Grenfell. 'Into Battle'. Text from *The Times*, 27 May 1915.

109. John McCrae. 'In Flanders Fields', *In Flanders Fields and other poems*. With an essay in character by Sir Andrew Macphail (1919).

118. Guillaume Apollinaire. 'Calligram, 15 May 1915', trans. O. Bernard, *Guillaume Apollinaire: Selected Poems* (1965).

119. Benjamin Péret. 'Little Song of the Maimed', trans. David Gascoyne, *Collected Verse Translations* (1970).

123. W. B. Yeats. 'Reprisals'. Text from Peter Allt and Russell K. Alspach, eds., *The Variorum Edition of the Poems of W. B. Yeats* (1957).

148. Wilfred Owen. 'Dulce et Decorum Est'. Compare Horace (I), p. 14 below.

153. Wilfred Owen. 'Strange Meeting'. Compare Shelley, p. 86 below.

173. David Jones. *In Parenthesis*, part 7, pp. 162–6.

175. Ezra Pound. 'Hugh Selwyn Mauberley', sections iv and v.

190. Louis MacNeice. *Autumn Journal*, section vi.

195. Anonymous. 'Eyes of men running, falling, screaming'. Text from Valentine Cunningham, ed., *The Penguin Book of Spanish Civil War Verse* (1980).

197. Sylvia Townsend Warner. 'Benicasim'. Text from Valentine Cunningham, ed., *The Penguin Book of Spanish Civil War Verse* (1980).

203. Louis Aragon. 'The Lilacs and the Roses', trans. Louis MacNeice, *Collected Poems* (2007).

219, 221. Sidney Keyes. 'The Foreign Gate', section iv; 'The Wilderness', sections i–ii.

226. Keith Douglas. 'Aristocrats'. I prefer this title and text, from Desmond Graham, ed., *The Complete Poems of Keith Douglas* (1978), p. 139, to the later version, entitled 'Sportsmen', on p. 110.

251. Ephim Fogel. 'Shipment to Maidanek'. Text from Edwin Seaver, ed., *Cross Section 1945. A Collection of New American Writings* (1945).

252. W. H. Auden. 'Sonnets from China', xii.

269. Andrei Voznesensky. 'I am Goya', trans. Stanley Kunitz. Text from Patricia Blake and Max Hayward, eds., *Antiworlds and the Fifth Ace. Poetry by Andrei Voznesensky* (1966).

ACKNOWLEDGEMENTS

The editor and publishers gratefully acknowledge permission to use copyright material in this book as follows:

Richard Aldington: 'Battlefield' from *Collected Poems 1915–1923* (Allen & Unwin, 1933), copyright © The Estate of Richard Aldington, reprinted by permission of the Estate of Richard Aldington c/o Rosica Colin Ltd, London.

Kenneth Allott: 'Prize for Good Conduct' from *Collected Poems* (Secker & Warburg, 1975); copyright holder not traced.

Aneirin: stanzas vi, viii, ix, x, xi and xxi from 'The Goddodin': see J P Clancy.

Anonymous Spanish poem by an International Brigadier c.1937: see Valentine Cunningham.

Guillaume Apollinaire translated by Oliver Bernard: 'Calligram for Madelaine (15 May 1915)' from *Guillaume Apollinaire: Selected Poems* (Anvil, 2004), translation copyright © Oliver Bernard 1965, 1986, reprinted by permission of Kate Bernard, Executor for the Estate of Oliver Bernard, and Anvil Press Poetry.

Louis Aragon: 'The Lilacs and the Roses': see Louis MacNeice.

Herbert Asquith: 'The Volunteer' from *Poems 1912–1933* (Sidgwick & Jackson, 1934); copyright holder not traced.

W H Auden: 'Spain 1937', Stanza xii from 'Sonnets from China, and 'The Shield of Achilles' from *Collected Poems* (Faber, 2007), reprinted by permission of Curtis Brown Ltd, New York, for the Estate of W H Auden and of Random House LLC.

John Balaban: 'After Our War' and 'In Celebration of Spring' from *Locusts at the Edge of Summer: New and Selected Poems* (Copper Canyon, 2003), copyright © John Balaban 1997, reprinted by permission of The Permissions Company, Inc, on behalf of Copper Canyon Press. www.coppercanyonpress.org.

John Betjeman: 'In Memory of Basil, Marquess of Dufferin and Ava' from *Collected Poems* (John Murray, 2006), copyright © John Betjeman, reprinted by permission of Estate of John Betjeman c/o Aitken Alexander Associates.

John Peale Bishop: 'In the Dordogne' from *Now With His Love* (Charles Scribners Sons, 1933) and *Selected Poems* (1941): copyright holder not traced.

Edmund Blunden: 'Two Voices', 'The Zonnebeke Road', 'Report on Experience', 'Vlamertinghe: Passing the Chateau, July 1917' and '1916 seen from 1921' from *Poems of Many Years* (Wm Collins, 1957), reprinted by permission of David Higham Associates.

ACKNOWLEDGEMENTS

Norman Cameron: 'Green, Green is El Aghir' from *Collected Poems and Selected Translations* edited by Warren Hope and Jonathan Barker (Anvil, 1990, 2011), reprinted by permission of Anvil Press Poetry.

May Wedderburn Cannan: 'Rouen', 'August 1914' and ' After the War' from *In War Time* (Basil Blackwell, 1917), reprinted by permission of Clara Abrahams for the Estate of May Wedderburn Cannan.

Joseph P Clancy: translation of Aneirin: stanzas vi, viii, ix, x, xi and xxi from 'The Goddodin' in *Medieval Welsh Poems* (Four Courts Press, Dublin, 2003), reprinted by permission of Joseph P Clancy.

Charles Causley: 'Armistice Day' and 'At The British War Cemetery, Bayeux' from *Union Street* (Hart-Davis, 1957) and *Collected Poems 1951–2000* (Macmillan, 2000), reprinted by permission of David Higham Associates.

Kevin Crossley-Holland: 'The Finnesburgh Fragment' and 'The Battle of Maldon' from *The Battle of Maldon and Other Old English Poems* (Macmillan, 1965), copyright © Kevin Crossley-Holland 1965, reprinted by permission of the author c/o Rogers Coleridge & White Ltd, 20 Powis Mews, London W11 1JN.

E E Cummings: 'My sweet old etcetera' and 'next to of course god america i', copyright © 1926, 1954, © 1991 by the Trustees for E E Cummings Trust, copyright © 1985 by George James Firmage; and 'i sing of Olaf glad and big' copyright © 1931, © 1959, 1991 by the Trustees for E E Cummings Trust, copyright © 1979 by George James Firmage; all from *Complete Poems 1904–1962* edited by George J Firmage (W W Norton, 1994), reprinted by permission of Liveright Publishing Corporation.

Valentine Cunningham: translation of anonymous Spanish poem 'Eyes of men running...' from *The Penguin Book of Spanish Civil War Verse* edited by Valentine Cunningham (Penguin Poets, 1980), reprinted by permission of Peters Fraser & Dunlop (www.petersfraserdunlop.com) on behalf of Valentine Cunningham.

R N Currey: 'Unseen Fire' from *This Other Planet* (Routledge & Kegan Paul, 1945), reprinted by permission of the Executors of the Literary Estate of R N Currey.

Elizabeth Daryush: 'Subalterns' from *The Collected Poems of Elizabeth Daryush* (Carcanet, 1976) *Selected Poems* (Carcanet, 1972), reprinted by permission of Carcanet Press Ltd.

Donald Davie: 'The Year 1812', translation of 'Pan Tadeusz' by Adam Mickiewicz from *Collected Poems 1922–1995* (Carcanet, 1990), reprinted by permission of Carcanet Press Ltd.

ACKNOWLEDGEMENTS

C Day-Lewis: 'The Stand-To' and 'Where Are All the War Poets?' from *Collected Poems 1954* (Jonathan Cape, 1970), reprinted by permission of The Random House Group Ltd.

Paul Dehn: 'St Aubin D'Aubigné' first published in *The Day's Alarm* (Hamish Hamilton, 1949), from *The Fern and the Rock: Collected Poems 1935–1965* (Hamish Hamilton, 1965), reprinted by permission of Berlin Associates Ltd on behalf of the Executors of J M Bernard.

James Dickey: 'The Firebombing', © James Dickey 1964, 1967, first published in *Poetry* 1964, and in *Poems 1957–1967* (Wesleyan University Press, 1967), from *The Complete Poems of James Dickey* edited by Ward Briggs (University of South Carolina Press, 2013), reprinted by permission of Wesleyan University Press,

Emily Dickinson: 'My Portion is Defeat today ' (J639) and 'My Triumph lasted till the Drums' (J1227) from *The Complete Poems of Emily Dickinson* edited by Thomas H Johnson (The Belknap Press, 1983), copyright © 1951, 1955, 1979, 1983 by the President and Fellows of Harvard College, reprinted by permission of the publishers and the Trustees of Amherst College.

Hilda Doolittle (HD): lines from 'The Walls Do Not Fall' from *Collected Poems of H D 1912–1944* edited by Louis L Martz (Carcanet, 1984), copyright © 1973 by Norman Holmes Pearson, copyright © The Estate of Hilda Doolittle 1982, reprinted by permission of the publishers, Carcanet Press Ltd and New Directions Publishing Corp.

Keith Douglas: 'John Anderson', 'Gallantry', 'Vergissmeinicht', and 'Aristocrats' from *The Complete Poems of Keith Douglas* edited by Desmond Graham (Faber, 2011), reprinted by permission of Faber & Faber Ltd and of Desmond Graham, the Executor of the Estate of Keith Douglas.

Douglas Dunn: 'War Blinded' first published in *St Kilda's Parliament* (Faber, 1981), from *Selected Poems 1964–2000* (Faber, 2003), reprinted by permission of Faber & Faber Ltd and United Agents on behalf of Douglas Dunn.

Richard Eberhart: 'The Fury of Aerial Bombardment' first published in *Collected Poems 1930–1976* (Chatto & Windus, 1976) from *Collected Poems: 1930–1986* (OUP, 1988), reprinted by permission of Oxford University Press.

W D Ehrhart: 'Beautiful Wreckage' from *Beautiful Wreckage: New and Selected Poems* (Adastra Press, 1999), copyright © W D Ehrhart 1999, reprinted by permission of the publisher, Adastra Press.

T S Eliot: 'Triumphal March' from *Collected Poems 1909–1962* (Faber, 1963), copyright © Houghton Mifflin Harcourt Publishing Company 1936, © renewed T S Eliot 1964, reprinted by permission of the publishers, Faber & Faber Ltd and Houghton Mifflin Harcourt Publishing Company.

ACKNOWLEDGEMENTS

James Fenton: 'Dead Soldiers' from *The Memory of War* (Salamander Press, 1982), reprinted by permission of United Agents on behalf of James Fenton.

Robert Fitzgerald: 'Book 22' from *The Iliad of Homer* (OUP, 1998), translation copyright © Robert Fitzgerald 1998, reprinted by permission of The heirs of Robert Fitzgerald.

Ephim Fogel: 'Shipment to Maidanek', copyright © Ephim Fogel 1945, first published in *Cross Section, 1945: An Anthology of New American Writing* edited by Edwin Seaver (L B Fischer, 1945), reprinted by permission of Daniel Mark Fogel, the Literary Executor of the Estate of Ephim Fogel.

Carolyn Forché: 'The Colonel', first published in *Women's International Resource Exchange* (May, 1978), from *The Country Between Us* (Jonathan Cape, 1983/ Harper & Row, 1981), copyright © Carolyn Forché 1981, reprinted by permission of the author, c/o William Morris Endeavor Entertainment LLC and HarperCollins Publishers, USA.

Robert Frost: 'Range-Finding' from *The Poetry of Robert Frost* edited by Edward Connery Lathem (Jonathan Cape, 1972), copyright © 1916, 1969 by Henry Holt & Company LLC, copyright © Robert Frost 1944, reprinted by permission of the publishers, The Random House Group Ltd and Henry Holt & Company LLC. All rights reserved.

Roy Fuller: 'The Middle of a War' from *Selected Poems* (Carcanet, 2012), reprinted by permission of Carcanet Press Ltd.

David Gascoyne: 'Ecce Homo', 'Spring MCMXL' from *Collected Poems* (OUP, 1965), and 'Little Song of the Maimed' translated from the French by Benjamin Peret in *Selected Verse Translations* edited by Alan Clodd and Robin Skelton (Enitharmon, 1996), reprinted by permission of Enitharmon Press Ltd for the Estate of David Gascoyne.

Allen Ginsberg: 'A Vow' from *Collected Poems 1947–1997* (HarperCollins, 2006), copyright © Allen Ginsberg, 1984, 1997, copyright © The Allen Ginsberg Trust 2006, reprinted by permission of The Wylie Agency (UK) Ltd and HarperCollins Publishers, USA.

Robert Graves: 'The Dead Fox Hunter', 'The Legion', Sergeant-Major Money', 'Recalling War' and 'The Persian Version' from *The Complete Poems* (Carcanet, 2000), reprinted by permission of Carcanet Press Ltd and United Agents on behalf of the Trustees of the Robert Graves Copyright Trust.

Thom Gunn: 'Claus von Staffenberg' first published in *My Sad Captains, and other Poems* (Faber, 1961), copyright © Thom Gunn 1961, from *Collected Poems* (Faber, 1993), reprinted by permission of the publishers, Faber & Faber Ltd and Farrar, Straus & Giroux, LLC.

ACKNOWLEDGEMENTS

David Harsent: 'Snapshots (1)' and 'The Piss-pail' from *Legion* (Faber, 2005), copyright © David Harsent 2005, reprinted by permission of the publishers, Faber & Faber Ltd.

Seamus Heaney: 'Requiem for the Croppies', and 'Whatever You Say Say Nothing' first published in *Selected Poems 1965–1975* (Faber, 1980); 'The Strand at Lough Beg' first published in *Field Work* (Faber, 1979); from *Opened Ground: Selected Poems 1966–1996* (Faber 1998), copyright © Seamus Heaney 1998, reprinted by permission of the publishers, Faber & Faber Ltd and Farrar, Straus & Giroux, LLC.

Anthony Hecht: 'More Light! More Light!' first published in *The Hard Hours* (OUP, 1967), from *Collected Earlier Poems* (Knopf, 1990), copyright © Anthony E Hecht 1990, reprinted by permission of Alfred A Knopf, an imprint of the Knopf Doubleday Publishing Group, a division of Random House LLC, and 'The Book of Yolek' from *Collected Later Poems* (Knopf, 2003/Waywiser, 2004), copyright © Anthony E Hecht 2003, reprinted by permission of the publishers, The Waywiser Press and Alfred A Knopf, an imprint of the Knopf Doubleday Publishing Group, a division of Random House LLC.

Geoffrey Hill: 'September Song', copyright © Geoffrey Hill 1968, first published in *King Log* (Andre Deutsch, 1968), from *Selected Poems* (Penguin, 2006), reprinted by permission of the author and Penguin Books Ltd.

Miroslav Holub translated by George Theiner: 'The Fly' from *Collected Later Poems 1988–2000* (Bloodaxe, 2004), translation copyright © George Theiner 1990, reprinted by permission of Bloodaxe Books.

Homer: 'Book 22' from *The Iliad*: see Robert Fitzgerald; *The Odes* see James Michie.

Ted Hughes: 'Six Young Men' and 'Platform One' from *Collected Poems* edited by Paul Keegan (Faber, 2003), copyright © 2003 by the Estate of Ted Hughes, reprinted by permission of the publishers, Faber & Faber Ltd and Farrar, Straus & Giroux, LLC

Victor Hugo: 'Russia 1812': see Robert Lowell.

John Jarmain: 'El Alamein' from *Flowers in the Minefields: El Alamein to St Honorine* edited by James Crowden (Flagon Press, 2012), reprinted by permission of Janet Coward, heir to the Literary Estate of John Jarmain.

Randall Jarrell: 'Eighth Air Force', 'The Death of the Ball Turret Gunner', 'A Camp in the Prussian Forest, and 'A Front' from *The Complete Poems* (Faber, 1971), copyright © 1969, renewed 1997 by Mary von S Jarrell, reprinted by permission of the publishers, Faber & Faber Ltd and Farrar, Straus & Giroux, LLC.

David Jones: lines from *In Parenthesis* (Faber, 1963), reprinted by permission of the publishers, Faber & Faber Ltd.

ACKNOWLEDGEMENTS

Lincoln Kirstein: 'Rank' from *Rhymes and More Rhymes of a PFC* (New Directions, 1966), reprinted by permission of the Estate of Lincoln Kerstein, c/o the New York Public Library.

Yusef Komunyakaa: 'Facing It' and 'Starlight Scope Myopia' first published in *Dien Cai Dau* (Wesleyan University Press, 1988), from *Pleasure Dome: New and Collected Poems* (Wesleyan University Press, 2001), copyright © Yusef Komunyakaa, reprinted by permission of Wesleyan University Press.

Stanley Kunitz: 'Careless Love' from *The Collected Poems* (W W Norton, 2000), copyright © Stanley Kunitz 2000, reprinted by permission of W W Norton & Company, Inc; translation of 'I Am Goya' by Andrei Voznesenksky first published in *Antiworlds and the Fifth Ace: A Bilingual Edition* edited by Patricia Blake and Max Hayward (Basic Books, 1966), translation copyright © 1963 by Encounter Ltd, reprinted by permission of Darhansoff & Verrill Literary Agents. All rights reserved.

Philip Larkin: 'MCMXIV' first published in *The Whitsun Weddings* (Faber, 1964), from *The Complete Poems of Philip Larkin* edited by Archie Burnett (Faber, 2012), copyright © The Estate of Philip Larkin 2012, reprinted by permission of the publishers, Faber & Faber Ltd and Farrar, Straus & Giroux, LLC.

Laurie Lee: 'A Moment of War' from *Selected Poems* (Andre Deutsch, 1983), copyright © Laurie Lee 1983, reprinted by permission of Curtis Brown Group Ltd, London on behalf of The Estate of Laurie Lee.

J B Leishman: translation of 'Last Evening' by Rainer Maria Rilke from *Rainer Maria Rilke Selected Works Volume ii, Poetry* (Hogarth Press, 1960), reprinted by permission of The Random House Group Ltd and the President and Fellows of St John's College, Oxford.

Denise Levertov: 'What Were They Like?', copyright © Denise Levertov 1966, first published in *To Stay Alive* (New Directions, 1966), from *Poems 1960–1967* (New Directions, 1983) and from *New Selected Poems* (Bloodaxe, 2003), reprinted by permission of the publishers, Bloodaxe Books and New Directions Publishing Corp.

Ngo Vinh Long: untitled poem 'On this land...', first published in *The Indochina Story: A Fully Documented Account* by Committee of Concerned Asian Scholars (Pantheon Books, 1970), reprinted by permission of the author.

Michael Longley: 'Wounds' from *Collected Poems* (Jonathan Cape, 2006), reprinted by permission of the publishers, The Random House Group Ltd and Wake Forest University Press.

Robert Lowell: 'Fall 1961' and 'For the Union Dead' first published in *For the Union Dead* (Faber, 1965), translation of Victor Hugo: 'Russia 1812' and translation of Arthur Rimbaud: Sonnets I, II, III, VII and VIII from

ACKNOWLEDGEMENTS

'Eighteen-Seventy' first published in *Imitations* (Faber, 1961), all from *Collected Poems* edited by Frank Bidart and David Gewanter (Faber/Farrar Straus & Giroux 2003), copyright 2003 by Harriet Lowell and Sheridan Lowell, reprinted by permission of Farrar, Straus & Giroux, LLC.

George MacBeth: 'The Land Mine' from *Collected Poems 1958–1982* (Hutchinson, 1989), copyright © George MacBeth 1971, 1989, reprinted by permission of Sheil Land Associates Ltd.

Hugh MacDiarmid: 'Another Epitaph on an Army of Veterans' from *The Complete Poems of Hugh MacDiarmid 1920–1976* edited by Michael Grieve and W R Aitken, Volume 1 (Carcanet, 1978), reprinted by permission of Carcanet Press Ltd.

Archibald MacLeish: 'Memorial Rain' from *New and Collected Poems 1917–1882* (Houghton Mifflin, 1985), copyright © The Estate of Archiblad MacLeish 1985, reprinted by permission of Houghton Mifflin Harcourt Publishing Company.

Louis MacNeice: 'The Streets of Laredo' and translation of Louis Aragon: 'The Lilacs and the Roses' from *Collected Poems* (2e, Faber, 1979); and lines from *Autumn Journal* (Faber, 2012), reprinted by permission of David Higham Associates.

Allen Mandelbaum: lines from *The Aeneid of Virgil* (Bantam, 1981), translation copyright © Allen Mandelbaum, reprinted by permission of Bantam Books, an imprint of The Random House Publishing Group, a division of Random House LLC.

John Manifold: 'The Tomb of Lt John Learmonth, AIF' from *Collected Verse* (University of Queensland Press, 1978), reprinted by permission of the publishers.

Adam Mickiewicz: 'The Year 1812': see Donald Davie

James Michie: translation of Homer's *The Odes* (Penguin Classics, 1967), reprinted by permission of David Higham Associates.

Czeslaw Milosz: 'A Book in Ruins' from *New and Collected Poems 1931–2001* (Penguin, 2006), copyright © Czeslaw Milosz Royalites, Inc., 1988, 1991, 1995, 2001, reprinted by permission of the publishers, Penguin Books Ltd and HarperCollins Publishers, USA.

Adrian Mitchell: 'To Whom It May Concern' from *Out Loud* (Jonathan Cape, 1964), reprinted by permission of United Agents on behalf of the Estate of Adrian Mitchell.

Marianne Moore: 'In Distrust of Merits' from *The Complete Poems* (Faber, 1968), copyright © 1944 by Marianne Moore, renewed 1972 by Marianne Moore, reprinted by permission of the publishers, Faber & Faber Ltd and Scribner Publishing Group, and for electronic use by permission of The Literary Estate of Marianne C Moore, David M Moore, Administrator of the Literary Estate of Marianne Moore. All rights reserved.

ACKNOWLEDGEMENTS

Andrew Motion: 'Now Then' from *The Customs House* (Faber, 2012), copyright © Andrew Motion 2012, reprinted by permission of Faber & Faber Ltd and the author c/o William Morris Endeavor Entertainment LLC.

Howard Nemerov: 'Redeployment' from *Collected Poems of Howard Nemerov* (University of Chicago Press, 1977), and 'The War in the Air' from *War Stories: Poems About Long Ago and Now* (University of Chicago Press, 1987), reprinted by permission of Alexander Nemerov for the Literary Estate of Howard Nemerov.

George Orwell: 'The Italian Soldier Shook My Hand', copyright © George Orwell 1938, from *Looking Back on the Spanish War* (Secker & Warburg, 1938) and *A Kind of Compulsion* (Secker & Warburg, 1998), reprinted by permission of Bill Hamilton as the Literary Executor of the Estate of the late Sonia Brownell Orwell, c/o A M Heath & Co Ltd.

Benjamin Peret: 'Little Song of the Maimed': see David Gascoyne.

Peter Porter: 'Your Attention Please' from *Collected Poems* (OUP, 1983), reprinted by permission of the Estate of Peter Porter, c/o Rogers, Coleridge & White, 20 Powis Mews, London W11 1JN.

Ezra Pound: lines from 'Hugh Selwyn Mauberley' and translation of 'Rihaku: Lament of the Frontier Guard' from *Personae: Collected Shorter Poems* (Faber, 1952), copyright © Ezra Pound 1926, reprinted by permission of the publishers, Faber & Faber Ltd and New Directions Publishing Corp, and of Pollinger Ltd.

F T Prince: 'Soldiers Bathing' from *Collected Poems 1935–1992* (Carcanet, 2012), reprinted by permission of Carcanet Press Ltd and The Sheep Meadow Press.

John Pudney: 'For Johnny' from *Collected Poems* (Putnam, 1957), reprinted by permission of David Higham Associates.

Herbert Read: 'To A Conscript of 1940' from *Collected Poems* (Faber, 1946), reprinted by permission of David Higham Associates.

Henry Reed: 'Naming of Parts', Judging Distances' and 'Unarmed Combat' from 'Lessons of the War' first published in *A Map of Verona* (Jonathan Cape, 1946), from *Collected Poems* edited by Jon Stallworthy (OUP, 1991/Carcanet 2007), reprinted by permission of Oxford University Press.

Edgell Rickword: 'Winter Warfare', and 'Trench Poets' from *Collected Poems* edited by Charles Hobday (Carcanet, 1991), reprinted by permission of Carcanet Press Ltd.

Rainer Maria Rilke: 'Last Evening' see J B Leishman.

Arthur Rimbaud: Sonnets I, II, III, VII and VIII from 'Eighteen-Seventy: see Robert Lowell.

ACKNOWLEDGEMENTS

Alan Ross: 'Off Brighton Pier' from *Open Sea* (London Magazine Editions, 1975), copyright holder not traced.

Carl Sandburg: 'Grass' from *Cornhuskers* (Harcourt Brace Jovanovich, 1946), and *The Complete Poems of Carl Sandburg*, revised and expanded edition (Harcourt, 1970), copyright © Lilian Steichen Sandburg, Trustee 1969, 1970, reprinted by permission of Houghton Mifflin Harcourt Publishing Company.

Vernon Scannell: 'The Great War' and 'Walking Wounded' from *New and Collected Poems 1950–1980* (Robson Books, 1980), reprinted by permission of the Estate of Vernon Scannell.

Siegfried Sassoon: 'They', 'The Hero', 'The General', 'Glory of Women', and 'Everyone Sang' from *Collected Poems* (Faber, 1961); and 'The Redeemer' and 'Christ and the Soldier' from *The War Poems* (Faber, 1983), copyright © Siegfried Sassoon, reprinted by permission of the Bargbara Levy Literary Agency for the Estate of George Sassoon.

Dorothy L Sayers: from *The Song of Roland: a new translation* (Penguin, 1957), reprinted by permission of David Higham Associates.

Louis Simpson: 'Carentan O Carentan' from *Arrivistes: Poems 1940–1949* (Fine Editions, 1949), 'Memories of a Lost War', 'The Heroes', and 'The Battle' from *Good News of Death and Other Poems* in *Poets of Today II* (Scribners, 1955), all from *The Owner of the House: New Collected Poems 1940–2001* (BOA Editions, 2001), copyright © Louis Simpson 2001, reprinted by permission of The Permissions Company Inc on behalf of BOA Editions Ltd, www.boaeditions.org.

Edith Sitwell: 'Still Falls the Rain' from *Street Sons* (Macmillan, 1942) and *Collected Poems* (Duckworth,2005), reprinted by permission of Peters Fraser & Dunlop (www.petersfraserdunlop.com) on behalf of The Estate of Edith Sitwell.

Robert W Service: 'Only a Boche' and 'Tipperary Days' from *The Rhymes of a Red-Cross Man* (Fisher Unwin Ltd, London, 1916); copyright holder not traced.

W D Snodgrass: 'After Experience Taught Me . . .' from *After Experience* (OUP, 1964), and 'Returned to Frisco, 1946' from *Heat's Needle* (Alfred A Knopf, 1959), both from *Not for Specialists: New and Selected Poems* (BOA Editions, 2006), copyright © W D Snodgrass 2006, reprinted by permission of The Permissions Company Inc on behalf of BOA Editions Ltd, www.boaeditions.org.

Bernard Spencer: 'A Thousand Killed', copyright © Bernard Spencer 1981, from *Complete Poetry, Translations and Selected Prose* (Bloodaxe, 2011), reprinted by permission of Bloodaxe Books.

ACKNOWLEDGEMENTS

Stephen Spender: 'Two Armies', and 'Ultima Ratio Regum' from *New Collected Poems* (Faber, 2004), copyright © Stephen Spender 2004, reprinted by permission of Ed Victor Ltd for the Estate of Stephen Spender.

William Stafford: 'At the Bomb Testing Site' from *Stories that Could Be True* (Harper & Row, 1960) and *The Way It Is: New and Selected Poems* (Graywolf, 1998), copyright © William Stafford1960, 1962 and The Estate of William Stafford 1998, reprinted by permission of The Permissions Company Inc on behalf of Graywolf Press, Minneapolis, www.graywolfpress.org.

Wallace Stevens: 'The Death of a Soldier' from *Collected Poems* (Faber, 1955, 2006), copyright © Wallace Stevens 1954 and renewed 1982 by Holy Stevens, reprinted by permission of the publishers, Faber & Faber Ltd and Alfred A Knopf, an imprint of Knopf Doubleday Publishing, a division of Random House LLC. All rights reserved.

James Tate: 'The Lost Pilot' from *The Lost Pilot* (Ecco Press, 1978, 1982), copyright © James Tate 1978, reprinted by permission of HarperCollins Publishers, USA.

George Theiner: translation of 'The Fly': see Miroslav Holub.

Dylan Thomas: 'The Hand That Signed the Paper' from *Collected Poems* (J M Dent, 1952), reprinted by permission of David Higham Associates.

Charles Tomlinson: translation of 'At Vshchizh' by Fyodor Tyutchev from *Selected Poems 1951–1974* (OUP, 1978), reprinted by permission of Carcanet Press Ltd.

Fyodor Tyutchev: 'At Vshchizh': see Charles Tomlinson.

Virgil: lines from *The Aeneid* : see Allen Mandelbaum.

Andrei Voznesenksky: 'I Am Goya' : see Stanley Kunitz.

Arthur Waley: translation of Anonymous Chinese poem 'Hymn to the Fallen' from *Chinese Poems*, translated by Arthur Waley (G Allen & Unwin, 1946), reprinted by permission of John Robinson for the Estate of Arthur Waley.

Sylvia Townsend Warner: 'Benicasim' from *New Collected Poems* edited by Claire Harman (Carcanet, 2008), reprinted by permission of Carcanet Press Ltd.

Bruce Weigl: 'Song of Napalm' from *Song of Napalm* (Atlantic Monthly Press, 1998), copyright © Bruce Weigl 1988, reprinted by permission of Grove/Atlantic.

Richard Wilbur: 'Advice to a Prophet' from *Advice to a Prophet and Other Poems* (Faber, 1962), copyright © Richard Wilbur 1961, © renewed 1989; 'First Snow in Alsace' from *The Beautiful Changes and Other Poems* (Harcourt Brace, 1947) and from *Poems 1943–1956* (Faber, 1957), copyright © Richard Wilbur 1947, © renewed 1975; and 'Terza Rima' from *Anterooms, New Poems and*

ACKNOWLEDGEMENTS

Translations (Faber, 2010), copyright © Richard Wilbur 2010, all reprinted by permission of the publishers, Faber & Faber Ltd and Houghton Mifflin Harcourt Publishing Company.

Peter Wyton: 'Unmentioned in Dispatches', copyright © Peter Wyton 1996, from *Even the Beggars Have Pearls* (Tempus Publishing, 2001), reprinted by permission of the author.

INDEX OF FIRST LINES

The references are to the numbers of the poems

INDEX OF POETS AND
TRANSLATORS

The references are to the numbers of the poems

INDEX OF POETS AND TRANSLATORS